WIV[...]

Here are three portraits of very different Victorian women, all of whom married men of exceptional talent, energy and genius. To be the wife of such frenetic, explosive characters as David Livingstone, Karl Marx or Charles Darwin, especially at this period in history, demanded rare qualities. Yet the late twentieth-century view of these women is perhaps best summed up in the frequently heard comment: 'I didn't know he had a wife.'

'Edna Healey has a gift for making history easy'
Literary Review

'Mrs Healey gives us a detailed and coherent factual account of the three lives, with apposite quotations from letters and diaries'
The Listener

'Not only poignant tales of women whose personal happiness would be overshadowed by their husbands' ambitions but vivid chronicles of lives and times in the mid-19th century'
Yorkshire Post

'A fascinating book and the interest in the subjects is enhanced by the persuasive eloquence of the author's writing'
Catholic Herald

About the Author

Edna Healey read English at Oxford and subsequently taught and lectured widely on literature and history in Europe, America and Japan. Now well-known as a broadcaster and film-maker, she wrote and presented for Scottish television a documentary film on one of the subjects of this book, *Mrs Livingstone, I Presume*, which won the Radio Industries of Scotland award and a silver medal at the International Film Festival in New York. Her book, LADY UNKNOWN, a biography of the Victorian philanthropist Angel Burdett-Coutts, received the Yorkshire Post Literary Award for the best first work of 1978.

Married to the former Labour Minister of Defence and Chancellor of the Exchequer Denis Healey, she has three children and four grandchildren.

WIVES OF FAME

**Mary Livingstone
Jenny Marx
Emma Darwin**

Edna Healey

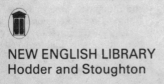

NEW ENGLISH LIBRARY
Hodder and Stoughton

To Denis
with love and gratitude

Copyright © 1986 Edna Healey
Picture research by Philippa
Lewis
Maps by Neil Hyslop

First published in
Great Britain in 1986 by
Sidgwick & Jackson Ltd.

NEL edition 1988
Second impression 1988

British Library C.I.P.

Healey, Edna
   Wives of fame: Mary
   Livingstone, Jenny Marx,
   Emma Darwin.
   1. Women—Biography
   2. Wives—History—19th
   Century
   I. title
   920.72'09'034   CT3203

   ISBN 0-450-42140-6

Printed and bound in Great Britain
For Hodder and Stoughton
Paperbacks, a division of Hodder
and Stoughton Ltd., Mill Road,
Dunton Green, Sevenoaks, Kent
TN13 2YA (Editorial Office: 47
Bedford Square, London WC1B
3DP) by Richard Clay Ltd.,
Bungay, Suffolk.

Contents

Author's Acknowledgements   x
Prologue   xiii

Mary LIVINGSTONE   1

Jenny MARX   81

Emma DARWIN   193

Epilogue   280
Bibliography   287
Manuscript Sources   293
Picture Acknowledgements   295
Index   297

The author and publisher gratefully acknowledge permission to quote from the following works still in copyright:

B. Andreas (ed.), *Briefe und Dokumente der Familie Marx aus den Jahren 1862–1873*, Verlag für Literatur und Zeitgeschehen, Hanover.

Bilddokumente über das Geburtshaus, Karl Marx Haus, Trier.

L. and D. Bottigelli, *Lettres et Documents de Karl Marx 1856–1883*, Annali dell'Istituto Giangiacomo Feltrinelli, Milan.

Bernard Darwin, *The World That Fred Made*, Collins.

Yvonne Kapp (ed.), *Karl Marx: Letters to Kugelmann*, Lawrence and Wishart, London.

David McLellan, *Karl Marx, His Life and Thought,* Macmillan.

Karl Marx, *Letters 1835–1871*, Progress Publishing Co., Moscow.

Karl Marx and Friedrich Engels, *Collected Works*, Lawrence and Wishart.

Olga Meier (ed.), *The Daughters of Karl Marx*, André Deutsch.

M. Müller (ed.), *Familie Marx in Briefen*, Dietz Verlag, Berlin.

Saul K. Padover, *The Letters of Karl Marx*, Prentice-Hall Inc., Princeton.

Robert Payne, *Marx, A Biography*, W. H. Allen.

Robert Payne, *The Unknown Karl Marx*, University of London Press.

F. Raddatz (ed.), *The Marx–Engels Correspondence*, Weidenfeld and Nicolson.

Gwen Raverat, *Period Piece, A Cambridge Childhood*, Faber and Faber.

I. Schapera (ed.), *David Livingstone Family Letters*, Chatto and Windus.

F. A. Sorge, *Correspondence Engels–Marx*, A. Costes, Paris.

P. S. Vinogradskaya, *Documentary Life of Jenny Marx*, MISL, Moscow.

Wedgwood Letters, The (extracts from), by courtesy of the Trustees of the Wedgwood Museum and Keele University Library where the papers are deposited.

Author's Acknowledgements

Too often fame is the Gorgon's head that turns the great to stone. In this book I have tried to show the human faces of three famous men and the predicament of the women who married them. I have not attempted to assess the work of Livingstone, Marx or Darwin: many brilliant writers have undertaken this task. I am grateful for their books, which have given me the essential background for this triple biography.

I have found the life of Jenny Marx the most difficult to write, for since I do not read German or Russian, I have been dependent on translations. I have been most grateful, therefore, to the editors of the English-language edition of the *Collected Works* of Marx and Engels; vols 1–3 (1975) and 38–40 (1983) have been my main sources. Two other works have particularly influenced and inspired me: Professor McLellan's comprehensive *Karl Marx, His Life and Thought*, and Yvonne Kapp's scholarly *Eleanor Marx*, one of the great biographies of our time.

I am deeply grateful for the help I have had, from so many quarters, in what has often been a frustrating search for three invisible ladies. Bill Cunningham, the curator of the Livingstone Memorial, Blantyre, has encouraged and helped me throughout. Scottish Television gave me the opportunity to follow in Mary Livingstone's footsteps in Africa and Scotland; to Dr Nelson Gray and the director, Jim McCann, who guided me in the presentation of the documentary film *Mrs Livingstone, I Presume*, I give my heartfelt thanks. Dr Oliver Ransford was my kind host in Bulawayo, and gave me his much-valued and expert advice on Livingstone in Africa. My special thanks go to Chief Sechele in Botswana, who allowed me to spend a day with his people. I am most grateful to the Rev. H. Thompson and the Rev. Butler in Kuruman, and Dr H. Moffat in Mochudi Botswana, who helped me to understand missionary life. The directors and librarians of the National Archives of Zimbabwe, in Harare, were extremely kind and helpful. To all the members of the Livingstone, Moffat and Stewart families who have written with help and encouragement I give my warmest thanks. In particular Tessa Wilson most kindly guided me in Kendal and gave me much valuable insight into the Braithwaite family. Jean Anderson, Stewart's granddaughter, kindly lent me useful material. Dr Sheila Brock, Dr Cecil Northcott and Mr Gary Glendennan are only three of the many kind advisers I have had.

In my research into the life of Jenny Marx I have been very dependent on my good friend Beatrice Griffiths, who translated German texts for me. Sheena Wakefield and Judy Robinson have been most competent and helpful in translating from Russian and German respectively. The director of the Karl Marx Haus in Trier gave me invaluable assistance, for which I am deeply grateful. On my short visit to the Institute of Marxism-Leninism in Moscow the deputy director and his staff were kindness itself; they gave me a sight of material in their archives and sent me Xeroxed copies of letters. Many Marx scholars have encouraged me, and I particularly thank Daniel Norman for all his advice at the beginning of my research, and Mr C. Abramsky for his interest and help.

I owe my deepest gratitude to Peter Gautrey, librarian at Cambridge University, for his exceptional kindness in guiding me through the Darwin archives and directing me to useful sources. Professor and Mrs Keynes allowed me to see Darwin material in their possession; to them and to Mrs Nora Barlow I give my thanks. I owe a great debt of gratitude to Mrs Hensleigh Wedge-wood, who generously lent me material from her own research in the Wedgewood archives at Keele University and offered help and advice. Sir Hedley Atkins, late of Down House, gave me invaluable guidance and aid, as did Mr Robin Price, librarian of the Wellcome Institute. Mr and Mrs Fradley were kind enough to allow me to visit Maer Hall.

A host of archivists and librarians have aided me. To all of the following I am grateful, and I apologise if I have inadvertently omitted some names: librarians and staff at the School of Oriental and African Studies; the Rhodes House Library, Oxford; the National Library of Scotland; the British Library; Malvern Public Library; the Marx Memorial Library; and Hamilton Museum. I am deeply grateful to Mr Douglas Matthews, librarian of the London Library, and his staff for their courteous and competent assistance.

To my patient editor, Esther Jagger, I give my warmest thanks and apologies for all my shortcomings. Mrs Watts-Jones has not only typed for me but is always a tower of strength and has constantly cheered and encouraged me.

Above all I am eternally grateful to my husband and family, who have loyally supported me and urged me on when my triple task seemed impossible.

Edna Healey
January 1986

Prologue

The summer of 1857 has been the most beautiful in memory. The last echoes of the Crimean War have died away a year ago, and here in the quiet Kentish countryside the horrors of the Indian Mutiny are far away. The garden at Down House, bright with summer flowers, is silent save for the distant voices of children, the rattle of the flywheel of the well, and from the great lime trees the murmur of myriad bees. A clock chimes twelve and Charles Darwin, stick in hand, comes out over the shiny, pebbled path to take his morning walk. Down the sunny side of the Sand Walk to the summer house he paces, rapping the marker stones with his stick. By a bank of wild flowers Emma, in her faded cotton gown, waits for him and quietly they walk back together through the wood. It is a tranquil scene, and a casual observer watching this quiet routine would not have guessed the tumult in Charles Darwin's mind. For the book he has been wrestling with for almost twenty years was to startle the world. When *The Origin of Species* was published in 1859 it would transform the thought of his and future generations.

That same summer, in the woods at Hadley Green on the edge of the peaceful Hertfordshire hamlet of Barnet, a man, lean and sun-tanned and wearing a battered peaked cap, plays with his children, leaping from the bushes and startling them with his lion's roar. David Livingstone is taking a break from the agony of writing of his missionary travels in southern Africa. Beside the path a small, sturdy woman watches. In her old-fashioned bonnet and plaid shawl she could be his housekeeper. It is four years since Mary Livingstone and the children last braved real lions at their home on the edge of the Kalahari desert, years of separation wandering through chilly Britain while Livingstone trudged across the unknown heart of Africa to return a hero. Now he is writing a book which is to be seminal in his own time and which still affects our own. 'We are sowing seeds', he would write, 'which will bud and blossom when our heads are low.' His description of the fertile highlands of Central Africa, which men had thought was arid desert, would encourage merchants, explorers and governments to scramble for the riches of the new country; while his searing account of the slave trade – 'the open sore of the world' – would inspire generations of missionaries to follow in his steps.

It is Sunday evening on Hampstead Heath. A group of picnickers singing German folksongs makes its way from the grassy heights of Hampstead Heath towards the city spread out beneath them. At the rear a sturdy maid humps the huge, empty picnic basket; in front of her run three pretty girls. At the head of the procession a powerfully-built man with a shock of greying hair and a black beard walks with his wife. Karl Marx and his family are heading home to their house in north London. His wife, Jenny, looks thin and ill but she strides beside him as one who is accustomed to walking. Her dress is simple, even poor, but her style is unmistakable. The singing stops and she begins to recite Shakespeare in a clear, musical voice. For a while she is Desdemona, then the girls call, 'Come on, Moor – your turn!', and Karl begins the long, long story that will hold them spellbound all the way home. He too is taking a break – from his work at the British Museum. For more than twelve years he has laboured at his mammoth *Critique of Political Economy*. On its publication, in 1859, it would hardly cause a ripple of interest. But it was to be the first instalment of his later work *Das Kapital*, which would disturb the whole world.

* * *

When Engels delivered his funeral oration at the grave-side of Karl Marx in Highgate Cemetery he spoke of Marx and Darwin as the two giants of the age, claiming that, 'just as Darwin discovered the law of development of organic nature, so Marx discovered the law of development of human history'. Livingstone, too, still towers above his contemporaries. He was, according to Florence Nightingale, 'the greatest man of his genera-tion', a supreme example of the hardy working-class Scots who dominated the sphere of exploration in the nineteenth century. Each of these men pushed back the frontiers of knowledge. Each in his different way changed the thought of their age and of ours, and each still arouses fierce controversy.

The figures of the great, who loom so grandly in the halls of fame, appear to stand alone. But shine a light into the darkness and slowly dim outlines emerge behind them. Few men achieve greatness in isolation. Somewhere in the background is a colleague, a sister, or even a housekeeper or valet, without whom they could not have endured the stress and loneliness. But often there stands a wife, invisible and forgotten, whose name is not recorded on the tablets of bronze and of whose famous husband it is so frequently said: 'I didn't know he had a wife.'

Only three such wives have been chosen here, but there are hundreds more throughout history who still await recognition. The reason for their obscurity may be in part that the followers of great men are jealous and resentful that their hero has a private world into which they may not intrude. Often they feel that marriage diminishes divinity. Many wives of famous men have been happy to be obscure. When asked if she took part in his work, the wife of the scientist Michael Faraday replied, 'I am content to be the pillow of his mind.'

Mary Livingstone, Jenny Marx and Emma Darwin were three very different but exceptional women, living in the same turbulent period and married to three of the most outstanding men of the century. To understand their problems it is necessary to try to understand the nature of those who are spurred on to go, in Livingstone's words, 'beyond other men's lines'.

Men and women who break through boundaries are unique, but they have much in common. There is an extraordinary energy that impels the great. This electrifying power often strikes with such force that they describe it as coming from outside themselves. Francis Darwin wrote that his father worked 'as if an outside force were driving him', and 'as though he were charged with theorising power'. Some believe, as Wellington did, that they were directed by 'the finger of God', while some are led by their 'star'. Missionaries have seen before them a pillar of fire which they are compelled to follow, and many religious men and women, feeling this power, have agonised over its source, wondering whether it comes from God or the devil. But whatever the source of the power it can lead to feats beyond the usual bounds of endurance, and woe to him who resists it. This force can make a man a fanatic. In his unfinished tragedy *Oulanem* Marx wrote:

> I must bend myself to a wheel of flame
> And dance with joy in the circle of eternity.

When the manic energy subsides it leaves black despair. He continued:

> We are the apes of a cold God.

Thomas Huxley believed that, as he wrote to Joseph Hooker in 1860,

> we have certain duties to perform to ourselves, to the outside world and to science. Don't flatter yourself that there is any moral chloroform by which either you or I can render ourselves insensible or acquire the habit of

doing things coolly. It is assuredly of no great use to tear
oneself to pieces before one is 50. But the alternative for
men constructed on the high pressure tubular boiler
principle like ourselves, is to lie still and let the devil
have his own way. And I will be torn to pieces before I
am 40 sooner than that.

Genius also demands exceptional powers of concentration. Darwin advised his son Francis to pursue his
theories 'to the death'. Dickens's biographer Forster
wrote of him, 'In all intellectual labour his will prevailed
so strongly when he fixed it on any object of desire that
what else its attainment might exact was never duly
measured . . . it may be doubted if any man's mental
effort cost him more.'

An extraordinary restlessness commonly accompan-
ies this energy and concentration. As Byron wrote in
his journal, 'My restlessness tells me I have something
within that "passeth show". It is for Him, who made it,
to prolong that spark of celestial power which illumi-
nates, yet burns this frail tenement.' Too often the
sword of the mind is too sharp for the body. As
Charlotte Brontë said of her sister Emily, 'The spirit is
inexorable to the flesh.'

Such intense mental effort often causes illness. Sometimes the stress produces the malady; sometimes the
malady is created to protect the vital energy. After a
period of intense physical activity both Charles Darwin
and Florence Nightingale became chronic invalids,
reserving their energy for concentrated thought. There
is a formidable list of famous invalids; were it not for
the discretion of doctors and the loyalty of partners
dedicated to preserving the legends, the list would be
even longer.

Coping with these problems is difficult in any age,
but there were additional stresses in the mid-nineteenth
century, when families were haunted by fear of the
cholera epidemics that swept through Europe. This was

a period of medical change when treatments such as blood-letting, by cupping or leeches, were being discarded in favour of new cures. Many became addicted to the opium and laudanum that were as easily available as aspirin is today. Apart from the notorious addicts such as Coleridge and de Quincey, devout men like William Wilberforce also took opium. Neither Lady Lovelace, Byron's brilliant daughter, nor Elizabeth Barratt Browning could do without what Browning called 'the red hood of poppies'. This was also a time of medical experiment. Dickens, Tennyson, Carlyle, Marx, Darwin, Florence Nightingale and many others flocked to Malvern for the new water cure, or travelled abroad to Spa or Karlsbad in search of health.

There were other problems, too, for wives at this period. Between 1801 and 1871 the population of England and Wales increased from nine million to twenty-two million. In human terms these statistics meant that wives had a life of constant child-bearing – and until the late 1840s without the relief of chloroform. Emma Darwin is not an isolated example – she married at thirty and then had ten children. At a time when birth control was considered immoral and merely to write about it was illegal, there was little alternative.

For women comfortably at home in a stable environment this was difficult enough, but there is no other period in which so many families were on the move. In 1815 fewer than two thousand people left the British Isles, while between that year and 1860 seven million emigrated. Many saw emigration as the only solution for overcrowding and poverty. In the 1850s two million were driven out of Ireland by the potato famine. Other emigrants, lured by gold fever, struggled across America to join the Forty-Niners in California, and as many as eighty thousand joined the gold rush to Australia in 1852.

For restless adventurers there were exotic lands to be discovered, and for missionaries there were heathen hordes to be converted. Their wives had to choose between suffering the loneliness of separation or packing up and following them – to share the dangers, but often without the faith that sustained their men. Yet frequently the wives' existence was only acknowledged in missionary records by an asterisk against their husbands' names. Year after year they bore their babies on crowded ships or ox wagons, and then trudged on into the unknown. Mary Livingstone was only one of the many thousands of uprooted wives. In the words of her sister Bessie, also married to a missionary, 'Wives act as organ blowers to the musicians.'

Jenny Marx, on the other hand, was one of the multitudes who were displaced by the political upheavals of the century. The earthquake of the French Revolution sent shock waves rumbling through Europe for decades, erupting in revolutions in 1830 and 1848 in France, Poland, Hungary, Italy and Germany, and even shaking the pragmatic British. Revolutionary ideas ricocheted from country to country. Not only politicians were involved: poets, artists and musicians – all were carried on the tide. In 1848 Wagner fought on the Dresden barricades; Heine and Lamartine took active parts in the revolutions in Germany and France; Byron and Shelley fanned the flames. When the revolutions failed many fled to the New World, and more took refuge in an already overcrowded Britain.

In this age of scientific discovery it was no longer possible to rest on the rock of religion. The newly awakened interest in archaeology and geology shook men's belief in the Bible. It is hard for the modern reader to understand the upheaval in religious thought during this time. Many of the Jews of the period were for political or social reasons cut off from their religious roots: Marx, born a Jew, was confirmed in the Lutheran Church and as a schoolboy wrote devout Christian essays. Engels came from a strictly religious Protestant family and wrote hymns in his youth. Darwin had intended to become a clergyman. Yet all three, like many of their generation, became atheists or agnostics. The Churches retaliated with revivalist movements which swept across Europe, but for many ordinary people it was a time of great uncertainty. When death struck there were many who could no longer take consolation from the belief that their loved ones had gone to a 'happy land far, far away'. The mementoes – withered flowers, faded portraits, and locks of hair treasured among family letters – are pathetic reminders of the Victorian need to hold on to something in the face of ever-present death.

Three of the men who made this an age of change, disruption and insecurity themselves demanded the reassurance of wife and family. Mary Livingstone, Jenny Marx and Emma Darwin gave their husbands the love and support that were so desperately needed. They deserve to be brought out of the shadows, to share their husbands' place in history.

Mary
LIVINGSTONE

The best spoke in the wheel

It was midsummer at the remote mission station of Kuruman, eight hundred miles from Cape Town in the South African interior. The low hills around were arid and bare; only the stunted thorn trees broke the monotony of the bleached landscape. But down in the Kuruman valley Robert Moffat had created an oasis by channelling the clear water from an underground spring, and had planted neat vegetable gardens and orchards of peaches and apricots, apples and pears. There, swallows skimmed the streams between tall willows, and by the great thatched stone church the mimosa was in full bloom. Beyond the square stone mission houses were clusters of thatched huts, ringed by rough-hewn stockades. These were the homes of the Batlapings and other tribes who, over the years, had settled at Kuruman.

On this day, 9 January 1845, the gardens were deserted as throngs of Africans, in Sunday dress, crowded into the cool dark of the church for the marriage of Robert Moffat's eldest daughter, Mary, to David Livingstone, the Scots missionary who four years earlier had come out to Africa. As the full-throated harmony of African voices swung to the rafters, transforming the old Scots hymns, there was general rejoicing – this was a royal wedding. In twenty-four years Robert and Mary Moffat had become as king and queen of the whole region. Robert had fought alongside them, protected them from their enemies, black and white, and had made their desert blossom. He had learned their languages, had patiently translated into their native Sechwane the Bible and the hymns that they were now singing, and taught them to read. This huge church, that could hold a thousand people, he and his mason had built with their own hands. He had stood for days in the swamps, cutting the reeds for the thatched roof, had laboured by slow ox wagon to distant Matabeleland and hauled back the great beams. Gardener and blacksmith, doctor, teacher, preacher and translator – there was nothing he could not do.

Tall, handsome, with piercing black eyes, Robert Moffat had an eloquence and a magnetic personality that had enthralled thousands who had heard him preach during his four years' leave in England, and had totally mesmerised Mzilikatze, the fierce chief of the neighbouring and hostile Matabele. Yet he remained simple and unaffected and, though his faith was rigid and uncompromising, with a firm belief in the Day of Judgement when sinners would perish in hellfire and white-robed saints rejoice in Heaven, he had a gentle sense of humour. Now, Mary was marrying a fellow Scot whose courage and energy and sense of mission matched his own, and he was well content.

Mrs Moffat, too, was glad that at last Mary had found a husband. Her keen blue eyes scanned the congregation, approving the clean cotton dresses – and woe betide any wife whose husband was not properly dressed. It was Mrs Moffat's indomitable will that had created not only a well-organised, comfortable home in the wilderness, but also a haven for all travellers to the far interior. There were old women in the congregation who, twenty-three years before, had, in the dust of their huts, clasped her baby to bosoms shiny with grease and red with ochre dust. She knew that there was a rough life ahead for her daughter, but she looked forward to teaching David and Mary how to run a mission station.

David Livingstone, standing beside Mary, stiff and

awkward in his black missionary suit, was more than content. His bride was not a beauty. As he told his brother, she was 'a little, black-haired girl, sturdy and all I want', always so clean and fresh in the dust and heat – 'always', he said, 'the best spoke in the wheel'. As she stood there, calm and modest in her crisp white dress and bonnet, he knew he could never find a better wife.

As they left the church. Mary Livingstone too was quietly happy. Finally she had found someone who could compare with her father. But she had no illusions about their future. Now it was high summer, the air heavy with the scent of syringa, the mimosa golden in the hard, bright sunlight. But she had said 'Yes' in July, in midwinter, when the African mimosa showed its cruel, long, silver thorns. Born and brought up in the beauty and harshness of Africa, she knew full well the rigours of mission life.

It takes some fortitude to live at rest in this tumultuous land amidst barbarians

Mary Livingstone was African-born, but it was only after years of study and toil that her father had been able to say, 'I am African.' And for her mother, brought up in a comfortable Lancashire home, the learning had been hard. At a Moravian school Mary Smith received an excellent education and also absorbed a deep and lasting faith. As a girl she was remembered as being 'ever active and attentive' in the Independent Chapel. Her father owned a market garden, and when Robert Moffat, a tall young Scot, came to work for him Mary was soon in love. Robert shared her religious zeal and after a visiting missionary, John Campbell, had spoken of his work in a place called Lattakoo in the Kuruman valley they were both determined to go out to Africa as missionaries. Robert, encouraged by a local minister,

William Roby, taught himself enough to be accepted by
the London Missionary Society, an ecumenical organisation, and sailed for the Cape in 1816. Having overcome
her parents' objections Mary followed him, and they
were married in St George's church, Cape Town, on 27
December 1819.

At this time on the maps of southern Africa the
interior was still mainly a blank, although the Cape of
Good Hope had been settled since King John of Portugal
named it in 1488. It remained the Portugeuese port of
call on the way to India until the British East India
Company took temporary possession of it as a refuelling
and victualling station for its own ships.

But it was the Dutch who had been the chief settlers,
who had built a fort and cultivated the land as farms. In
1795 Holland was defeated by France during Napoleon's Revolutionary Wars, and to forestall French occu-
pation of the Cape Britain took possession in the name
of its ally, King William of Holland. In 1814 William
sold the Cape to Britain, which appointed a governor
who was directly responsible to the Secretary of State
for War and the Colonies. The administration was now
British, but the white population was still mainly Dutch
– in 1819 there were forty-seven thousand Dutch inhabitants but only four thousand British. The neighbouring
tribes – the Hottentots – provided slave labour.

Until 1819 the British government regarded the Cape
as a halfway house to India and discouraged settlers.
But at this time a great Zulu army was on the march on
the colony's eastern border. To protect the frontier,
therefore, the government now changed its policy and
actively encouraged emigration to the eastern Cape. In
1820 whole families and even entire villages from England and Scotland uprooted themselves and settled
along the frontier.

When the Moffats started their work they found a
number of missions, but they were scattered and badly
organised, and many disheartened missionaries had

deserted their flocks. Mission wives often could not stand the strain in the remote villages; some died in childbirth, while many left their husbands and escaped back to Cape Town or took ship for Britain. Missionaries were in any case unpopular. The London Missionary Society sent out a deputation under Dr Philip to report and reorganise. He stayed there, to become the Society's superintendent, and built a reputation as a fierce champion of the Africans.

At this time the British government saw nothing to gain by increasing its responsibilities in the barren lands beyond the boundaries of the Cape Colony, and it was some time before Robert Moffat was allowed to start for Lattakoo to become superintendent of a mission there. With John Campbell, the missionary who had himself been stationed there, they trekked by slow ox wagon from Cape Town across the barren, sandy Karroo plateau to Beaufort West, then comprising only a few houses and almost the last outpost of the Cape Colony. Their trail took them across the colonial boundary through country unexplored by white men except for hunters and missionaries. Luckily the Orange river was low. Had it been in flood they could have been marooned on the bank for weeks. They forded the Orange and the Vaal, their oxen straining and stumbling across the rocks, until finally they reached the Kuruman valley.

Both Robert Moffat and his young bride were convinced that they had been divinely called to Lattakoo, but until the mission authorities at the Cape gave them permission to settle there they went to Gricqua Town, ninety miles away, where their daughter Mary was born on 12 April 1821. Gricqua Town was the nearest approach to civilisation for hundreds of miles. It was a small community, inhabited by people of mixed descent; there were coloureds, half-castes, and escaped Hottentots from the Cape Colony. But it had a number of prosperous farmhouses, including some, as Mrs

The Livingstone and Moffat Families

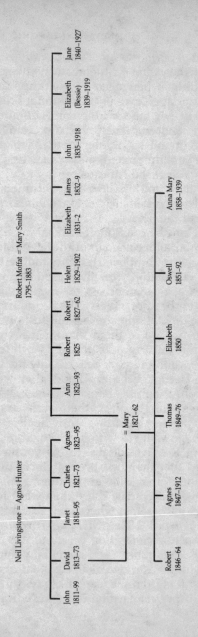

Moffat reported home, 'even with wagons before the door'. When their daughter was a year old they were finally given permission to settle at Lattakoo, and for the next twenty years Mrs Moffat was to need every ounce of her indomitable spirit. Diminutive but determined, she organised them in Lattakoo as she had bossed them back at the chapel in Lancashire.

She came to accept the strange and dangerous life, but it took time. The reality was far from the romanticised story of mission life with which old Johnny Campbell had first fired Mary's imagination in far-off Lancashire. Though the valley here was open and beautiful as she had imagined, under a burning sun the stream dried up and clouds of fine white dust filled the air. At first they lived among the Batlaping tribe in a hut, built by Robert in the traditional manner. It had no furniture: they slept on the mattress from the wagon laid on goatskins on the mud floor, and their seats were ledges moulded into the clay of the walls. She cooked over an open fire, and in summer the air in the smoky hut was suffocating.

Mary had no privacy. To the women of the tribe this blonde, blue-eyed little creature with the delicate, fair skin was a strange curiosity. They pressed into her hut, squatting on her floor, watching every movement, clutching and fondling her precious baby Mary. She had watched them with horror mixing with their hands the cow dung and clay with which they built the walls and floors of their huts, seen them climbing up to thatch roofs, heard them chant of their aching backs as they threshed the corn or hoed the fields. She started to pick up their language, Sechwane, and she became, in the traditional way, 'Ma Mary', the mother adopting the name of the eldest child.

Their customs still appalled her: polygamy in her eyes was a mortal sin, yet as she looked at the wives of the chief – each in her little hut around the master's – she realised in despair how woven it was into the fabric of

their lives, how long it would take to change them. She
began to appreciate, however, that some of their seem-
ingly barbarous habits made sense. The nights were
long and in winter – surprisingly – bitterly cold; yet by
the light of the candles they made themselves Mary
Moffat wrote vivid letters home.

You will perhaps think it curious that we smear all our
room floors with cow dung once a week at least. At first
when I saw Sister Helm do it I thought to myself, 'but
I'll do without that dirty trick or I will try hard'. However, I had not been here long but was glad to have it
done and I had hardly patience to wait till Saturday. It
lays the dust better than anything, kills the fleas which
would otherwise breed abundantly and is a fine clear
green . . . it is mixed with water and laid on as thinly as
possible. I now look upon my floor smeared with cow
dung with as much complacency as I used to do upon
our best rooms when well scoured.

There was, however, no sign that they were succeed-
ing as missionaries. 'Could we but see the smallest fruit
we could rejoice amidst the privations and toil which
we bear,' Ma Mary wrote to her parents; 'but as it is,
our hands do often hang down.' Robert's eloquent
sermons fell on deaf ears. His favourite theme – the Day
of Judgement – was received with incredulity. Did he
mean that their enemies, slain in battle, would rise
again? 'Alas!' Robert wrote home, 'we still hang our
harp on the willows, and mourn over the destiny of
thousands hastening with heedless but impetuous
strides to the regions of woe. They turn a deaf ear to
the voice of love, and treat with scorn the glorious
doctrines of redemption.' Ma Mary was as much a
missionary as Robert – she had, as she put it, 'heard the
call' back in Lancashire, and the absence of any converts
weighed heavily on her. But, like Robert, she firmly
believed that their reward would come when, on the

Day of Judgement, they would sit beside the King in all his glory. 'The Day will tell,' was her repeated consolation.

Though it took time for Mrs Moffat to adjust to this life, Mary grew up absorbing from earliest childhood the sounds, sights and smells of an African village. She chattered in Sechwane and even picked up the difficult clicking language of the Bushmen. Her earliest nurse, Sarah Robey, had been a little Bushman girl rescued by Mrs Moffat from being buried alive with her dead mother.

The Moffats experienced danger in these early years; Ma Mary wrote home, 'It takes some fortitude to live at rest in this tumultuous land amidst barbarians.' Many times, as a little child, Mary had been awakened, wrapped quickly in her kaross, a skin cloak, bundled into the wagon and jolted, half asleep, the ninety miles to the comparative safety of Gricqua Town. Often, when her father was away, she had seen her mother, in her nightgown, rallying the frightened Africans in the face of approaching bandits or hostile tribes. At this time the Zulu army in the east, led by their powerful chief, Shaka, threatened both whites and blacks. His victorious troops scattered enemy tribes, who fled across the country, pillaging as they went. In 1823 one such tribe, the Mantatees, led by a woman warrior who could wield her axe as powerfully as a man, terrorised the country in the vicinity of Kuruman. In this battle, Robert Moffat, immensely tall beside the little commandant from Gricqua Town, walked nonchantly between the battle lines of the warring tribes. His courage had turned the tide and saved Kuruman. From that day onwards, he, his wife and family could travel hundreds of miles protected by the shield of the Moffat legend. Now his congregation would listen to his sermons.

When Mary was three she was taken on her first long ox wagon journey to Cape Town, where Ma Mary needed to see a doctor. During the next seventeen years

Ma Mary had nine more children. Ann, Robert (who died in infancy), another Robert and Helen came in quick succession, and then Elizabeth, James, John, Bessie and Jane. It was remarkable that, born under such difficult circumstances, only two babies should have died. In her letters home Ma Mary told of these long trips by ox wagon with small children.

very positive!

> But you can form no idea how comfortable our waggons are. They are very light vehicles, and in them we carry all necessary comforts. If there are children, they play on the bed or lie asleep. The length of our day stages is about eight or twelve hours on an average, riding about three and a half miles an hour; we are chiefly guided by the water, riding from one fountain to another, that our oxen may be refreshed as well as ourselves. Sometimes the water is too distant and we make two stages of it, but we always take with us a keg of water in case of an accident in the wilderness. When we span out (or unyoke), a fire is immediately made, the kettle set on, and coffee or tea made, I would here notice that that missionary must be very regardless of his wife's comfort who does not see to that being done without her troubling herself. For my own part I never think of coming out of the waggon till there is a good fire, for it is comfortless work indeed turning out in a cold night in the wilderness with a child or children before there is a fire.

On Ma Mary's return Robert prepared to move from drought-stricken Lattakoo to a site near the Eye of Kuruman, a spring of clear water bubbling up into caves, which even in the severest droughts never failed. Gardens were planted and flourished, the church begun, and solid stone houses built. The Moffat's house was built on the same plan as the mission houses that Ma Mary had stayed in on the journey from the Cape, and which she described:

> Those who have tolerably good houses have generally what is called a forehouse. It is the place of entrance.

The outer door renders it cool and comfortable, which door is in the middle, as in a hall; and this place is generally the largest in the house. It is the houseplace of the family, where they eat, fold and iron their clothes, prepare victuals for the fire, &c. At each end of this place is a small room, one of them the bed-room, the other the private sitting-room, study, or whatever you may call it. Behind are detached pack-houses, where everything is kept. This is the plan of a good missionary house here, and I approve it, only I would have both kitchen and pack-houses attached to the dwelling house. If I want a little coffee, sugar, or butter, I like to have it at least a little nearer the house than they have it. Custom seems to have established this awkward system, which is productive of many evils; for instance, it ruins servants, and there is such a propensity in all the natives of this country to assist each other to food, when they have it in their power, that you cannot keep them from it whilst the kitchen is out of your sight.

Before long visiting hunters were reporting on the exquisite order of the Moffat home. Some of the furniture made by Robert Moffat still exists in Bulawayo, and is surprisingly elegant. At last Robert had a study, where he could settle to his life's work of translating the Bible into Sechwane. For the first time young Mary knew comfort and was safe behind stone walls, but the insecurity of those early years was to leave its mark.

When she was ten, she was abruptly uprooted and taken with her younger sister, Ann, to the Wesleyan mission school at Salem, five weeks' journey away. Though Ma Mary twice made the long journey to see them, it was to be many years before Mary saw her father again. At Salem, as at Kuruman, there was always danger on the horizon, for it was one of the emigrant communities financed in 1820 by the British government to act as a buffer between the Cape Colony and the warring Zulus of Kaffirland. Tension was now building up that would eventually lead to yet another Zulu war.

Although Salem had only been settled for such a short time it had already, under the leadership of men such as the Rev. William Shaw, head of the school at Salem, built up a reputation as an educational centre called, with exaggerated pride, 'the Athens of South Africa'. The school was cheap but well run, and it was, to Ma Mary's pleasure, strictly religious. Mary had excellent teachers during her six years there and was happy enough at school. But at Salem and nearby Graham's Town violent hostility was shown to missionaries. Like other mission children, Mary was called, 'white African' and was often lodged during the holidays with unwilling hosts. Shy by nature, she learned at an early age to set her face to hide her feelings.

In 1836, at the age of fifteen, she was once again uprooted and sent with her sister Ann and brother Robert to school at Cape Town, to be trained as an infant teacher. Mrs Moffat had once more made the long journey down from Kuruman, this time alone with the younger children, making a dangerous crossing of the Orange river in flood. She collected Mary, Ann and Robert from school and took them down to Port Elizabeth where they were to take ship for the Cape – the overland journey was too difficult.

Here Mary fell desperately ill; Mrs Moffat wrote to her husband, 'Her symptoms were so violent that she was twice bled, and had to take much medicine.' The other two children were taken on board, but the ship was delayed and Mary recovered enough to be carried in a chair over the sands to a small boat from which she was hauled aboard the sailing ship. 'Mary bore it well,' Mrs Moffat reported composedly to her husband. There was a perilous eleven days' voyage ahead in stormy seas, but they were 'well and in good spirits'. This was the first report of a series of illnesses which might well have been psychosomatic.

Whatever the school was like, the sea air suited her, and Cape Town was pleasant. Certainly her brother

John enjoyed his schooldays there later, watching the troops drilling and the ships below in the harbour. It is possible that at this time Mary, Ann and Robert saw the *Beagle* sail into the harbour from its voyage round the world. It is even possible that they saw the young Charles Darwin, who came ashore and was escorted into the interior by Dr Andrew Smith, whom Mary knew well. For in 1835 she had been recalled from her school in Salem to Kuruman to help her mother when her brother John was born. Ma Mary was seriously ill and Robert Moffat was due to leave Kuruman to accompany a government scientific expedition, led by Dr Smith, into Matabeleland – only Moffat could give the expedition safe conduct to the warlike chief Mzilikatze. Dr Smith saved Ma Mary's life, and reluctantly Robert set out, leaving young Mary in charge.

From extreme youth Mary had learned to shoulder responsibility and had seen the sober reality of missionary life. She had observed the loneliness and isolation of the mission wives, she had watched them endure constant child-bearing in primitive conditions, and she had known the agony of separation from her family. She had also experienced from earliest childhood the difficulties of travel by ox wagon.

In 1839, when she was eighteen, she had expected to return to Kuruman to teach in the school there. So when her parents came down to Cape Town she thought she would be going home with them. It was an emotional reunion with the father she had not seen for so many years, but she would have to wait even longer before she saw Kuruman again. Robert Moffat had brought the manuscript of his great work, the translation of the New Testament into Sechwane, to be printed, but since Cape Town lacked the proper facilities he now decided to take Ma Mary, the six children and their black servants, Sarah Robey and John Mokateri, to England.

The family managed to get berths on a crowded troopship returning to England from India. Life aboard troopships was uncomfortable – they carried horses for transport and cows and poultry for provisions, and at the best of times the din and smell were unbearable. But this was a nightmare voyage. Ma Mary was, at the age of forty-four, pregnant again; the sea, even in harbour, was rough – they were all seasick; and James, the six-year-old, had measles. Amid the tumult Ma Mary gave birth to her ninth child – Elizabeth, known as Bessie. Three days later, James, the most beloved of her children died. Mary, as the eldest daughter, must have borne much of the responsibility for the distressed family on board ship.

It was a bad beginning to what was, for Mary at least, not a happy four and a half years' stay in England. She never forgot the raw cold, nor that the family always seemed to be just outside the glowing warmth which surrounded Robert Moffat, who with his magnificent presence and eloquent oratory took England by storm. Immense audiences listened in rapture while he told them of the thousand campfires beckoning in the dark interior of Africa. Victorian England was ready for missionary heroes, and Robert Moffat was the prophet they wanted.

Moffat's words changed one young man's life. David Livingstone was in London training to be a missionary and, caught by Moffat's eloquence, decided to ask to be sent to join him in Africa. He had worked in a cotton mill in Blantyre on the banks of the Clyde until he was twenty-three. Here he had taught himself Greek and Latin by 'placing the book on a portion of the spinning jenny', thus acquiring that gift of concentration which, he claimed, enabled him to work in Africa amid 'the songs of savages'. Livingstone qualified as a doctor in Glasgow, and studied theology with the London Missionary Society. As he later explained, he chose that organisation because 'it sends neither episcopacy, nor presbyterianism, nor independency, but the gospel of Christ to the heathen'.

Livingstone may have met Mary at this time, but she clearly made no impression on him for the awkward, gruff and graceless young man took no notice of Mrs Moffat's advice that a missionary needed a wife. In any case, at some time during that period Mary was half-engaged to a cousin. Livingstone went ahead to Kuruman and began his work while the Moffats were still in England.

The Moffat children saw little of their father in England. The younger ones were cared for by two kindly spinsters, the Misses Eisdell, while Mary and Ann were lodged with friends. Ma Mary, pregnant yet again, went back to her father's home in Lancashire for the birth of her tenth child, Jane.

When the time came to return home they were all delighted – relieved to escape the gushing of the comfortable ladies who loaded them with unsuitable gifts for their 'sable friends'. Boxes of ball dresses and stiff collars and even a phaeton had to be packed for the voyage. Sarah Robey had become a star turn on missionary platforms and was often away, and John, their other servant was useless; his head had been completely turned by his stay in England. He had become the token African, on whom sentimental ladies lavished their adulation. Mary, helped by her sister Ann, had once more to take charge of the arrangements for their departure.

So, on 30 January 1843, the family embarked in the snow at London Bridge for a rough voyage home. Aptly was their ship named *Fortitude*. They would need it in the year it took them to get back to Kuruman. They also had to suffer the pain of leaving Robert and Helen behind at school. It would be ten years before Mary saw her sister again, and Helen, who married at eighteen, did not see her mother again for twenty-seven years.

*You are as dear to me as ever and will be so long as our lives
are spared*

They sailed into Table Bay on 10 April, but it was
difficult to find enough oxen to haul their massive array
of possessions. Moffat's New Testament, stores and
equipment for the mission station, and bulky gifts as
well as their own trunks and boxes had all accumulated
during the years in England. It took months to organise
the trek back north, and it was December before they
reached the Vaal river – the last river to ford before
home. Then in a cloud of dust, scudding across the
barren veldt, came a horseman. David Livingstone had
raced out to meet them. And if little John Moffat
thought him a queer figure in his home-made suit,
Mary would never see him in a more romantic light.
'Few', wrote Robert Moffat later, 'can conceive of the
hallowed feeling his presence produced, direct from the
station and people to whom all our fondest affections
were bending.'

As the slow wagons rumbled over the brown scrub,
there was time for Mary and Livingstone to get
acquainted; time to stroll ahead of the straining oxen,
time to watch the spectacular sunsets over the rolling
veldt, and time to talk in the starlit nights when Ma
Mary and the girls came down from the wagons to join
the men round the campfire for the evening hymns.

At the end of December the long train of ox wagons
jolted down from the barren hills to the flowery slopes
of Kuruman, where ecstatic black crowds thronged,
singing and leaping in anticipation. Robert Moffat, his
fine head held high and Ma Mary beside him, rode
home in triumph. In spite of himself David Livingstone
was caught up in the excitement, and from that time to
the end of his life his admiration for Moffat never
flagged. This was a family he felt he could happily join.

For Mary it was a moving homecoming, back to the
stream with the skimming swallows, the scented syr-

inga trees and the long-remembered stone house she had left at the age of ten. She quickly adapted to the new life and enjoyed teaching in the Kuruman school, but eagerly awaited the letters that came down to her parents from Livingstone, who had settled at the Mabotsa mission. One day, having rashly joined the villagers on a lion hunt, he was attacked and mauled. His arm was broken; with difficulty he had set it himself, but the wound had not properly healed. The news of this encounter filled her with alarm, and when he came down to Kuruman to see her, with his arm in a sling, she had decided. She would be glad to be married, for living with Ma Mary had its problems. Though her rule was benevolent, she was also, as Livingstone once remarked, 'given to fault-finding'. In the orchard by the stream he proposed. Mary's answer under the almond tree was a swift 'Yes'.

Livingstone returned to Mabotsa to build their house with his own hands, in spite of his crippled arm. He wrote with enthusiasm to Mary:

> The walls are nearly finished, although the dimensions are 52 feet by 20 outside, or about the same size as that in which you now reside . . . If you will not laugh at my drawing, I shall give you the plan . . . It is pretty hard work, and almost enough to drive love out of my head. But it is not situated there; it is in my heart, and won't come out unless you behave so as to quench it . . . You must excuse soiled paper, my hands won't wash clean after dabbling in mud all day and although the above does not contain evidence of it, you are as dear to me as ever and will be so long as our lives are spared.

Ma Mary, meanwhile, was happy to offer advice. Livingstone wrote:

> Give Mother my kindest salutations. I suppose I shall get a lecture from her too about the largeness of the house. If there are too many windows she can just let

me know. I could build them all up in two days and let
the light come down the chimney if that would please.
I'll do anything for peace except fighting for it.

He could not wait to get into his own house. Bachelor
life at Mabotsa had been uncomfortable, and his colleague Roger Edwards was uncongenial. While Livingstone had been cooped up as a lodger in the Edwards's
hut their mutual irritation had grown into a frenetic
hostility. Mrs Edwards couldn't cook and the house
was dirty – in his unmade bed were fleas which 'danced
the reel of Tulochgorum as I drew the clothes over me'.
For her part Mrs Edwards clearly had had enough of
the gruff, awkward Scot who had got himself mauled
by a lion and expected her to clean and bandage the
suppurating wound, crawling with maggots.

To the London Missionary Society director, the Rev.
Arthur Tidman, Livingstone wrote stiffly:

> Various considerations connected with this new sphere
> of labour . . . having led me to the conclusion that it was
> my duty to enter into the marriage relation, I have made
> the necessary arrangements for union with Mary, the
> eldest daughter of Mr Moffat, in the beginning of Janu-
> ary 1845. It was not without much consideration and
> earnest prayer that I came to the above decision and if I
> have not deceived myself I was in some measure guided
> by a desire that the Divine Glory might be promoted in
> my increased usefulness.

Early in the new year they were married at Kuruman,
and in the last week of March they arrived at Mabotsa
to begin their life together.

Missionaries' wives have not time to knit stockings

The name 'Mabotsa' means 'marriage feast', and later
David would remember these days as 'the sweet time',

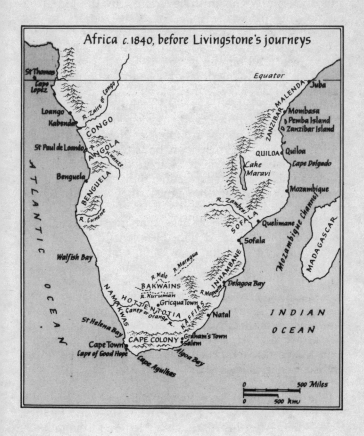

Africa c. 1840, before Livingstone's journeys

but there was in fact little festivity in the early months of their marriage. By day he toiled – building, irrigating and doctoring – and in the evenings, by the guttering candlelight, he wrote long, obsessive letters to his father-in-law. The quarrel with Edwards, caused by such little thorns, festered. Did he criticise Edwards to the natives? Call him an old man? Take for himself the credit for the new mission? Choose the best plot for his garden? It was as well that Mary, as he wrote to his mother, was amiable and good-humoured.

Had it not been for David's restless irritability, Mary could have been happy at Mabotsa. Her infant school, which she held in their own house, thrived and the children loved her. Robert Moffat's daughter had also inherited his talent for gardening; they had 'scotch kale, lettuces and carrots in abundance', they wrote to Kuruman with some pride.

Part of David's trouble was that missionary life in enclosed Mabotsa irked him. He went to his services with a heavy heart, for he was no orator in his own tongue and in this unfamiliar language he made no impact at all. His father-in-law had faced similar difficulties in the early days, but David was appalled at the thought of the years of slow, patient toil that had erected Kuruman. Driven by his dynamic temperament, he decided that Africa needed missionaries who would train native teachers, then leave them and press on to undiscovered fields. Mary would long in vain for a settled home.

Like his mother, Mary was fastidious; she brought order and some peace – and clean sheets – into Livingstone's life. After his marriage his letters to his mother were gentler than they had ever been. Mary was comforting and maternal, reminding him of the warmth of his early life.

> I often remember you, how you used to keep us all cozie and clean. I remember you often assisted me, my dear

Mother, to put on my clothes on dark, cold wintry mornings, and later in life made a good breakfast for me on Monday mornings before I went away down to College. A thousand things rise up in my memory when I think of you. May God bless you.

Desperate to get away from Edwards and to be sole master of his own mission, Livingstone decided to move forty miles north to Chonwane, where the Bakwain tribe had now settled with their chief, Sechele. Livingstone had a high regard for this intelligent man, had taught him to read in two days and hoped that here he could make another Kuruman.

Mary had to be left at Mabotsa while he built yet another house – again with his own hands. She was pregnant and lonely, so her sister Ann came up to look after her, travelling the two hundred miles with only a maid and a couple of wagon boys. Ann returned to Kuruman and, as the dust cloud of her sister's wagon disappeared on the horizon, Mary was left once more alone. And Ann had before her a terrifying journey through lion-haunted hills. 'The oxen had been unyoked, and were grazing close to the waggon,' her brother John later wrote; 'a fire had been lighted and the kettle put on, and the tired travellers were sitting in the peaceful twilight. A sudden rush was heard . . . and one of them [the oxen] fell with a lion on his back, not fifty yards from where Miss Moffat was sitting.' She and her maid leaped into the wagon and lay all night listening in terror as the lion crunched the beast's bones outside.

When Mary's baby was due, Livingstone left his house-building and returned to Mabotsa. In January 1846 Robert was born, and from now on, after the Sechwane custom, Mary was called Ma Robert. After their return to Chonwane together all went well for a while, but their arrival coincided with the beginning of a period of drought. Their garden dried up and was finally destroyed by the wild animals that infested the area.

In September 1846 Mrs Moffat came up from Kuruman, bringing food and comfort. It was with reluctance that she returned to Kuruman, leaving her daughter, son-in-law and grandson to face months of drought and hunger. By March 1847 they were totally exhausted. In low spirits they returned to Kuruman to recuperate and to wait for the birth of Mary's second child. 'Bless me! How lean she is!' the old women at Kuruman cried. 'Has he starved her?' After the birth, David wrote to his mother, 'Have been favoured with a little girl, named Agnes; not a pretty name but it is that of My dear Mother . . . Thanks to God.'

They went back to Chonwane, but it was clear that they could never make it into another Kuruman. Because the springs were drying up, Sechele and the Bakwain were moving to Kolobeng, forty miles north-west of Chonwane, where the stream was said to be never-failing. Livingstone followed and began building a house, his third, once again leaving Mary with the children in deserted Chonwane. 'Mary', wrote Livingstone, 'feels her situation among the ruins a little dreary, and no wonder, for she writes me yesterday that the lions are resuming possession and walk round our house at night.' Understandably she refused to wait for the new house to be finished, and in September 1847 joined Livingstone in a temporary hut.

Kolonbeng was, and still is, a place of exceptional beauty. Low, rounded hills rise from rolling plains that sweep to a limitless horizon. Among the stunted shrubs and long-thorned mimosa bushes the ruins of the Livingstone house remain, and there is still a path leading through the undergrowth to the pile of stones that is all that remains of Mary's school. At first Kolobeng had its attractions, 'the blessed sound of gurgling water' and 'merry midnight frogs' that made 'sweeter music than nightingales'. But October brought intense heat. It was

a difficult year 'in a little hut through which the wind
blew our candles into glorious icicles (as a poet would
say) by night, and in which crowds of flies continually
settled on the eyes of our poor little brats by day.' Mary
and the children were once again ill, so, even before it
was finished, they moved into their square stonehouse
among the round huts of the Backwain. At least now
they had some protection from the lions and jackals –
Livingstone called the latter wolves – that prowled
around. Livingstone wrote:

> I am still making doors for it. A big wolf came the night
> before last and took away a buffalo's skin from the door.
> Mary wanted me to go and see whether the room door
> were fastened, but . . . I advised her to take a fork in her
> hand and go herself, as I was too comfortably situated
> to do anything of the sort. HA !

There would be many times in their lives when Mary's
courage drove the wolf from the door.

It was the third home for Mary, and perhaps the only
settled one she would ever have. At last she began to
acquire possessions: a desk, even a sofa with 'air cush-
ions' – Livingstone, as he sent for it, was astounded by
their 'awful extravagance. What next!' Not that Mary
had much time to relax on her sofa. Life at Kolobeng
was hard. She had not been well since Robert's birth,
and since then she had been constantly on the move.
At Chonwane there had been weeks 'itinerating' to
neighbouring tribes by slow, jolting ox wagon with an
increasingly restless husband. Yet Mary found time to
teach, and here at Kolobeng she had a new school to
start. Sechele and his young wives were their best
pupils and were becoming close friends. And even if
they did not make much headway with their religious
mission – David was, after all, a poor preacher – her
school was to be a great success. 'The children love her,'

he wrote to his brother Charles in America, 'and so do
I!' She deserved his love.

School began in the early morning and finished at
eleven. Then came domestic chores. Mary brought in
Bakwain girls and trained them; once they were profi-
cient, she sent them back to the village and began over
again with new ones. Like her mother, she was an
efficient housekeeper; visiting hunters wrote with admiration of their well-run home and Mrs Livingstone's
delicious home-made bread. It was baked – as Livingstone was proud to point out – in his patent stove, a
hollowed-out anthill for which he had made a door. He
told his sisters:

Shocking! Adams Rib

> My rib bakes all our bread, and I built an oven for her
> one morning. We had an anthill near, so having made
> an iron door we made a large hole in the anthill and put
> on the door, and then we had a good oven in a
> twinkling. Previously we baked in a flat-bottomed pot,
> which, by the by, you may do by putting coals on the lid
> as well as under.

Livingstone sometimes allowed himself a rest in the
afternoon, but Mary more often than not toiled up and
down the hill in the broiling sun to the school or to the
women's sewing class. It is not surprising that there are
few letters from Mary – an occasional postscript scribbled on David's letters, or a brief message. But she was
glad to thank Livingstone's sisters in Scotland for bon-
nets sent from Agnes and Janet's hatshop in Hamilton,
near Glasgow, and, though she had no time for vanity,
a tartan shawl gave her great pleasure. Their clothes,
sent from tailors in Hamilton, had to be tough and
thornproof – Mary's needle had to be pushed hard into
sailcloth and strong calico. 'Missionaries' wives have
not time to knit stockings,' she scribbled on one of
David's letters to his sisters, 'they are domestic
drudges.'

They had not been long at Kolobeng before the sound of the musical frogs ceased. The springs in which they had placed so much hope began to dry up, and the whole area was stricken by drought. By January 1849 a fierce sun had withered their corn; there were no vegetables, and although Sechele supplied them with meat, 'breast of young buffalo' or 'that of the cameleopard', had it not been for supplies from the Moffats at Kuruman they would have starved. Thin and ill, Mary gave up her school – the Bakwain children in any case were away searching for food. She was expecting her third child. Livingstone thought with longing of the new chloroform that Queen Victoria was trying – even in this remote station he kept in touch, through the *Lancet*, with medical news; his library, too, was well stocked with books, sent from Hamilton or borrowed from Kuruman. In January 1849 he wrote to Moffat:

Wish I had some chloroform. From the accounts I see of its operation I expect the old ladies will be wishing they could begin again. It is uniformly safe for both mother and child and the recovery is much accelerated. It is much more speedy in its operation than ether, and has not any of the disagreeable effects of that drug. Half a teaspoonful sprinkled on a handkerchief and held to the nose is all that is required. There is no lividity, no coughing, but a calm and gentle sleep, and the mothers will scarcely believe when they awaken that they have a child. Should have attempted to make some by a makeshift retort, but fear the heat is too great here and it is very volatile. Could we not procure some chloral from England and a retort? Professor Simpson of Edinburgh had used it in 50 cases with entire success.

But, though she had been starved during her pregnancy, Mary came through well. Thomas Steele was born on 7 March after 'only three hours' labour' and without any of the usual complications. In a fortnight, as Livingstone reported to Robert and Ma Mary, she was at church for the baby's christening.

Domestic difficulties and drought were not their only problems. To Livingstone's chagrin the tribal rainmakers sometimes achieved results. A charcoal made of 'burned bats . . . jackal's livers, baboon's and lion's hearts . . . and the bowels of old cows' or pounded roots 'converted into smoke' did the trick, and rain descended. The Backwain knew perfectly well why they were afflicted now. Sechele had caught the Christian madness, and would not play the chief's part in their rainmaker's ceremonies. Why else would the rain pour down on the heathen tribes on the distant hills while at Kolobeng there was not a drop? After Tom's birth, it was true, rain fell, but by April the heat was as intense as ever, and had it not been for the locusts they would have starved. For six months the people lived on them. They were 'rather like shrimps', Livingstone wrote without enthusiasm.

For some time Livingstone had found the tribe unreceptive, and in April the worst blow fell. Sechele, their model pupil and only true convert, had, with much anguish, put away his young wives and reluctantly accepted his ugly and disagreeable senior wife as his only partner. Finding it difficult to remember to be faithful to one, Sechele visited a pretty young ex-wife in her hut. When she became pregnant, Livingstone felt compelled to ban him 'for a season' from communion. All this was totally incomprehensible to the Bakwain and cruel to the young wives who had to return in disgrace to their fathers' kraals. They were Mary's friends, she could speak their language 'like a native', Livingstone said, and she sympathised with their predicament: Victorian morality was so inappropriate here. What would become now of the rejected wives?

Yet another worry was that Kolobeng was under constant threat of attack by the Boers. By 1834 England had made slavery illegal in her colonies, and those

Dutch settlers who resented their loss of freedom to make slaves packed their ox wagons and trekked beyond the Orange river. From now on many of them would make miserable the lives of missionaries in their path, believing that it was here at the mission stations that the dangerous doctrines of racial equality were fostered, doctrines which would destroy their way of life. The Boers' real fear was that missionaries such as Livingstone and Moffat were supplying their African friends with guns. And though Livingstone denied it, it was true that missionaries often mended guns for the chiefs and gave them as presents, or in exchange for food, protection, or even ivory.

So the Boers eyed Livingstone and Moffat warily. Kuruman was tempting, fertile; but Moffat was too powerful – his friendship with the dreaded chief of the Matabele and his legendary courage in the defence of Kuruman in 1824 made him a difficult target. Kolobeng was more vulnerable, even if Mary was a Moffat – the Boers kept watch, waiting for an opportunity. Once again, Livingstone felt hemmed in. To the west was the Kalahari desert, on the east the Boers prevented missionary activity, and south lay discovered country. God had shut all other roads. Now He was guiding him north. Hunters and tribesmen had brought him news of a great lake and, further north, of a legendary chief, Sebituane, who ruled the Makololo people and a vast kingdom. Sechele, whose life Sebituane had once saved, was full of enthusiasm for the wise old chief and anxious to visit him. A hunter, William Cotton Oswell, proposed that Livingstone should accompany him on an expedition towards the great lake. Disheartened by the setbacks that were impeding his work at Kolobeng, he readily agreed. His missionary zeal was diminishing, though his faith in his own mission drove him as hard as ever.

Oswell was at this time on leave from the Madras Civil Service, recuperating after a serious illness. He

was rich and brave – his courage as a hunter was a
legend among the Africans. His gentleness and sincerity
charmed Mary, and reluctanty she agreed that she
would go to Kuruman while Livingstone went exploring
across the Kalahari.

At Kuruman the children were no problem – her
young sisters, Bessie and Jane, looked after them; they
had dolls' tea parties with grandma's miniature teaset,
and toys arrived from their grandparents in Scotland –
a barking dog, a toy cart. Ma Mary enjoyed having her
grandchildren. One of them remembered her always
with a child on her knee, gently stroking the little bare
feet. Thomas, the baby, born in such lean times, would
always be delicate. Agnes was a happy child, laughing,
her father wrote, before she opened her eyes in the
morning. But Robert must have found Ma Mary's strict
discipline irksome. From early days he had been a little
difficult – life had not been easy as the one little white
boy among the sea of black faces, and he was constantly
switching from English into Sechwane. As a small boy,
his father once wrote, he had been brave – but then
something or someone had frightened him, and after
that he always ran away from the oxen and panicked
the other two children.

So Livingstone set off in search of the lake. His
success brought him fame, and for the discovery of
Lake Ngami twenty-five guineas from the Royal Geographical Society. Until that time it had been assumed
that the centre of Africa was a burning desert, but here
on the shores of Lake Ngami the expedition heard of a
country beyond, where great rivers flowed through
forests of gigantic trees. But there were also reports of
extensive slave-trading by the Arabs, whose captives
were taken to the east coast and sold in the slave
markets of Zanzibar.

It was at this point that Livingstone changed. Once,
he had hoped to set up centres of missionary activity
from which native teachers would go as Christian

agents to the surrounding country. Now there came a new vision, appealing both to his idealism and to his restless temperament. He would explore the country to the north, and find a route through to either the west coast or the east which would lead into this new-found, fertile land, where missionaries could settle and where they would be out of reach of the menacing Boers. Above all, he was now determined to root out the slave trade at its source. This was his new mission.

Mary and the children, meanwhile, were regaining their strength at Kuruman; but good food and care could not totally restore her. The plump and placid girl who had left home in 1845 was thin, weary and exhausted, and perhaps in that state could not take her mother's dominating presence. In October she went back to Kolobeng with the children to find that Livingstone had not yet returned. They suffered two months alone, then, ill and desperate, she sent an anguished message north to hurry him home. He thought it important enough to travel on a Sunday, normally unthinkable for a religious Scot.

The discovery of the river Zouga had excited Livingstone more than that of Lake Ngami. He was a man for restless rivers, not enclosed lakes. 'It is a glorious river,' he wrote to a friend, 'you never saw anything so grand. The banks are extremely beautiful, lined with gigantic trees . . . and then the Bukoba in their canoes – did I not enjoy sailing in them? Remember how long I have been in a parched-up land and answer.' He planned to return the following year, sending Mary to Kuruman.

When the time came, however, Mary baulked at the idea of a year at Kuruman, though to stay at Kolobeng was impossible. The Bakwain were on the move, searching for land where no missionary would dry up the heavens. Without their protection she would be vulnerable to an attack by the Boers. The Kalahari, she thought, could not be much worse than Kolobeng, withered under an angry sun, where there was not a single flower and the grass crumbled to powder in one's hand. Mary had caught Livingstone's enthusiasm. 'The emotions', he later wrote, 'caused by the magnificent prospects of the new country . . . might subject me to the charge of enthusiasm, a charge which I wished I deserved, as nothing good or great has ever been accomplished in the world without it.' From this time onwards an obsessive urge to explore took hold of him. God, he told himself, was pointing the way. And Mary accepted this, following the man whose fate it was to be driven 'beyond other men's lines'.

I must again wend my weary way into the far Interior,
perhaps to be confined in the field

So, in April 1850, he and Sechele set off on the long trail, and this time Mary and the family went too. Robert was four, Agnes three, and Tom barely a year old. Ahead, the scrub stretched flat and featureless to a horizon invisible in the immense distance. There was often no track, and at two miles an hour the journey seemed interminable. But in spite of the difficulties, there was much that was agreeable in their gypsy life. She could sit with the baby high on the mattresses, while the other two played in the wagon, as Mary had done as a child, or trotted with their father along the dusty track. 'We were happy as a family,' Livingstone wrote; and they were happier still to reach the river and the shade of tall trees.

But, as they pushed their way along the river bank, news came of a party of traders ahead of them in great distress. Sam Edwards, known as 'Far Interior Sam', the son of his old colleague and adversary, was down with fever; Wilson, his companion, was dangerously ill; and a young artist had died. Mary and Livingstone nursed the stricken party to health. The local chief, unwilling to open up his territory, made difficulties.

But, attracted by Livingstone's favourite gun, he was finally prepared to look after Mary, who, with the children, agreed to remain with the wagons by the river while Livingstone pushed ahead in search of Sebituane.

Mary, wrote Livingstone, was 'a heroine', reminding him of her father. She had need of courage, for she was pregnant yet again and her time was nearly come. But here, by the river, at least there was water and shade and the promise of food. She understood the native dialect, and she had her African girls to help her. Livingstone took the family to see Lake Ngami and watched with delight while the children 'paidled [sic] like ducks'. But the next day Tom and Agnes contracted fever and their parents decided to return to Kolobeng. With Livingstone's patent remedies – his 'rousers', as he called his fever pills – the children got better, though Mary would never quite recover from the strain.

Her baby was born at Kolobeng in August, 'a tiny thing no bigger than Ma Mary's middle finger,' she wrote. But six weeks later the Moffats heard that

> our sweet little girl with blue eyes was taken from us to join the company of the redeemed of whom she never heard. It is wonderful how soon the affections twine round a little stranger. We felt her loss keenly. We could not apply remedies to one so young except the simplest. She uttered a piercing cry, previous to expiring, and then went away to see the King in his beauty and the land – the glorious land and its inhabitants.

She was buried among the mimosa trees; they marked her grave and carried to the end of their days the memory of that piercing cry. Elizabeth's grave is still there, but the thorn bushes have closed over it.

This was the nadir. They had little food, Kolobeng was deserted, and when the heavens opened it was to batter their windows with rocks of hail. Livingstone, himself sick and dispirited, did not have the energy to

mend the broken windows – good ventilation, he
morosely observed. But, worst of all, Mary developed
Bell's palsy, a paralysis of the face, and for long afterwards she suffered severe headaches and recurring pain
in her side. Ma Mary came to the rescue, grumbled at
the broken panes, packed them into the wagon and
brought them back to Kuruman. Here, though all the
surrounding country was stricken by drought, the
stream still ran clean and cool from its deep, bat-
haunted caves.

In time, Ma Mary was able to send them back to
Kolobeng 'with roses in their cheeks'. Mary's face was
still partially paralysed, but Livingstone was eager to go
once more across the desert to the great rivers and lakes
of the north. The Zouga must lead – either to east or
west – to the sea, and he must be the first to open up
God's highway. Ma Mary feared that the explorer was
taking over the missionary, though, with unusual reti-
cence, she did not speak out while they were at Kuruman. But when in April 1851 she heard that Mary, who
was yet again expecting a baby, was proposing to go
with him, she exploded.

Before you left the Kuruman I did all I dared to do to
broach the subject of your intended journey, and thus
bring on a candid discussion, more especially with
regard to Mary's accompanying you with those dear
children. But seeing how averse you and Father were to
speak about it, and the hope that you would never be
guilty of such temerity (after the dangers they escaped
last year), I too timidly shrunk from what I ought to
have had the courage to do. Mary had told me all along
that should she be pregnant you would not take her, but
let her come out here after you were fairly off. Though I
suspected at the end that she began to falter in this
resolution, still I hoped it would never take place, i.e.
her going with you, and looked and longed for things
transpiring to prevent it. But to my dismay I now get a
letter, in which she writes, 'I must again wend my weary

way into the far Interior, perhaps to be confined in the field?' O Livingstone, what do you mean? Was it not enough that you lost one lovely babe, and scarcely saved the others, while the mother came home threatened with Paralysis? And will you again expose her & them in those sickly regions on an *exploring* expedition? All the world would condemn the cruelty of the thing to say nothing of the indecorousness of it. A pregnant woman with three little children trailing about with a company of the other sex, through the wilds of Africa, among savage men and beasts! Had you *found a place* to which you wished to go and commence missionary operations, the case would be altered. Not one word would I say, were it to the mountains of the moon. But to go with an exploring party, the thing is preposterous. I remain yours in great perturbation. M. Moffat.

But Mary was resigned. She could not spend a year under Ma Mary's dominant rule, she could not stay at Kolobeng, and at least on the trail Livingstone would help with the other children and be there with his medicine chest when her time came. So once more she accepted that she must 'wend my weary way', and they set off. This time, however, thanks to Oswell, it was a well-heeled expedition: he provided the best equipment and went on in advance to open up the wells. Sechele, the Bakwain chief, did not accompany them this time.

They followed their old trail, through flat scrub land until they came to the Kalahari. As the weary ox team dragged ever more slowly through the heavy red sand, 'it was', Livingstone wrote, 'as bleak a land as I have ever seen'. In the shadeless, featureless landscape even Shobo, their merry Bushman guide, grew disoriented and despaired. They lost track of Oswell and his party and were running dangerously short of water. Then their spirits lifted when the quickening oxen picked up the spoor of rhinoceros, and the men set them loose to follow the trail that must lead to water. As their dust clouds disappeared on the horizon, the family settled in the shade under the wagon to wait.

For four days there was no sign, no sound. It was a dead land – no bird, not even an insect, stirred. Their water was nearly gone – the last bottle had been spilt. The children cried themselves to sleep, and Livingstone wrote:

> This was a bitterly anxious night; and next morning, the less there was of water, the more thirsty the little rogues became. The idea of them perishing before our eyes was terrible; it would have been a relief to have been reproached with being the entire cause of the catastrophe, but not one syllable of upbraiding was uttered by their mother, though the tearful eye told the agony within.

When, to their 'inexpressible relief', on the fifth day the men returned with water, their decision had been taken. Never again must they put the children in such danger. If they got through this expedition, Mary must take them to Britain.

Eventually they reached the welcome shade of the great trees along the Chobe river. This time Sebituane, the chief of the Makololo, had come to the edge of his territory to meet them. Leaving Mary and the children with the wagons, Livingstone and Oswell canoed up the river for thirty miles to meet him, and brought him back to meet her. The daughter of Moffat was of great interest to Sebituane, for was not Moffat the bosom friend of his mortal enemy – the formidable chief of the Matabele, Mzilikatze? If Livingstone and his family settled with him they would bring immunity, for Mzilikatze would not endanger the life of Moffat's daughter. The meeting was historic. It was Mary's presence that had made possible the first step towards her father's dream – that his family should unite the two warring tribes, the Makololo and the Matabele, and bring peace to the heart of Africa.

Alas, the friendship between Livingstone and Sebituane, deep and immediate though it was, was short-lived. Within two weeks of their meeting Sebituane was dead. Livingstone's grief was profound: 'Poor Sebituane,' he later wrote, 'my heart bleeds for thee . . . I will weep for thee till the day of my death.'

Now they would have to wait upon Sebituane's heir – a woman – to get permission to settle in her territory. Livingstone, who could be so prickly and abrupt with his own people, showed delicacy and patience with Africans. For two months they waited on the reedy banks of the Chobe. Meanwhile he and Oswell explored the surrounding country on horseback – horses were not susceptible to tsetse fly – and discovered that it was too fever-haunted and swampy for a mission settlement. But he and Oswell discovered the Sesheke river, the main branch of the Zambesi, broad and rolling like the sea. And he sent to his father-in-law the first reports of the distant waterfall, called by the natives Mosewatunya, 'The Smoke That Thunders'. Livingstone would later see it for himself and name it Victoria Falls.

These months cannot have been easy for Mary, left alone with her children for much of the time. She was still suffering from severe headaches and her baby was almost due. Only the memory of parched Kolobeng would have reconciled her to the discomfort. Here at least she would watch Robert, Agnes and Tom shouting and laughing and paddling in the river.

Her third son was born on the return journey, in the shade of a thorn tree on the banks of the Zouga river. 'Never had an easier or better time of it,' Livingstone reported. There would have been no fuss, no cries during labour. Mary had been brought up among a tribe where women do not cry – not even in childbirth. So Oswell was puzzled when Livingstone insisted that they waited for a few days in obviously unsuitable terrain, and it took some time to extract the explanation

that Mrs Livingstone had had a little son the previous
night. Livingstone wanted to call the baby Zouga, but,
he wrote, 'the mother rebelled'. Instead he was called
Oswell, after their benefactor and friend – though for
many years the child kept the nickname Zouga. The
journey back was easier – rain had brought a miraculous
crop of wild melons to the desert – and they reached
Kolobeng in good spirits. Livingstone wrote: 'Thomas
had fever three times but is now as merry as possible
and getting fat. Little Zouga is dancing in his mother's
arms.'

*The mark of Cain is on your foreheads. Your father is a
missionary*

Having made the decision that Mary and the children
must go to England, the family did not stay in Kolobeng
but made for Kuruman. There, too, they rested only
long enough to prepare for the tedious and lengthy
journey to the Cape.

On a Monday morning in mid-March 1852 the Livingstones' dusty wagon rolled up to the mission house in
Cape Town. They had been on the trail for nearly a
year, with just short breaks at Kolobeng, Kuruman and
Gricqua Town. The children were ragged and shaggy-
haired, and Mary and Livingstone looked like gypsies.
They spoke English with difficulty, and found even
using stairs a strange experience. Fortunately, with
characteristic sensitivity Oswell had gone on ahead and
bought new outfits for them at a smart store in Cape
Town, so that Mary could face the fashionably dressed
ladies. Indeed, settled for six weeks in a comfortable
house with a large garden on a hill overlooking the sea,
Mary blossomed. She knew Cape Town and had friends
there; rested and in her new clothes she was, her
husband wrote, 'never better'.

Livingstone, on the other hand, who had a swollen
uvula which was giving him much trouble, became
increasingly depressed. Back at Kuruman he had tried
to persuade his father-in-law to cut off the end of the
uvula with a pair of scissors. Moffat, brave man though
he was, refused. Livingstone would have to have an
operation in Cape Town.

He now had time to appreciate the wife and children
to whom he was soon to bid farewell. He could see no
alternative but separation for a number of reasons,
quite apart from the one that had been revealed to
them so horrifyingly in the burning Kalahari. If they
stayed in Africa the children would, he thought, be
increasingly exposed to the evil influences of their
heathen friends, 'those sad captives of sin and Satan
who are the victims of the degradation of ages'. And,
as he pointed out in a letter to the Rev. A. Tidman at
the London Missionary Society, separation was the
only way to prevent 'the frequent confinements which,
notwithstanding the preaching of Dr Malthus and Miss
Martineau, periodically prevail'. But to lose them, he
wrote, was like 'tearing out his bowels'. The children
asked: 'When shall we return to Kolobeng . . . When
to Kuruman?' only to receive the reply: 'Never . . . the
mark of Cain is on your foreheads. Your father is a
missionary.'

There is no doubt of Livingstone's deep love and
admiration for Mary, who on the Chobe had been, as
he wrote to her father, 'a heroine'. When they halted
on their way south at Gricqua Town he could not help
remarking how much better his wife was than other
mission wives.

Mary had earned that admiration. In her seven years
of marriage she had borne five children, one of whom
died. She had travelled thousands of miles by ox
wagon across deserts hitherto believed impassable for
white men. She had journeyed through swamps and

forests into the deep interior, to regions where no white woman had been before, and on those journeys she had been accompanied by a young family and almost continuously pregnant. Throughout she had remained calm, courageous and competent. Visiting officers from the Indian Army remembered her bravery. Captain Webb, who had known them at Kolobeng in the autumn of 1851, wrote in glowing terms of the 'sturdy little dark-haired lady with the bright, kind smile' who was 'scrupulously neat and tidy in her dress and person even when journeying'. He never forgot the composure with which she had smothered a scorpion with a pillow, holding it in place until Livingstone came to the rescue, nor her self-command when a dangerous, six-inch centipede was observed on her bare arm. With a 'quiet word of reassurance she stood perfectly still till it reached her dress and then shook it off'. Webb thought it the most surprising example of nerve in a woman.

Once, as a little girl of ten, she had been praised for her cool-headedness when rescued from an overturned wagon. She had waited, rolled up in a mattress and protecting her baby brother, until she was found. The dread of experiencing a similar accident was all her life a recurring nightmare. But when it happened on the journey of 1851, even though she was pregnant at the time, she could calmly say, 'Is that all?' After her death Oswell wrote,

After spending two years in the company of Mrs Livingstone I am qualified to speak of her courage, her devoted attention to her husband, and her unvarying kindness to myself. In regions thousands of miles away from a white person she cared for her children and encouraged the prosecution of the expedition. To myself she ministered many acts of kindness with a delicacy and consideration that only a woman can exhibit.

But that composed exterior hid a sensitive, shy woman often near to breaking point, as was evident from her recurring headaches and paralysis. The Mary Livingstone who left Africa in 1852 was therefore an even more courageous woman than her admirers realised.

She left behind a husband who loved her deeply. In spite of all their difficulties their marriage was a happy one. And it was not just, as Ma Mary later wrote, that they were 'comfortable together'. During the two months he spent at Cape Town Livingstone wrote by almost every mail, and for that introverted Scot they were passionate letters.

Capetown
5 May 1852

My dearest Mary,

How I miss you now and the dear children! My heart yearns incessantly over you. How many thoughts of the past crowd into my mind! I feel as if I would treat you all much more tenderly and lovingly than ever. You have been a great blessing to me. You attended to my comfort in many, many ways. May God bless you for all your kindnesses! I see no face now to be compared with that sunburnt one which has so often greeted me with its kind looks. Let us do our duty to our Saviour and we shall meet again. I wish that time were now. You may read the letters over again which I wrote at Mabotsa, the sweet time you know. As I told you before, I tell you again, they are true, true; there is not a bit of hypocrisy in them. I never show all my feelings; but I can say truly my dearest, that I loved you when I married you, and the longer I lived with you I loved you the better.

He went on to remind her to 'Love Him more and more and diffuse His love among the children.' Mary would not have found the moralising odd – it was their language, and the language of the time.

*Do you think I·would reproach you with the sorrows that I
bore?*

While Livingstone was making his way back to Kuruman, Mary was on the high seas with four children and
no help: her two African girls had come down to the
Cape with her, but had returned with Livingstone. One
hopes that Livingstone was right in thinking that the
Indian Army officers' wives returning home would be
helpful. Mary had last been in England in the days of
sail and stagecoaches; now she landed in the hubbub of
the age of steam and railways. For one accustomed to
travelling – at two miles an hour – thousands of miles
in clear air and desert silence, the cultural shock was
immense.

The Rev. Tidman made sure she was met and seen
off on the train to Manchester, where she broke her
journey to see her mother's friends. Then, on a raw
October day, she struggled on by rail to Glasgow,
burdened with bags and boxes and her young family.
Oswell was barely a year old, Tom only three, and
though Agnes was a happy little girl, Robert was always
a handful.

Livingstone's parents had moved to a comfortable
little house in Hamilton. His brother John was in
Canada, and Charles was a pastor in America. Now
that his parents were, as he facetiously wrote, 'Laird
and Lairdess . . . landed proprietors', he had trusted
that they could look after the family until Mary could
find a cottage.

But life in the little grey village of Hamilton was a
disaster from the start. The children, accustomed to the
freedom of the veldt, did not take kindly to the constraints imposed by a stern grandfather and spinster
aunts. But they adapted more easily than Mary. She
would certainly have found the Livingstones' broad
Scots accent incomprehensible, and the bitter cold of
Hamilton brought on her paralysis again. And they,

who had expected an impressive daughter of the great Moffat, found a dark, dumpy little lady with a stiff manner and a foreign accent. Unaccustomed to dealing with money, she was soon penniless. Livingstone's letter to little Tom must have caused her a wry smile: 'Tell mamma that she is to buy plenty of meat for you in cold weather to make you warm, and you must take care not to get wet.' How could she have kept them dry? This year was exceptionally rainy, and under the leaden sky of Hamilton Mary longed for the African sun.

Her letters to the Rev. Tidman were at first competent and businesslike. She was given thirty pounds a quarter, a generous allowance, the directors considered.

6 Almada Street
October 1852

Dear Sir,

As you kindly gave me permission to write to you I now sit down to let you know how I am situated and to tell you of my difficulties. My health has been very poor since my arrival in Scotland but I am now a little better. We are in lodgings at £15 per quarter, independent of food and other expenses. Now that will never do for me. There is a cottage being built which the owner will let me have at £7 the year, but it is not furnished, which I shall have to do, my parents are unable to assist me at present. The furnishing of the cottage will be £20 at least if it is ever so plain and simple. My friends will buy it from me when I leave. I shall at present give you an account of the £30 I received from you. First I paid £5 for custom house dues. The journey from London to Manchester and Scotland including luggage, £12. And £5 for house rent and £2 for other expenses. Now there are only £5 left. This will be sufficient for me this October. The reason I am so explicit is this, that you may see how the money has gone. Now I shall require to get winter clothing for the rest of the family. Therefore I think it will be necessary to let me have £26 of the next quarter's

allowance for the house. I trust you will be satisfied with
the explanation I have given of my affairs. If you should
think of any other plan your advice will be thankfully
received.

The following month, writing from her new address at
46 Almada Street, she was clearly homesick for Africa.

> 18 November 1852
> I just write a few lines to ask if you could kindly favour
> me with a missionary chronicle every month, it is very
> difficult to get it here. The cold is exceedingly severe but
> the children seem to bear it well, better than we did
> when we first visited this country, the only one suffers
> from it is myself. Have you heard anything of Mr L this
> mail? I hope he is far in his travels in Sebituane's
> country. I have had some trouble in procuring lodgings
> but I have at last succeeded in getting one room at £5 a
> year.

But to bring up four children in one room was difficult,
and that winter was a particularly hard one.

From the beginning the Livingstones had found her
strange and difficult. During the winter they quarrelled;
and in January Mary left bleak Scotland without telling
her father-in-law where she was going. Disturbed, Neil
Livingstone wrote to the directors of the London Missionary Society asking if they knew where Mary and
the children were. He explained that on three separate
occasions Mary had forbidden the children to speak to
them, though 'we do love them dearly'.

Mary had in fact gone to Hackney, then a respectable
village on the outskirts of London with a mixed population of shopkeepers, bank managers and City workers; it is likely that she had known it on her previous
visit. At that time it was a centre of Noncomformity,
and many of her father's friends were there. But Mary
was finding it difficult to manage on her allowance: not
many people were ready to take in a penniless stranger
with four children. There were in these years too many

refugees flooding into London from a Europe torn by revolution. From now on her letters became increasingly desperate. In February she again asked the directors for an advance on her allowance. 'I trust', she wrote, 'you will not refuse as I have no-one else to look to.' In fact she had a sister, Helen, who had stayed behind in England when the rest of the family went back to Africa, and who at eighteen had married a silk merchant named James Vavassour. But Helen, who was already taking care of her two youngest sisters in her large, rambling, turreted house at Knockholt in Kent, presumably did not want to take in Mary and her four children.

So the summer was spent in poverty in Hackney. In great anxiety, she wrote to the directors enclosing her accounts. Unused to money and to the dirt of London, she incurred expenditure such as a ten pound bill from a laundress which would have been unthinkable in Africa, where clothes were beaten on stones by the river and dried in the blazing sun.

Finally, on the verge of a breakdown, she returned to her mother's friends in the Manchester area. Here one of them took charge and arranged for her to have room and board in a village outside Manchester. Even so, she found Lancashire as expensive as London and by November she was at the end of her tether. She sent Agnes to another of her mother's friends, Miss Braithwaite, at Kendal, and later she and Oswell followed. Mary was now penniless, and Miss Braithwaite had to pay their fares to Kendal. The importance to Mary of the Braithwaites, a Quaker family, during this period cannot be underestimated. Their doctor treated her without payment, they gave her clothes and money, and they took charge of the children, whom they sent to the Quaker school. Years later Livingstone wrote that the Quakers were very good with 'wayward boys like Robert'.

Old Mrs Braithwaite was perhaps one of the few

women who could really understand Mary's problems. As a young wife she too had left her children and husband to follow her 'inner light' in the wilds of America, had travelled with her Quaker message hundreds of miles alone on horseback. Now, in her old age, she and her husband presided over a successful family. Their son, Charles, a lawyer, was of great assistance both to Mary and later to Livingstone; and their daughter Anna, sweet-natured and crippled, looked after Mary and the children during their worst times. As the rain swept unceasingly over the little grey market town Mary could relax in their comfortable house. And now she could break down. We shall probably never know the nature or course of Mary's illness, but it is not difficult to guess. Livingstone had feared that the paralysis of her face indicated chronic disorder. The accumulated stress of years of privation, the cultural shock and bitter chill of Scotland, the worries over the children – Tom's recurring illness, Robert's wildness – were enough to break any woman. Then, unfamiliar as she was with money, the worry of poverty in a land where African-style hospitality was rare, and to be without help when she had been used to servants in Africa, were additional burdens. She was also increasingly disturbed by the scepticism and religious controversy of the period. Even the Quakers of Kendal were riven by dissension. It was a far cry from her parents' simple, certain faith. Above all, she who had been a crown princess among the Africans had no place in Victorian society.

For two months she was severely ill, and in January 1854 the doctor declared that she would not be perfectly restored until May, when she expected to return to Africa. Gradually she recovered. When the incessant rain ceased and the spring came she could walk up Kendal's narrow lanes and look out over the grey stone walls to the wide, lakeland landscape that so reminded her of the country round Kolobeng. And when from the hilltop she saw the gleam of the river winding to the distant sea she ached for her husband and Africa.

She hoped that Livingstone could be at the Cape to meet her in August. But letters from Africa took months to reach her and brought little comfort. They carried news of his return to Kolobeng, of an attack by the Boers in November and the sacking of their house. Her desk, their books, their furniture – everything had been destroyed. It was the only real home she had had in their married life, and that news must have been the last straw in a dreadful year.

She learned that he had pushed his way from Linyanti in the centre of Africa to the west coast. But, instead of sailing down the west coast to meet her at Cape Town, he intended to attempt to cross Africa again and follow the course of the Zambesi to the sea on the east coast.

Not even the Braithwaites could help her now. In the summer of 1854 she took rooms near Epsom, where an old friend, Miss Eisdell, lived; desperate for money, she wrote from here to Tidman asking for five pounds, 'as I have now set up house'. For the rest of the summer her letters were broken and tear-stained. The 'gallant little lady' who had so impressed the hunters in Africa had completely disintegrated. Those who had known her then would not have recognised her as the same woman.

By now she knew that she would have to stay in England until Livingstone returned from his expedition. Somehow she got through the year, and when Tidman wrote to Livingstone in August 1855 he could report that he had seen Mrs Livingstone in good health, and added, with masterly understatement, 'Of course she is looking forward to your return.'

Livingstone's reappearance on 20 May 1856 on the east coast at Quelimane was an immense relief. Yet the slow pace of Victorian travel meant that it was six months before she travelled to Southampton to meet him on his return. Unfortunately he arrived at London Bridge; his ship had broken down and he had come overland by express train to Paris and London. So Mary had to wait yet one more lonely night for their reunion on 11 December.

The news of his return from the interior had inspired her to write this poignant verse:

A hundred thousand welcomes, and it's time for you to come
From the far land of the foreigner, to your country and your home.
Oh, long as we were parted, ever since you went away,
I never passed an easy night, or knew an easy day.

Do you think I would reproach you with the sorrows that I bore?
Since the sorrow is all over now I have you here once more,
And there's nothing but the gladness and the love within my heart,
And hope so sweet and certain that never again we'll part.

A hundred thousand welcomes! How my heart is gushing o'er
With the love and joy and wonder just to see your face once more.
How did I live without you all those long years of woe?
It seems as if t'would kill me to be parted from you now.

You'll never part me darling, there's a promise in your eye:
I may tend you while I'm living, you will watch me when I die.
And if death but kindly lead me to the blessed home on high,
What a hundred thousand welcomes will await you in the sky!

Glad I am that I am to be accompanied by my guardian angel

Their next two years in England were much like those that Mary had spent as a girl in the shadow of her father's fame, but from time to time she was thrust into the full glare of publicity. On 15 December 1856, when Livingstone was presented with the Royal Geographical Society's Victoria Medal, Oswell and Colonel Steele, Livingstone's old friends from Africa, praised Mary for her great kindness and hospitality to travellers in the wilderness. Now Mary, who for years had been invisible, moved into the limelight. At the end of the meeting Lord Shaftesbury spoke in her honour:

> That lady was born with one distinguished name, which she has changed for another. She was born a Moffat, and she became a Livingstone. She cheered the early part of our friend's career by her spirit, her counsel and her society. Afterwards, when she reached this country, she passed many years with her children in solitude and anxiety, suffering the greatest fears for the welfare of her husband, and yet enduring all with patience and resignation, and even joy, because she had surrendered her best feelings, and a sacrifice of her own private interests to the advancement of civilization and the great interests of Christianity.

The Livingstones made a brief visit to Hamilton, where, as David's sisters told his biographer, Blaikie, 'his father's empty chair deeply affected him'. Neil Livingstone had died while his son was making his way back to England, and the quarrel with Mary seems to have died with him. Certainly David's sisters visited them later at their lodgings in Chelsea.

Livingstone had hoped to take Mary back within a few months, but John Murray, the publisher, persuaded him to write an account of his travels and they retreated to a little white house at Hadley Green, a village north of London, where Mary's youngest sister, Jane, came to join them. Here, at last, they had the kind of family life Mary had always yearned for. Local residents remembered how devoted Livingstone was to his children, how he would play with them in nearby Barnet woods.

He took his children with great pride to visit his distinguished friends: 'It was beautiful to observe', Sir J. Risdon Bennett remembered, 'how thoroughly he enjoyed domestic life and the society of children.' With these wealthy friends Mary was quiet and composed but not always at ease. But there were great ladies such as Lady Murchison and Miss Coutts, the wealthy philanthropist, who were particularly kind to her.

The gentle Miss Coutts, granddaughter and heiress of the banker Thomas Coutts, was one of the richest women in England. Deeply religious, she had been inspired by the accounts of Livingstone's travels in *The Times*, and immediately offered practical help in spite of discouragement from her friend Charles Dickens. For him, 'the history of all African effort hitherto, is a history of wasted European life, squandered European money and blighted European hope'. But like many others Miss Coutts, excited by the prospects of new cotton plantations which would make Europe independent of America, and by the expectation of mineral wealth, welcomed the prospect of bringing both trade and the Christian religion to the heathen. To aid his medical researches she sent Livingstone the most modern microscope available, and loaded them both with other gifts. Miss Coutts and Mrs Brown, her companion, now delighted in packing boxes for them to take to Africa; equipment for the school Mary intended to set up, shawls and rugs which were later to be worn with great panache by African chiefs, and a little silver mug which finished up at the bottom of the Zambesi.

Nothing better illustrates Mary's difficulties in Victorian society than the account given by the famous naturalist, Professor Owen, of her appearance in public.

After the lecture by Livingstone at the Society of Arts Colonel Sykes asked me if I had a ticket for the Photographic Soirée at King's College. I had, so had he, and as each ticket admitted two he took the Doctor and I, Mrs Livingstone. It was a dress assembly in the Grand Hall. Mrs L., with a straw bonnet of 1846 and attired to match, made a most singular exception to the brilliant costumes. Who could that odd woman be that Professor O. is taking round the room and paying so much attention? . . . I caught sight of Will's countenance . . . Disgust and alarm most strongly portrayed. He could not conceive what badly dressed housemaid I had picked up to bring to such a place . . .

Poor Mary had to undergo

the extraordinary scrutinies of many fine ladies as they shrank at first from contact as far as the crowd permitted. But when the rumour began to buzz abroad that it was Dr and Mrs Livingstone, then at the acme of their lionhood, especially with the Church party through Lord Shaftesbury's speech of the day before – what a change came over the scene. It was which of the scornful dames could first get introduced to Professor Owen to be introduced to Mrs Livingstone and the photographs were comparatively deserted for the dusky strangers.

But with Frederick Fitch and his wife, Mary was completely comfortable. She and Livingstone stayed at their Highbury home for some time and Mrs Fitch became one of Mary's closest friends. Mr Fitch, a merchant who was to provision Livingstone's next expedition, remembered how careful both Livingstone and Mary were 'as to dress and appearance' and how 'Dr and Mrs Livingstone were much attached, and thoroughly understood each other. The doctor was sportive and fond of a joke and Mrs Livingstone entered into his humour . . . In society both were reserved and quiet. Neither of them cared for grandeur.'

In November 1857 *Missionary Travels* was published, and it had an immediate success. John Murray was, he said, torn to pieces for copies, and at a guinea a time the edition of twelve thousand was quickly sold. It brought Livingstone not only wealth but an influence beyond his dreams. Young men and women were inspired to become missionaries. Students flocked to his farewell meeting in Cambridge and heard a lecture that would transform the lives of many of them. 'I know', he told them, 'that in a few years I shall be cut off in that country which is now open; do not let it be shut again. I go back to Africa to make an open path for commerce and Christianity . . . I leave it with you.' As a result, an Oxford and Cambridge Mission to Central Africa was set up, a mission with which in due course he would become deeply involved.

During these years Livingstone had gradually dissociated himself from the London Missionary Society, and now they were unwilling to finance his next expedition – to explore the Zambesi river. They regarded it as a risky venture which, even if successful, would exhaust their resources. Livingstone, nettled by their lack of encouragement, believed that they had neglected Mary in her lonely exile, refusing financial aid because, they claimed, she had been receiving gifts from her rich Quaker friends. The government, on the other hand, was, thanks to Livingstone's book, at last taking a real interest in African exploration. If there were, as he promised, copper, coal and cotton on the Zambesi, then it was in the national interest for the British to take their share. This time he went as Her Majesty's Consul to Central Africa, with a commission to explore and report on the geographical and commercial possibilities of the area. Nothing was to be spared to make this expedition a success. On the eve of Livingstone's departure *The Times* reported with pride:

The Government has advanced £5,000 for this fresh expedition into the interior of Africa. A Government vessel will take them to the mouth of the Zambezi – they will travel 300 miles up the Zambezi in a steam launch and not until the travellers are about to explore will the watchfulness of the British Government be withdrawn.

Queen Victoria granted him an interview, and on Saturday, 13 February 1858 a great farewell banquet was held in the Freemasons' Hall. Sir Roderick Murchison, President of the Royal Geographical Society, was in the chair and more than three hundred people crowded to get into places for 260. Behind Murchison a great map of Africa showed Livingstone's travels. The President toasted Livingstone, praised the competent assistants he was to take with him, and then, amid loud cheering, raised his eyes to the gallery. There in the front row, filled 'with the fairer sex', sat Mrs Livingstone, on one side of her Professor Owen, on the other Miss Coutts and her companion. To applause from the assembly, Murchison announced that 'the daughter of that faithful missionary Mr Moffat' would accompany her husband, and 'will lend materially to the success of the expedition'. As Murchison sat down, a gentleman in the body of the hall called for three hearty cheers for Mrs Livingstone. The explorer rose to thank his hosts and added his praise for her tolerance in forgiving him his delayed return. To further loud cheers he declared: 'My wife is familiar with the languages of South Africa, she is able to work, she is willing to endure and she well knows that in that country one must be able to put one's hand to everything . . . glad I am that I am to be accompanied by my guardian angel.'

As the cheers rose once again from the assembled guests, the 'guardian angel' sat impassively with her companions. Mrs Owen remembered that

Poor Mrs Livingstone was in a stout lindsey dress and thick bonnet and, as the heat was overpowering, even the rest of us (who were in evening dress) suffered considerably from it. I persuaded her to take off as much as she could. She bore the scene wonderfully well but I saw she kept her eyes intently fixed on her husband the whole time.

When the whole assembly looked up and cheered her,

the honours paid with three times three to one woman by such an assembly would have been almost too much to bear for most people, but no Hottentot could have betrayed less emotion under the trying circumstances than she did. There is doubtless much activity of mind hidden under her extreme quietness. She betrayed by a slight twinkle in her dark eyes that she was gratified at the Duke of Wellington's speech about her, as the true helpmate of her honoured husband and also at his drinking to her in a glass of wine. After the whole room had risen to salute her, and when the cheering and waving of handkerchiefs had subsided, I told her she ought to acknowledge the attention in some way and she did it at once with a calm curtsey . . . After the speeches were over as we had gone into the tea room I had to introduce many people to her . . . Mrs Livingstone seemed pleased . . . at my explaining the names of the Scotch airs the band were playing in honour of their Scotch birth. She did not recognize any of them for I suppose that music was never heard in her father's house. She however expressed her liking to me much as she might speak of some new and rather extraordinary thing. After the band had ceased playing, she whispered, 'I think I like music.'

Even after two years, English society was more strange and foreign to Mary than the wildest of African scenes, and the music of the Scots Guards more exotic than the chants and drums of Africa.

A queer piece of furniture

They spent their last night with the three oldest children at the Braithwaites' home in Kendal. Mary had the consolation that she was leaving them in good hands: Livingstone's sisters were to take charge of them, and he left his now considerable fortune to be handled on their behalf by reliable trustees, his old colleagues Professor Buchanan, James Hannan and James Young. At the station there were, Livingstone wrote to Miss Coutts,

> bitter parting ceremonies with each of our children. I tried to get them to let the last look be a smile, but no it would not do. I braced myself up tightly but the last boy stood at the railway and the carriage would not move off quick enough and the tears came in spite of me. But now all is over and I'll do my duty whatever betide.

At least they had one child with them, Oswell, now a lively little boy.

The screw steamer *Pearl*, which was to take them to the Cape, carried on board the steam launch *Ma Robert*, named after Mary, which they were to use on the Zambesi. They sailed out of Birkenhead in rough seas and 'it snowed and how it did snow', Livingstone wrote to Miss Coutts. But, basking in the warm sunshine off Senegal on the west coast of Africa, he could reflect with pleasure that there was 'no cross-grained specimen' among his comrades, who came 'regularly and cheerfully to prayers'. Mary saw little of them, since she and Oswell were seasick all the way to Senegal. Commander Norman Bedingfeld, RN, was an old friend, and as yet showed no sign of the quarrelsome nature that would later cause him to be sent home. The Scot, Dr John Kirk, remained throughout calm, competent and an accurate observer. At twenty-five he had already been toughened by service in the Crimea, but he was also a skilled botanist and it was for this as much as for his medicine that he was on the expedition. Kirk, it was hoped, would prospect for cotton, and a brilliant nineteen-year-old geologist,

Richard Thornton, was detailed to look for coal.
Thomas Baines was the official artist. At thirty-eight he
was much travelled and he had had considerable
success. His South African paintings were greatly
admired. George Rae, the engineer, was from Blantyre,
Livingstone's home town, and spoke the same language. Dour, but efficient and loyal, Rae had a malicious steak that would later cause trouble.

Livingstone's younger brother, Charles, was
regarded from the beginning with jealous suspicion.
He had emigrated to America in 1839, studied theology
in Ohio, been ordained as a Nonconformist minister
and was with the expedition as 'moral agent' and
photographer. The rest of the party was rightly scepti-
cal of his ability as a photographer; he certainly left
little record. But he had left behind a wife and children, and was the only one who had the least understanding of Mary's difficult position. For the others, a
seasick matron and a little boy were a couple of
nuisances who would divert Livingstone's attention
from the mission. Oswell was a plucky little lad but
always in trouble – on one occasion he chopped his
finger badly in the cook's galley. The young men
found Mary difficult to place – she was 'cut out for
rough work' or 'a queer piece of furniture' and even 'a
coarse and vulgar woman'. Like many others, they
found it difficult to place her in rigidly stratified
Victorian society. None of them had any idea of her
brave past or of how invaluable she could be as a
nurse, interpreter and a competent member of the
expedition. Many misleading impressions of Mary
came from the journals of these fellow explorers. She
had known hardship, neglect and obscurity during the
struggling days, she had experienced the pleasures
and pains of fame, and now she was to discover that a
man of genius attracts acolytes who do not have room
for his wife.

In Sierra Leone they landed briefly, and Mary and Livingstone stayed in comfort with the Governor; but by now they had realised that Mary was not only seasick – she was again pregnant. As the *Pearl* steamed on towards the Cape she became feverish and was, as Livingstone wrote to Miss Coutts, 'reduced to such a state . . . that it was thought impossible that she could reach the Zambezi'. Mary was never one to complain, and with typical Victorian modesty she concealed in her letters the real reason for her sickness. At this time she was confident that she would be able to join the expedition later. Luckily, her parents were at the Cape and could escort her back to Kuruman.

In the short time that they spent together at the Cape, the Livingstones were fêted and presented with medals and prizes. 'Eight hundred guineas were presented in a silver box by the hand of the Governor, Sir George Gray,' Livingstone wrote. How different, Mary thought, from their last visit, when her husband had had the greatest difficulty in getting any help with the expedition that was to bring him this fame. 'Poor man,' she wrote to Miss Coutts, 'he is quite worn out.'

God's highway

But at last, on 1 May 1858, Livingstone and his party left Simon's Bay for the Zambesi. Mary, in tears on the quayside, waved her bonnet until the ship steamed out of sight.

For Mary and the Moffats there were long delays while they waited for Mary's brother John Smith Moffat and his bride Emily to arrive from England; it was not until August that the long train of ox wagons rolled out of Cape Town. The journey to Kuruman was a nightmare; it began with floods, and Mary's wagon foundered in a river. Once again Mary found it not the most comfortable way to spend the last months of pregnancy;

but at least she could advise and support her sister-in-law Emily who had come out, young and also pregnant, straight from a comfortable home in Brighton. As Livingstone wrote to his brother-in-law, Ma Mary would be in her element dishing out thin gruel to her pregnant daughters-in-law.

Though Emily's child did not survive the rough journey, Mary's baby, Anna Mary, named after Miss Braithwaite of Kendal, was born at Kuruman on 16 November 1858; Livingstone did not get the news until a year later. Throughout the following months Kuruman was a hive of activity. The new arrivals buzzed with preparations for their departure in June. John and Emily, accompanied by Moffat himself, were to go north to establish a mission with Mzilikatze and the Matabele, and another expedition, led by an experienced pioneer missionary, Holloway Helmore, taking with him his wife and children, was to follow Livingstone's old route across the Kalahari and north to the Makololo on the Zambesi. He was accompanied by Roger Price and his wife. Livingstone's original plan for Mary was, as Livingstone wrote to Miss Coutts, for her 'to remain at Kuruman till her period of trial is over, then join me at the Zambesi by going overland'. She was expected to go north either with her brothers or with the Helmores.

It was as well that Mary had not planned to stay at Kuruman, for the Moffats were at this time in a very unsettled state themselves. Robert Moffat had received information that the Boers were planning to make an attack on the mission station in May, and it was only after he wrote a letter to the Governor at the Cape that they were warned off. Moffat was equally most unhappy at Mary's original intention to go north. Livingstone had run up against an insurmountable obstacle on 'God's highway' – the Kebara Basa rapids – and it was unlikely that he would be able to reach the Makololo headquarters by the Zambesi route. Besides, remembering Livingstone's difficult journeys the Moffats were also against the Helmore expedition, and Mary herself must have had enough of the Kalahari desert. With a little boy, a baby and no Livingstone she would not have wanted to tread the path for the fifth time.

Had she gone, however, the Helmore party might not have met its tragic fate. The chief of the Makololo was expecting Mary – Moffat's daughter – and when she did not appear, the tribe made life impossible for the strange missionaries. They were robbed, possibly poisoned, and in 1860 Roger Price and two Helmore children returned to Kuruman. Mrs Price and three children had died, and as Livingstone reported to Miss Coutts, the Makololo themselves were perishing in the 'hot, steamy valley. They would remove at once to the Highlands if Mrs Livingstone were here'.

Mary, however, had decided to return to her other *WOW* children in Scotland. She could not go north, and Kuruman and the Cape were alive with rumours of the quarrels on the Zambesi. Livingstone had dismissed Bedingfeld, who returned to the Cape with jaundiced accounts of the expedition, and Mary was, Livingstone wrote, 'much distressed' because he had 'turned round after his dismissal and said all he could against us'. So Mary and her two smallest children once more set out for the Cape – once more eight hundred miles by ox wagon – and thence to Scotland.

Her third voyage was less traumatic than before. This time, Livingstone's success with *Missionary Travels* guaranteed that there would be no repetition of her earlier poverty. On her return from the Cape, Mary had called on Mr Marjoribanks, the kindly banker at Coutts and Co., who assured her that they would supply what money she needed. Nevertheless, there were problems; no one ever understood what happened to Mary's money at this time, but it must be remembered that now, as the wife of a famous man, she moved in different circles and had new needs, such as clothes for herself and for the children. She had lived rough for so long, had been starved and deprived of luxuries, that it would not be surprising if, now that she knew they were comparatively well off, she indulged herself a little. It may be, too, that Robert, who, though only fourteen, had been getting into bad company, had incurred debts. Tom, now ten, was also a worry and an expense – he had always been delicate and Mary had taken him away from his first school. Mary herself still suffered periods of black depression. Many of their friends were scientists, involved in the arguments over Darwin's *Origin of Species*. Often her faith was badly shaken.

In Scotland she found a tutor for Tom and a friend for herself. James Stewart was training as a medical missionary for the Free Kirk of Scotland. He was obsessed with the Livingstone legend, knew *Missionary Travels* by heart and, inspired by it, determined to go out to Livingstone and with his help found a mission of the Free Kirk on the Zambesi. Serious and devout, he had been involved in religious controversy from boyhood. His father, a farmer, had been one of those who in 1843 had broken away from the established Church to found the Free Church of Scotland. James, as a boy, held the candle for services in their barn, carried stones to build their church. As a youth he firmly believed he was called by God to some high mission; during his eleven years at Edinburgh and St Andrews Universities he studied theology and began his medical training.

Mary was charmed, as were others, by this immensely tall, handsome young Scot. Part-Norwegian, with a shock of lustrous auburn hair and beard, a Viking of a man, to Mary he must have seemed a tower of strength; though, as she later told him, she found him at first rash and hot-tempered. In fact, Stewart was fundamentally unsure, a self-regarding, self-conscious young man whose emotional life had been blocked, first by the early death of his mother and then by the death of a stepmother whom he extravagantly adored. Mary was comfortingly maternal, and indeed his feeling for her was then, and remained throughout, filial. But Mary could also open his road to Livingstone, and so she was useful to him. Mary herself, lonely and disoriented, was touched and flattered by his attention.

Meanwhile, Livingstone's expedition on the Zambesi was continuing to go badly; his boat, the *Ma Robert*, was full of holes. So he sent Rae back to Scotland to inspect her replacement, the *Pioneer*, which Livingstone persuaded the Government to build. Rae was also to supervise the construction of a steamship which could be sent out in parts, reconstructed on the Zambesi beyond the Murchison Falls and taken up to Lake Nyasa, which Livingstone had recently discovered.

While in Glasgow Rae met Stewart; he became suspicious of his friendship with Mary and wary of his obvious ambition. He also picked up the gossip about Robert's wild behaviour. Livingstone, reading Rae's letters, was beginning to feel guilty about Mary. The Zambesi was obviously not going to be God's highway into the heart of Africa. Yet if he tried a new way in from the Rovuma river it would mean another three years' absence. Finally – spurred on by a sharp letter from Miss Coutts complaining of his neglect of his wife – he sent for Mary. She could be escorted to the Zambesi by Rae, who had chartered in Scotland a brig, the *Hetty Ellen*, to bring out the iron sections of the *Lady Nyasa*. But Mary was delayed because the baby, Anna Mary, was ill, so Rae went ahead in the *Hetty Ellen* and she persuaded Stewart to wait a month and accompany her. On 6 July 1861 they sailed from Southampton in the Royal Mail ship *Celt*, reaching Cape Town on 13 August.

During the long voyage she and Stewart were constantly together, talking at first about the problems of setting up missions, then, as the weeks went by, more freely about themselves. Though Mary's increasing admiration pleased him, it is clear from Stewart's journal that he grew impatient with her, finding her difficult to understand and moody. He was also beginning to suspect that she drank.

Stewart's medical training had only just started, he was young, and he had not yet learned to understand the problems of a woman of forty facing a dangerous life. Mary had left behind five children – the youngest only two – and she knew it was likely that she would never see them again. It was not surprising that she was depressed. As for her drinking, it is probable that Mary, like her mother, had found brandy a cure for seasickness. 'You would smile to see me', Ma Mary had written home from the sailing ship that had first taken her to Africa as a girl in 1818, 'sitting on deck with my tumbler of brandy and water before dinner. Nothing would have kept on my stomach had it not been for that very thing.' If Mary had discovered that it was also a cure for heart-sickness, who can blame her? Except for Stewart's later declaration that she was sometimes 'besotted', there is, however, little evidence that she drank heavily. But certainly he often found her in black despair. To Mrs Fitch she wrote of her seasickness, but

> I must not complain . . . I am as comfortable as I can be . . . but I long to hear of my darling children. It is with the utmost difficulty that I keep up heart. Mr Stewart is kind and attentive and will not allow me to mope, he will not let a fly hurt me if he can help it. My dear baby, how my heart yearns for her. I miss her much.

Was it the rough seas, as she told Mrs Finch, that shook her handwriting?

As the ship sailed into the tropics Mary began to understand the young man who was so attentive to her – it was almost the first time in her life that she had been so cared for. Night after night they sat after dinner on the moonlit deck and talked, he worrying about his fitness for the tasks ahead, about the poor response to his sermons on board. Each night he recorded painstakingly his fears – first, would the Portuguese hamper him, then '. . . 2. The climate . . . 3. The distance . . . 4. Dr L.'s feelings'. In his energy, his determination, his driving sense of mission he was so like Livingstone. But Mary must have feared that his idealism would end in disillusion. Little by little she tried to show him the reality behind *Missionary Travels*. Kuruman was not all idyll, the missionaries were not all saints.

In August 1861 they sailed into Table Bay. Mary wrote back to Mrs Fitch of her pleasure at being in Cape Town once more. She was delighted to be received 'so cordially by all my friends and many that I never knew'. As she showed Stewart round Cape Town, strolled with him in the botanic gardens and took him to the Portuguese fort and the observatory, her friends noticed how well and happy she looked. But the gossips raised their eyebrows. So handsome a young escort must be her lover. The rumour took hold and was never totally silenced. In fact their relationship was undoubtedly innocent. Stewart was appalled and amazed when he heard these tales; he had thought of Mary as his mother, and she had always treated him with the same openness and ease as she had the young men who visited the Livingstone family in the interior.

They were delayed at the Cape for three months, waiting for the *Lady Nyasa* to be brought from Glasgow. Meanwhile another mission party was to sail to the Zambesi. The Universities' Mission to Central Africa, inspired by Livingstone's Cambridge speech, had already sent out a team led by Bishop Charles Mackenzie. They were establishing their mission in the Shire Highlands in the Zambesi area, and had sent for their ladies to join them. 'Here we are,' Mary wrote to Mrs Fitch,

and here we remain until November . . . and there is a regular cargo of ladies going to the Zambesi . . . I just fancy I see his look of surprise when he sees what a lot of women . . . should come upon him . . . I have been expected to teach them and inculcate them in the matters of housekeeping. Well I shall do my best to be agreeable to all.

But relations with the Mackenzie party were soon strained. They were High Church Anglicans, suspicious of Stewart whose motives they mistrusted. It was bad enough that he was scouting for a site for a Free Church mission, but in his methodical way he was also making enquiries about trading. They became convinced he was a trader in disguise, and persuaded the Bishop of Cape Town that he should not be allowed to join them. Tactfully Bishop Grey offered to pay Stewart's fare home; but Mary stood firmly by her companion, refusing to budge unless Stewart came too. And she won. When finally they sailed for Durban, Stewart went too. They were infinitely relieved to be leaving Cape Town – now, as Stewart thought, 'a foul-mouthed scandal mongering place'. He had foolishly told Mary that the gossips had accused him of being 'too intimate' with her, and Mary – speechless with anger – had left him 'without bidding goodnight'.

The Bishop's sister, Miss Mackenzie, had lapped up the scandal. An elderly, sick but indomitable old lady, she had responded to her brother's frenzied appeal to come and help him deal with the native women, who were obviously causing the handsome bachelor some embarrassment. She was bringing her housekeeper, Jessie Lennox, and a maid called Sarah, whose surname no one remembers. They were two pretty girls, 'rather fond of dress but a little steadied by belonging to the mission'. Then there was Mrs Burrup, the young bride of the Bishop's aide; eager and blithe, she was earnestly training herself for the ardours ahead by taking long walks. They were escorted by a limp and affected young curate, Edward Hawkins.

This ill-assorted party arrived on 21 November in Durban, where they were to meet Rae and make the rest of the voyage in the *Hetty Ellen*. For almost a month they were delayed in Durban, where Mary stayed with her brother Robert and his wife. Stewart occupied his time riding around in the interior, prospecting for a possible site for his own mission. But he called frequently on Mary, and walked with her along the sandy beach. One evening was 'delightfully pleasant, the fireflies gleamed through the trees . . . The air filled with all the murmur of insect life'. Though Mary was increasingly concerned by the thought of the Cape gossip, she was determined not to dismiss Stewart. But concerned as he was with his own problems – his lack of money, his threadbare coat, and the hostility of the Anglican party who were trying to prevent him boarding the *Hetty Ellen* – Stewart was irritated and unsympathetic. 'She is one thing one day and another the next. She is to give her life for mission work today . . . and to live altogether for that for the future: tomorrow she cares for nothing.' One night he was awakened by a coolie shouting through the darkness: 'Mrs Livingstone ill, *shake, shake!*' Half asleep, angry and confused, Stewart opened the note Mary had sent and believed that she was merely hysterical. He dressed and went over to the Moffats' house where he found them 'all in alarm . . . I gave some laudanum and returned about one with feelings I am not disposed to chronicle'. Mary is likely to have been genuinely ill. She certainly had bouts of malaria, and it is more than probable that her moods were aggravated as much by Stewart's prescriptions as by drink. Laudanum by itself could have caused her depression. But however annoyed he had become, Mary continued loyal to him. As the *Hetty Ellen* prepared to sail the Anglican party refused point-blank to allow him on board, until Mary sent her written authority for him to do so. At last, on 23 December, the brig set sail for the Zambesi.

An uncomfortable journey it was. The ship was cluttered with 160 tons of stores for the Magomero mission; the iron sections of the *Lady Nyasa*; and Miss Mackenzie's boxes and furniture, a mahogany wardrobe, a farm cart, two mules, a pony trap and Miss Mackenzie's donkey called Kate. The ladies slept on the floor in the captain's cabin, ate salt rations, and shared mugs and plates. The men slept in the hold, as one of them later described: 'The hay was stowed in the hold, the bits of the steamer on the top and a few planks on that formed our beds – a leaky pump certainly threw a damper on our feelings.' The Rev. Hawkins's fixed clerical smile faded early. He and Stewart bickered over the Bible, and the party soon divided into the High Church sect and the Low Church sect. Miss Mackenzie was snobbish and frosty to Mary.

Not surprisingly, Mary, as Stewart complained to his journal, 'took one of her queer fits and disappears like one of the ancient goddesses'. The physical discomfort would not have worried her – she was accustomed to that; but she saw the difficulties in store. Sectarian differences would make mission life impossible. How could these well-off Anglicans cope with the rough life ahead? As for the helpless Rev. Hawkins – he would be as much use on the Zambesi in his white surplice as one of her own babies. If she could have seen the good Bishop, a crozier in one hand and a gun in the other, waging war on the tribes he had come to convert, her state of mind would have been blacker still.

Her anxieties increased when they arrived off the mouth of the Zambesi and found no Livingstone. The captain made for Mozambique, through a hurricane, where they refuelled and picked up news. The rumours were worrying; gunfire had been heard around the Mackenzie mission, and there were confused tales of

dead missionaries. Once again, Stewart found Mary –
not surprisingly – out of sorts. She was, he wrote, 'dull,
dumpy and discontented'. Stewart was also disturbed
that Mary had so many long talks with Rae – was he
spreading new scandals? After Stewart went ashore in
Mozambique he returned to find Mary in a mood, 'I
suppose because I hadn't spent the last shilling I had
and bought every conceivable thing that passing whim
might suggest to her to eat and drink.'

In Mozambique, Captain Wilson of HMS *Gorgon* took
charge. His commission from the British government
was to search out and destroy slaving ships; dedicated
to his work, he was also much interested in the Livingstone expedition. When he heard that Mrs Livingstone
was on board the *Hetty Ellen*, he offered to tow the brig
back to the Zambesi, where his sailors would help
unload it and he would deliver Mary and the others
safely into the hands of Livingstone. Captain Wilson,
crisp and efficient unlike Captain Davies of the *Hetty
Ellen*, inspired confidence. He invited the ladies aboard
the *Gorgon* – the High Church party accepted, while
Mary and the Low Church Stewart preferred to stay on
the dirty little *Hetty Ellen*.

The paymaster of the *Gorgon* was named Cope Devereux – young, sensible and tolerant – and his journal
recorded his first impression of Mary Livingstone as a
kind and motherly lady of about thirty-eight or forty.
Captain Wilson and his officers were appalled that this
helpless band should be setting out into the perils of
unknown Africa. They tried by every means to dissuade
the ladies from embarking on what was in their view a
'death march'. In a final, vain attempt, as HMS *Gorgon*
steamed towards the Zambesi they played 'Home Sweet
Home' on the phonograph every night. But for Mary,
listening from the deck of the *Hetty Ellen* as the tinkling
music drifted back across the still waters of the Indian
Ocean, 'Home Sweet Home' was Africa or wherever
David Livingstone was.

My dearie, my dearie, you are going to leave me

This time when they anchored off the Zambesi, among the mangrove trees of the delta was a low, white-painted paddle steamer, and on the paddle box a distant figure – the great explorer himself. Early next morning Livingstone steered the *Pioneer* across the rough waters of the bar. Devereux, on HMS *Gorgon*, remembered the 'great African traveller in his consul's faded gear', lifting his silver-laced cap (it was gold-laced in fact) to the ladies; 'having passed us makes for something more interesting, the ladies in the brig astern'. The doctor looked 'a great swell', Stewart told Mary as they leaned over the rail to hail him. She gave him a playful slap and a gratified smile, and then had eyes for no one except Livingstone. 'It must be confessed', wrote Stewart, 'that in his white trousers, frock coat and naval cap he looked uncommonly smart and really had a commanding air. All the troubles and work of many years seemed compensated for in the romance of this morning. Then he brought them the photographs and portraits and the L.'s went below – L. to marvel at his grown-up children.'

Stewart tactfully retreated as Mary Livingstone embraced. It was three and a half years since Mary had been left behind at the Cape, yet their mutual understanding had borne the strain. Mary need not have worried about the gossip, for her husband made light of it; it was 'madness . . . nonsensical'.

Captain Wilson, glad of the chance to meet the famous doctor and his companions, invited them all to breakfast on the *Gorgon*. It was decided that Wilson and fifty sailors should escort Livingstone and the Mackenzie party up the Zambesi, then up the Shire river to the Murchison Falls, and see them safely to Magomero. Since fighting was obviously in progress between Mackenzie and the slave traders, Captain Wilson could claim that it was his duty to protect the Livingstone party;

and it was a legitimate extension of his commission to destroy the slave trade.

Leaving the *Gorgon* at anchor at four o'clock the next day, Captain Wilson joined Livingstone in the *Pioneer*, which towed the *Hetty Ellen* and two paddle boats containing the ladies and fifty sailors across the bar to the swamps and mangrove trees of the delta to Expedition Island, where the mission stores were to be unloaded from the *Hetty Ellen* and stowed on the *Pioneer*. Now the officers and men looked with new respect at Mary Livingstone. She was indeed, as they had said, cut out for rough work. At 5 a.m. She was working in 'easy déshabillé', surrounded by packages and parcels, numbering and arranging. The sight of the mass of goods, 'necessaries and luxuries', strewn on the shore made even the tolerant Devereaux angry. Mary, remembering their poverty in Africa and in England, must have found the extravagance of the High Church expedition 'gorged with luxuries regardless of expense', infuriating. There on the sand with the mules and the donkey stood the mahogany wardrobe, expensive chairs for the *Lady Nyasa* and an enormous pile of cans and bottles, much of which would never reach the mission.

It took a week's hard work to unload the *Hetty Ellen*. After the enforced leisure of the ship, Mary was happy to be at work and too busy to understand Stewart's increasing bad temper. He, who had worshipped Livingstone, now saw him as an ordinary mortal who could be bad-tempered, and the river Zambesi and its treacherous delta looked hopeless as a 'highway for commerce'. Though Stewart was shocked that Livingstone worked on Sunday he was careful not to antagonise him. The 'godless Sundays' continued to worry him, but he remained silent. From then onwards he avoided the Livingstones – though he was glad enough for Mrs Livingtone to take care of his possessions in their

already overcrowded cabin. In the long weeks ahead
Mary and her husband were to swelter in this little
cabin – the boat was so overloaded that the portholes
could not be opened, and a hole bored in the roof was
their only ventilation.

The other ladies made themselves as comfortable as
they could on the deck, under the upturned hull of the
Lady Nyasa, for which they had made mosquito net
curtains. As the *Pioneer* throbbed slowly up the river,
officers, men and missionaries became more and more
depressed. Their nights were sleepless, for mosquitoes
swarmed in their millions, reducing even the sailors to
near hysteria. By day the heat was intense, and the
water looked like bad ale; along the slimy banks croco-
diles lurked. Until Captain Wilson took command,
Livingstone repeatedly ran the *Pioneer* aground; a boiler
burst, they ran out of coal and had to chop down trees
as they went. Almost everyone suffered from dysentery
and intermittent fever.

Yet Livingstone would later remember this as being
as happy a time with Mary as he had ever known.
Certainly there were moments when, as the ship
throbbed through the dark jungle, Mary thought of her
distant children and wept, or when she reflected gloom-
ily that she would never find a home again and foretold
her own death. But Livingstone laughed her out of her
black moods, and the river broadened and ran through
wide, grassy savannahs, 'park-like and fringed with
trees . . . delightful country made for some favoured
race'. They took long walks on these open plains, where
Livingstone and Mary could be at last alone and watch
the stunning magenta sunsets mellow to gold.

Then there were days when the men went hunting,
and in the evening they picnicked on the river banks
and made delicious curry from their day's killing. The
ladies made themselves chef's hats and helped at the
campfire, while the pretty maids basked in the admiration of sailors and visiting African chiefs. And in spite
of mosquitoes and the fever that attacked all of them,

there were even jolly dinners in the crowded cabin when the officers made beer and punch and the ladies clamoured for more; Livingstone, with Mary at his side, could be amusing, telling them tales of his African adventures. And there were hilarious evenings, as when their daft old bulldog fell through the cabin skylight onto Mary's plate. Stewart's first acquaintance with Log had been when he awoke one morning to find himself pinned down by the great paws. Sometimes the shore parties were boisterous, and Livingstone and the officers would leap from the bush, frightening the ladies with a lion's roar. 'We old bodies ought now to be more sober, and not play so much,' Livingstone said, and Mary replied, 'O no, you must always be as playful as you have always been, I would not like you to be as grave as some folks I have seen.' Stewart, the upright Scot, found this frivolity distasteful.

But for Captain Wilson, who longed to get back to the *Gorgon*, their slow progress and the inefficiency of the expedition were torture. At last, on 18 February, he decided in despair to take Miss Mackenzie and Mrs Burrup on ahead in an open boat. He hoped to escort them himself upstream to the confluence of the Shire and the Zambesi, then up the Shire and overland to the Magomero mission.

Six days later the *Pioneer* reached Shupanga, where Livingstone, after much vacillation, decided to unload the *Lady Nyasa*, fit her together and tow her upstream. So Mary had a welcome break during which she and Livingstone found time to walk round the old Portuguese settlement, admire the view of the mountain from the porch of the deserted old stone house, measure the girth of the giant baobab tree and watch the canaries and squirrels playing in its ancient branches. Mary, it was observed, looked well and was putting on weight; the sea air had obviously agreed with her.

On 18 February Captain Wilson had gaily waved goodbye as he set off with the ladies upstream in the

open boat. But on 14 March they returned. Captain
Wilson, drawn and wasted, silently watched the
stricken Miss Mackenzie and Mrs Burrup carried on
board the *Pioneer*. The Bishop, they had discovered,
had been dead since 31 January, and Mr Burrup had
died of the same fever three weeks later.

Mary did what she could for Miss Mackenzie, who
appeared to be near death, and consoled the young Mrs
Burrup. But Livingstone, whose response to distress
was often one of awkward anger, spoke within the
hearing of Miss Mackenzie of the need for 'better men'
next time. And as he sat in the dim cabin, head in
hands, his thoughts were of his mission: 'This will hurt
us all.' Once again Mary, whose own irritation with the
Mackenzie mission had now subsided, had to be the
appeaser and the comforter.

As the *Pioneer* made swift progress down to the sea,
it was to Mary that young Mrs Burrup turned as she
sobbed through the night of her wedding anniversary.
There were more delays while they waited for the
Gorgon to return from Mozambique, but at last they
watched the bereaved ladies carried silently aboard the
Gorgon on the crossed arms of the dejected sailors; Miss
Mackenzie and Mrs Burrup would return to their
homes, and with remarkable resilience would survive.
Jessie Lennox, Miss Mackenzie's housekeeper, a tough
Scot, lived to 102.

Stewart meanwhile had remained in the stone house
in Shupanga, depressed and lonely. There he was
joined by a survivor of the Bishop's mission, the Rev.
Horace Waller, and later by Rae. The nights were
moonless, their candles were gone; there was nothing
to do but talk over the past, renewing the gossip and
worrying over the future. In fact some of the missionaries would come back to serve in Africa. Charles
Livingstone and Dr Kirk both became HM consuls, the
former in Fernando Po, off the coast of West Africa, and
the latter in Zanzibar; and well pleased Dr Kirk must
have been to have a continent between them. Waller, in

spite of these miserable months, was to keep the legend of Livingstone alive in his writing.

As for Stewart, though he was now dispirited he was none the less determined to make his mark in Africa. In the dark stone house he brooded over the mistakes and learned the lessons of the doomed Zambesi expedition. The time was not yet ripe for a mission here, but after completing in Scotland the medical training that he now realised was absolutely essential, five years later he was to return to the eastern Cape and run with great efficiency a training college for Africans at Lovedale. And because, in spite of everything, Livingstone was still his hero, he did not rest until he had helped to found the missions of Blantyre and Livingstonia in Nyasaland.

Impatiently, Stewart and his companions now waited long weeks for the Livingstones' return. But the *Pioneer* had been held up in the delta by engine trouble and it was not until 14 April that it was heard chugging through the mangrove swamps. For Mary, the delay in the sweltering heat of the delta among the swarming mosquitoes proved fatal. Stricken with fever, she was brought ashore to their tent in the long, dank grass. Dr Kirk had noted, as early as 9 April, that Mary suffered repeated attacks of fever. Stewart noted unsympathetically: 'Mrs L *said* she was ill.' Mary did not fuss, for Livingstone's 'rousers', his famous pills, had always worked in the past.

By 26 April she had become so ill that they moved her to the old stone house. Stewart gave up his room and there she lay on a makeshift bed – a mattress laid on tea chests – while Livingstone and Dr Kirk battled to save her. But she was no longer the stalwart Mary of old, and it is probable that she was once again pregnant. In spite of her happiness with Livingstone, in these last months she was often, as he said, a fearful and dejected Christian; and, as her mother had written, she had come home to Africa as a lamb to the slaughter. Now

she became delirious, feverishly worrying over her
children: 'See, Agnes is falling over a precipice!' The
two doctors tried all remedies, but neither 'powerful
doses of calomel blisters or even a strong enema could
act for her'.

Racked by guilt that she might be dying without faith,
Livingstone tried desperately to rouse her. 'My dearie,
my dearie, you are going to leave me. Are you resting
on Jesus?' Did she hear? He would never know; he
could only find consolation that 'she looked thoughtfully up'. As her face changed in death the watchers
saw how she resembled her father. Long ago Livingstone had said, 'Mary is a heroine – like her father.'

And tragically, so ill and dispirited were the men
around her that, except for Livingstone and his brother,
all were past caring. The locks of her hair that Livingstone later sent to friends were matted and uncombed.
Dr Kirk was competent and professional as always, but
he had never really understood Mary and now only
wanted to leave the expedition. Rae, ill, and in pain,
was, the others remembered, 'like a madman in his
complaining'. At this desperate time he was mostly
concerned with the massive iron lumps of his steamship, lying on the river bank, still waiting to be assembled. Mary's death was a hindrance. Waller, whose
pencilled notes describe the scene, had sympathy for
'poor Mrs Livingstone' – but his main concern was for
Livingstone himself.

Stewart was detached. 'This has been an eventful
day,' he recorded. 'At 7 this evening Mrs L. breathed
her last.' With medical precision he described her symptoms and their treatment, noting clinically that 'her face
after death was infused with bile and was even more
yellow than in an ordinary case of jaundice. Mrs L.'s
case was a good instance of the insidious nature of the
fever of this country. It requires to be carefully
watched.' But the sight of 'the Dr weeping like a child'

affected him and 'I found my own eyes full before I was aware'.

Stewart was disappointed that it was Charles Livingstone who was asked to read the prayers on deck. Now that Mary was gone, his position was at risk. But he was reassured when

> out of all the ship's company except Dr Kirk who was attending all day, I alone was sent for to be with the Dr in his hour of sorrow . . . there was Waller and Young but no, I who was supposed by most on board to be *nobody* come in at the trying hour. It was altogether a day to remember, this long bright hot and clear Sabbath day at Shupanga.

Throughout the long night the wild geese screamed and the hyenas howled, while Rae hammered her coffin and the sailors dug her grave. Livingstone wandered around the house, broken, uncomprehending. She had seemed so strong; she had been so much a part of him – his 'rib', he had so often called her, his better half, sometimes his 'worse half'. Now and to his dying day he would regret that, with his eyes so fixed on his own mission, he had not seen what was happening to Mary; that he had not helped her failing faith or cured the sicknesses that destroyed her. Missionary and physician, he had failed his own. And for the first time in his life he wanted to die. He could only console himself that saints too had their times of spiritual blackness – as had Mary. He found a simple prayer among her papers, and was comforted: 'Take me O Lord as I am and make me what thou wouldst have me be.'

They buried her next day at one o'clock. Twelve years later three of the men who carried her then would bear Livingstone with pomp and ceremony to his own grave in Westminster Abbey. But here, on the banks of the Zambesi, while the squirrels and canaries still played in the great tree, was where he would have wished his

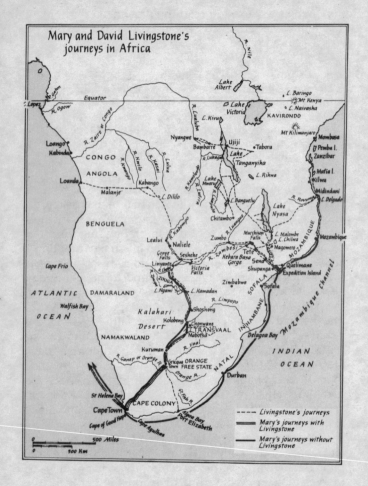

Mary and David Livingstone's journeys in Africa

grave to be. Stewart read the prayers and was sufficiently composed to observe the Portuguese commander kneeling and crossing himself.

Afterwards, Livingstone wrote through streaming tears to his children. To eleven-year-old Oswell, who must have known Mary best, he wrote as to himself:

Shupanga
28 April 1862

Mr dear Oswell,

With my tears running down my cheeks I have to tell that poor dearly beloved Mama died last night about seven o'clock. She has gone home to the House of many mansions before us. She was ill seven days but moved about for the first few days, and no alarm was taken, but at last continued vomiting came on every ten minutes or so, which nothing could stop. I was with her night and day and trust that she was tended by an all powerful arm besides. I did not apprehend danger till she lost the power to swallow. She was so deaf from quinine that I could not converse about the rest for the soul, but on asking loud if she rested on Jesus, she looked up towards Heaven thoughtfully. I think it meant yes. I very much regret that I did not use writing as when I asked her if she were in pain, she several times replied 'No'. She saw me shedding many tears in prospect of parting with my dear companion of eighteen years, and must have known that her bodily case was hopeless. She answered my kisses up to within half an hour of her departure. It was only after we had commended her soul to Him who himself passed through the gate of death, that she took no notice of me. She was then breathing with her mouth a little open, shut it quietly and breathed no more.

She has got home sooner than we – this earth is not our home. She loved you dearly and often spoke of you and all the family, especially little Baby. You must think of her now as beckoning you from Heaven, never to let the pleasures of sin cheat you out of a happy meeting with her, and above all, with Jesus who died bearing our sins on his own body on the tree.

She gave me the comb and toothbrush you kindly sent

us. We find in her notes evidence that she meant to try
and make us all comfortable. She is not lost but gone
before . . . She was collecting some curiosities for you.
There are two ostrich egg shells and other shells she
brought from Mozambique . . . you must let Agnes
divide them. She was pleased at the idea of your being a
missionary of the Cross and will be pleased still if you
hold steadfast to your resolution. You must all love each
other more than ever now. May God our Father be your
guide . . . Into his care I commend you.

That night he measured the stars above her grave,
doggedly determined to fix for ever its place in the
shifting jungle. Nothing would be the same again,
neither his simple faith in Heaven nor his confidence in
his own mission; and the zest for the Zambesi expedition slowly died. Mary's epitaph – in English and
Portuguese – was brief, and Livingstone's account of
her death in his book misleadingly curt. To his friend
Lady Murchison he wrote with deep feeling of

My dear departed Mary Moffat, the faithful companion
of eighteen years . . . At Kolobeng she managed all the
household affairs by native servants of her own training,
made bread, butter and all the clothes of the family;
taught her children most carefully; kept also an infant
and sewing school – by far the most popular and best
attended we had. It was a fine sight to see her day by
day walking a quarter of a mile to the town, no matter
how broiling the sun, to impart instruction to the
heathen Bakwains. Ma Robert's name is known throughout all that country and 1800 miles beyond . . . A brave,
good woman was she.

Livingstone never quite recovered. The next months
were haunted by death and disillusionment, for struggling once more up the river Shire towards Lake Nyasa
he found that the way he had opened had been followed by slavers. On the banks there were scenes of
devastation and slaughter, and the stench of death

hung over the river. Each morning the paddles of the boat had to be cleared of the clogging dead bodies.

Soon the Zambesi expedition was recalled and Livingstone returned to a Britain no longer enthusiastic. But first he had crossed the Indian Ocean to Bombay in the little *Lady Nyasa*, an extraordinary feat achieved by pushing himself to the uttermost limit.

He stayed only long enough in England to settle the older children, now grown out of recognition, and to meet for the first time little Anna Mary. Then he returned to die in Africa. The story of his last years and of the journey of his body to its resting place in Westminster Abbey has been often told. He was buried with high ceremony in an Abbey thronged with the rich and famous. Oswell and Steele, Young, Webb, Waller and Kirk were his pallbearers. Behind the coffin walked old Robert Moffat and two of his sons. David Livingstone lies among the great. But, as he wrote in the language of his childhood, 'poor Mary lies on Shupanga brae and beeks fornent the sun'.

Jenny
MARX

I have been engaged for more than seven years

On 19 June 1843 the famous roses were in full bloom in the fashionable German spa of Bad Kreuznach, and along the green lawns by the clear river elegant crowds strolled and listened to the band outside the Kurhaus. But in the Protestant church among the willows by the river it was quiet, broken only by the murmur of voices from a small wedding group. There were few present to witness the marriage of Jenny, daughter of the late Baron von Westphalen, to Dr Karl Marx, the lawyer's son from Trier. The Baroness was there – pretty, elegantly dressed – with her son Edgar and a few friends. But no member of the Marx family was there. The bridegroom, a striking figure, broad-shouldered beneath a shock of black hair, stood alone. Yet no bride could have been more radiant in her silk gown that matched her brilliant green eyes, a wreath of pink roses on her shining chestnut curls. There had been years of opposition from both families. It was to avoid more fuss that Jenny choose to be married here instead of fifty miles away in Trier, the town where both she and Karl had grown up.

After the ceremony they returned to the Baroness's house for a celebration; and if, as her carriage jingled along the Bad Kreuznach roads, she sighed for the wedding that might have been, she would have concealed her regret. For then and always she would give her daughter her loyal support.

Had the marriage taken place in Trier, the church would have been crowded, rustling with finery, for the

Westphalens were well-known and respected, and Jenny's stepbrother, Ferdinand von Westphalen, was a high-ranking government official there. But he and his wife strongly disapproved of Jenny's marriage to a man of twenty-four, four years her junior, without prospects and, worse still, with revolutionary tendencies. There was another reason, too: though in later life Karl Marx would vehemently deny it, there was undoubtedly an element of anti-semitism in the opposition of Jenny's family.

Karl's mother, Henrietta, also disapproved. Her husband had died while Karl was at university, leaving her with a large family to support. Her eldest son should have been helping her, and she certainly would have been reluctant to see him 'marrying out'. The Marxes had formally renounced their faith so that Heinrich could retain his legal position, for, after a period of comparative freedom, Jews were not allowed to hold high office in Prussia. But the Jewish heritage was not lightly to be shrugged off.

So it was before the main door of the town hall of Bad Kreuznach on 21 May and 28 May 1843 that the banns were called. And it was at the Baroness's Bad Kreuznach house that the legal contract was signed on 12 June, giving them common ownership of property, each partner promising to pay those debts that the other had contracted before marriage. The witnesses were one Johann Rickes, a private gentleman, and Peter Beltz, a tailor. Henrietta Marx had signed the contract, though she wrongly wrote Jenny's father's name as Ferdinand instead of Ludwig. The witnesses at the wedding itself were Bad Kreuznach citizens, a local innkeeper, their lawyer and a Dr Engelmann. For this moment Karl Marx, as he wrote to a friend, had waited long. 'I have been engaged for more than seven years, and my fiancée has been involved on my behalf in the toughest of struggles that have ruined her health.'

The Baroness presented the couple with wedding

gifts of jewellery and family heirlooms of gold, silver plate and fine linen. And she sent them off in a coach with a coffer of money for a honeymoon trip to the Rhine Falls. They met friends on the way, and in their hotels, with a generosity that was to be disastrously typical, they left the box open so that friends in need could help themselves. When they returned to Bad Kreuznach the coffer was empty.

The tradition of all the dead generations weighs like an Alp on the minds of the living

When in 1865 Jenny von Westphalen wrote her *Short Sketch of an Eventful Life*, she began with her marriage to Karl Marx in 1843 as though nothing had gone before. In fact a happy, secure childhood helped to form her character, giving her a stability and resilience that she would need in the tumultuous days ahead; just as the intellectual training of her youth prepared her mind. She would never quite forget her background or the attitudes of a small country town.

Jenny was born in Salzwedel in Saxony in 1814, the daughter of Ludwig, Baron von Westphalen. She came to Trier, a pretty town on the banks of the Moselle, when she was still a small child. Though her father was a baron, he was not, as has often been assumed, an aristocrat, but a distinguished lawyer, the equivalent of a Privy Councillor. He was a leading citizen in Trier and much esteemed for his erudition and for his upright and liberal character.

He had inherited his title from his father, Philipp von Westphalen, who was the Duke of Brunswick's chief of staff in the Seven Years' War and accepted the title of baron when he married Jean Wishart, the daughter of an Edinburgh minister and related to the third Duke of Argyll. She had come to Germany to visit her sister, the wife of General Beckwith, commander of the British troops, and had fallen in love with the handsome Philipp. Jenny von Westphalen was to inherit not only her grandmother's name but some of the Argyll crested silver, damask and linen, as well as a romantic interest in her Scottish ancestry. From her earliest childhood English was spoken in the home.

Her father had married twice. By his first wife, Louise von Veltheim, he had two sons and two daughters: Ferdinand, Karl, Lisette and Franziska. When Louise died, Lisette and Franziska were brought up by their mother's sisters, while Ludwig took charge of his two sons. His second marriage, to Caroline Heubel, seems to have caused a lasting resentment, for when Ferdinand wrote his memoirs late in life he avoided mentioning her, although Jenny remembered that her mother had cared for her stepchildren as few mothers care for their own.

Ferdinand and his younger brother Karl spent much time on the great estate of his mother's family at Hohenersleben in north Germany, or visiting their sister Lisette, who had married a wealthy landowner, Adolf von Krosigk. This high life suited the clever and ambitious Ferdinand, who soon fell out of sympathy with his liberal, progressive father. When Jenny was two years old Ludwig sold his estate in Salzwedel and moved to Trier, where two more children were born – Laura, who died young, and Edgar. Even as a child Edgar had more charm than character, though he was an amusing and lively boy, whereas Jenny was from her earliest years not only beautiful but highly intelligent.

It was a happy childhood, with picnics on the hills and long walks with her father through the vineyards that combed the sunny hillsides. The Roman remains of Trier awakened in her an interest in history. Near their home the great Roman gateway, the Porta Nigra, loomed, a visible reminder of Trier's past glory as the capital of the Roman province of Germania. But, as her father taught, Trier could take pride too in its more recent history, in its radical traditions inherited from the French who had occupied the area during the Napoleonic Empire.

Though Jenny's family was never wealthy, their home was comfortable and they had many servants; but Ludwig's salary was not high, he had sold their Salzwedel estate to pay their debts, and he had two families to support. The Westphalens lived hopefully, in constant expectation of small inheritances. The real excitement in Jenny's childhood happened in 1826, when they heard that a fabulously rich uncle, Wilhelm Storch, who had made his fortune in America, had died intestate in London. Now, apparently, the lawyers were searching for heirs for the fifty thousand pound inheritance. For years the favourite fantasy of the Westphalens was that some portion of the wealth of this Croesus would come to them. When it did not happen, Caroline was philosophical. The dream, she wrote to her relations, had given them 'hours of innocent pleasure'.

> This castle in the air had brought us much material for amusement; for sitting at our round table of an evening, each one tells of the first thing he would buy or do, if the inheritance arrives, the children especially amuse us, with their modest wishes, which could indeed be fulfilled even without the inheritance; for instance Edgar said the other day he would at once buy a copy of *Robinson Crusoe*, and when, the day after, my husband fulfilled his wish, he thought the treasure had already come.

Caroline's dream was that she would be able to buy the most lovely clothes and lace caps. Perhaps it was the example of Uncle Wilhelm that inspired Edgar with a romantic vision of the New World, where he was vainly to seek for his fortune in later life. Often, in the years to come, Jenny too was to look for a non-existent pot of gold at the end of a vanishing rainbow.

Jenny was adored by her mother and an aunt who lived with them. When she was four her parents reported: 'Jenny is very droll and gives us much amusement, she sings very nicely and speaks the Trier dialect like a native – a completely un-German gibberish that she can only have learned from the servants.' She suffered at that time from some kind of rash that confined her to the house, so the servants were her friends. Later on she was to show the same quick ear for languages and the same easy relationship with people of all kinds.

At thirteen Jenny was said to be 'full of spirit, beautiful in body and soul, the real joy of the house'. But as she grew up she was also, according to Lisette's grandson, 'not an easy girl to control, with a sense of fairness that led to passionate outbursts and a thirst for knowledge which made her love books from her childhood onwards'. She was developing radical, progressive ideas which her father and mother encouraged, but which perturbed her stepsisters. Lisette, who later became a lady-in-waiting at the Prussian Court, had been caught up in the religious revival that swept through Germany at this time. Although she could not share Jenny's politics she was nevertheless, as she wrote, 'drawn to her by martyr-like conviction, her passion for justice and burning enthusiasm which brought her nearer to the proletariat whom she believed had been betrayed by destiny'.

But Ferdinand, her stepbrother, disapproved of her politics and such furious arguments ensued that their meetings were discouraged. Ferdinand was an ambitious, slightly pompous lawyer who was gradually working his way up the legal ladder in Trier, first as a junior pleader, then as a junior magistrate. In 1826 he became a Provincial Counsellor in nearby Bitburg until he moved back to Trier as Principal Legal Counsellor. He reached the pinnacle of his career when he became Prussian Minister of the Interior in 1850. Jenny's hostil-

The Marx Family

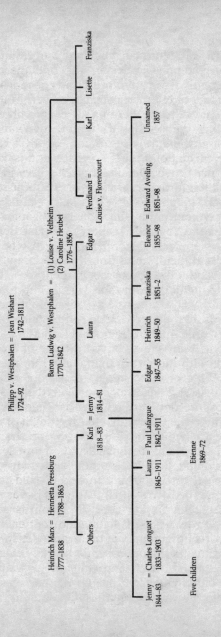

Philipp v. Westphalen = Jean Wishart
1724–92   1742–1811

Baron Ludwig v. Westphalen = (1) Louise v. Veltheim
1770–1842   (2) Caroline Heubel
                                  1776–1856

Heinrich Marx = Henrietta Pressburg
1777–1838   1788–1863

Others

Karl = Jenny
1818–83 1814–81

Laura   Edgar

Ferdinand =
Louise v. Florencourt

Karl   Lisette   Franziska

Jenny = Charles Longuet
1844–83 1833–1903

Laura = Paul Lafargue
1845–1911 1842–1911

Edgar   Heinrich   Franziska   Eleanor = Edward Aveling   Unnamed
1847–55   1849–50   1851–2   1855–98   1851–98   1857

Five children

Etienne
1869–72

ity to him was returned, for Jenny, sporting her tricolour as the representative of the political movement called Young Germany, must have been a constant embarrassment to the respectable lawyer. In 1830, when Jenny was sixteen, Ferdinand married Louise von Florencourt, whose relations with Jenny were affectionate, even gushing, on the surface; but there was always an undercurrent of mutual suspicion and jealousy.

Jenny may have attended a girls' school in Trier, but whatever her formal education, her real teacher was her father, who taught her Greek and Latin and read Homer with her. Above all, he taught her English and gave her a passionate love of Shakespeare that lasted all her life. It was an intellectual storehouse which would sustain her in the difficult years ahead. Like many liberals of his generation, the Baron was influenced by Rousseau, and his daughter's education was as important to him as that of his sons. Edgar was a disappointment, so the Baron was all the more impressed by one of his school friends, a brilliant little boy called Karl Marx.

Karl was born a Jew, but at the age of six had been baptised, with the rest of the family, into the Lutheran Church. One of his commended school essays was a devout dissertation on 'The Union with Christ'. His mother, more devoutly Jewish than her husband, did not abandon her faith until after the death of her father; even then it would appear that she became merely a nominal Christian. Both she and her husband came from distinguished Jewish families: there had been rabbis in Heinrich's family from the sixteenth century onwards; in her own Dutch family, as her granddaughter later claimed, 'the sons for centuries had been rabbis'. 'The tradition of all the dead generations weighs like an Alp on the minds of the living,' Karl wrote later.

Henrietta was, in fact, a quintessential Jewish mother, warm-hearted, direct and full of common sense. Because of her Dutch origins her German was poor, but she could not have been as illiterate as is usually suggested. To Heinrich she was 'incomparable' and to the young Karl she was 'angel Mother'. As a student Karl wrote to his father praising, as Heinrich gratefully acknowledged, 'so beautifully the life of your excellent Mother, so deeply felt that her whole life is a continued sacrifice of love and loyalty'.

At this time the two families were neighbours, though later Heinrich refers to the Westphalens as having moved some distance away. Sophie, Karl's elder sister, was one of Jenny's best friends, Edgar and Karl were classmates, and the two families saw a great deal of each other. The Baron and his family attended the Protestant church, which made both families minorities in a predominantly Catholic town where an annual festival was celebrated for the Revelation of the Holy Coat, a seamless tunic said to have belonged to Christ. Though Jenny and Karl must have shared the throbbing excitement of festival time, both of them were outsiders – Karl, in spite of his professed Christianity, doubly so. For although Heinrich was officially no longer Jewish he still on occasions spoke on behalf of the Jewish community, and there is no doubt that Henrietta would have created a typically Jewish home.

The Baron was much taken with the brilliant Karl, and he was often invited to the Westphalen house to share the readings of Shakespeare and Homer. Together they climbed the hills around Trier, reciting Homer as they walked through the vineyards. Marx never forgot the Baron's teaching: the measured wisdom of the Greeks was to give some balance to the fierce young man. It was a priceless heritage, and throughout his stormy life the world of the ancients shone, in the words of Aeschylus, as a 'citadel of light'. When Karl wrote his doctoral thesis in 1841 he dedicated it to 'His dear fatherly friend, Ludwig von Westphalen . . . as a token of filial love'. It was to

an old man who has the strength of youth, who greets every forward step of the times with the enthusiasm and the prudence of the truth and who with that profoundly convincing sun-bright idealism, which alone knows the true word at whose call all the spirits of the world appear, never recoiled before the deep shadows of retrograde ghosts . . . but rather with Godly energy which burns at the heart of the world.

He followed this convoluted tribute with the hope that he would 'follow soon this messenger of love which I send you and roam again at your side through our wonderfully picturesque mountains and forests'.

From the beginning of their friendship he had been bowled over by the beautiful, green-eyed girl who shared their walks and who could recite Shakespeare as well as her father. But Jenny, four years his senior, seemed unattainable. As a precocious adolescent Karl must have watched Jenny's coming out with fascination, seen her swept into a whirl of gaiety, heard the carriages clattering down the Römerstrasse as night after night she set off brilliantly dressed for yet another ball. For Jenny this was, as she later recalled, 'the golden time of maidenhood', and as 'Queen of the Ball' she was never forgotten in Trier. Her pious stepsisters also watched and were shocked by her giddy behaviour.

Is that Demon heavenly or Faustian?

In 1830 Jenny was an impressionable sixteen, not only fond of dancing but also with a lively interest in politics. These were stirring times, for Trier was caught up in the revolutionary storm sweeping through Europe. In France, the successful revolt of July 1830 against the reactionary Bourbon king, Charles X, triggered off similar rebellions in other countries. In England it was only after the passage in 1832 of the bill granting parliamentary reform that the rioting subsided; in Brussels, a successful revolution secured independence; and in the

German states of Saxony, Brunswick, Hesse-Cassel and Hanover the rulers were deposed and some constitutional reforms were gained. In Poland, Russian domination was thrown off in 1830, but in the following year the patriots were once again defeated. In Italy insurrections in Modena, Parma and the Papal States were suppressed by the Austrians.

Although the revolutionary drive was checked or crushed, some of the standard bearers achieved lasting fame. In particular the Italian patriot, Giuseppe Mazzini, fired the imagination of the young throughout Europe. His Young Italy and Young Europe societies, with their libertarian and humanitarian ideals, were copied in Ireland and Germany. Jenny von Westphalen was one of the leaders of the Young Germany movement in Trier, and here there was plenty of fuel for the flames of unrest.

Germany at this time was not a unified country but a collection of self-governing states. Trier was in the Confederation of Rhineland States which had been occupied by the French during the Napoleonic Wars and which, after the fall of Napoleon in 1814, had been taken over by the dominant Prussia. The citizens of Trier, conscious of their own more liberal history, resented Prussian rule and their hostility was fanned into rebellion by high taxes and the failure of the wine trade. In 1830 and 1831 there were riots with which the liberal middle classes, lawyers and teachers, were sympathetic. In the eyes of the Prussian authorities, Trier was a potentially troublesome town. At banquets attended by leading citizens demands were made for freedom of speech and constitutional reform. Even the schoolchildren, encouraged by their teachers, wore the tricolour. In response, and to forestall trouble, the Prussian government sent troops to Trier.

The influx of young officers seems to have enlivened the social life of the small town. Jenny was surrounded by suitors and one officer, Second Lieutenant Karl von

Pannewitz, fell deeply in love with her. Louise, Ferdinand's wife, at that time travelling with her husband,
wrote back to her parents, the Florencourts, eager for
gossip. In October she was 'displeased and surprised
. . . by your news of Jenny's recently begun affair. It is
as yet completely unclear to me how the mother has so
soon changed her mind about her . . . and, in particular, how disappointment can follow in such a short
time'. Caroline, who had at first encouraged the romance, had second thoughts when she realised that
Pannewitz, eleven years older than Jenny, had no
money and little prospect of advancement. Louise
hoped that 'the poor, infatuated girl already regrets this
over-speedy step', for Jenny, impetuous and passionate, had become engaged and had thrown herself with
wild abandon into the excitement of the season. Louise
read her parents' censorious letters with relish and
replied:

> This gadding about to casino balls in such circumstances
> can almost be called a public shame, and however little I
> can understand how a really happy, loving couple can
> wish themselves to be in such a place of diversion, all
> the less can I understand how an engaged couple can
> expose themselves . . . to the eye and quick blame of the
> public.

Louise blamed Caroline who, by her 'vain promotion of
this mad engagement', added to her husband's problems, for Ludwig's health was at this time causing
concern. Ferdinand and Louise thought that he should
have retired, but now he would be chained to his office
in order to pay for Jenny's wedding.

By Christmas-time Jenny had regretted her rash
commitment and broken off her engagement. Even that
did not wholly satisfy Louise and her strictly pious
parents, the Florencourts. The Westphalen family
apparently spent a noisy and hilarious Christmas which

'excited our united disapprobation. No spark of feeling can exist in Jenny's soul either, otherwise out of sympathy with her unfortunate lover who has shown her so much love she would have resisted such an unsuitable celebration'. How long, they asked, would Jenny go on like this? How long would it be before a better successor would step into Pannewitz's shoes – if he were not put off by the treatment given to his poor predecessor.

Karl Marx certainly was not put off. Indeed as a fourteen-year-old schoolboy he must have been much intrigued by the gossip surrounding the beautiful Jenny. During adolescence, meeting her often at her father's house, he became increasingly infatuated and determined to win her. By the time he left home for the university at Bonn, he had secured Jenny's affection. She who had considered herself a rational girl was caught by his extraordinary energy and brilliance. Karl was her 'dark little savage', her 'little wild boar', but she could never quite understand how this young man, four years her junior and still only seventeen, had managed so to sweep her off her feet.

In fact Jenny was a child of her age and a romantic. Her formative years in the 1820s were dominated by the events of the preceding half century; the French revolution and the Napoleonic Wars left long shadows out of which loomed giant figures larger than life. And the books she read fired her imagination. Her heroes were men battling for liberty, hurling defiance at oppressors, standing up even to God himself. Lucifer's pride was forgiven, Faust's passion for divine knowledge was understood; man triumphant was the vision that inspired Young Europe. Above all Prometheus was the symbol of the age, and Shelley's 'Prometheus Unbound' was a battle hymn. It was ironical that a poet who in his own country was dismissed as a 'beautiful and ineffectual angel' should so have inspired the rebellious young. Shelley's Prometheus was chained to a rock and tortured by the supreme God because he dared to bring

fire and self-knowledge to man. His defiant challange
echoed throughout Europe.

> Thou who art the God and Lord O Thou
> Who fillest with thy soul this world of woe
> To whom all things of earth and Heaven do bow
> In fear and worship all prevailing foe
> I curse thee!

In Jenny's eyes Karl was made of the stuff of heroes;
sometimes he was like Lucifer, sometimes like Faust,
but always he was her Prometheus, doomed to suffer
for mankind. And so overwhelmed was she that she
was prepared to suffer by his side.

Karl remained at Bonn for a year before moving to
the University of Berlin. At Bonn he studied jurisprud-
ence, the history of Roman law, Greek and Roman
mythology, and the history of modern art. In all those
subjects, according to the certificate granted in the
summer of 1836, he showed himself 'a diligent and
attentive student'.

But his father was distressed to learn that Karl was
imprisoned for a day for rowdiness and drunkenness,
was accussed of carrying forbidden weapons and had
taken up duelling. Heinrich was puzzled too by the
strange, obscure poetry that Karl sent them. And his
parents could make neither head nor tail of his accounts:
without appearing to be extravagant, Karl had got
himself deeply in debt. It was as well that Heinrich
could not see into the future. These were the first signs
of Karl's lifelong incapacity to cope with money.

Karl's failings were understandable in a young, single
student, but when in the summer vacation of 1836 he
and Jenny decided to become secretly engaged, Heinrich became seriously concerned. Jenny was twenty-
two, while Karl was only eighteen and still had no
career in sight. He was not sure whether he wanted to
be a lawyer, a professor, a drama critic or a poet.

No one understood Karl Marx better than his father. 'I love you above everything except your Mother,' he wrote, 'but I am not blind.' He recognised the 'uprightness, frankness and loyalty' of his son's character, but was concerned at his 'violent outbursts of passion' and his 'morbid sensitivity'. In March 1837 he wrote with prophetic insight,

> I cannot rid myself of ideas which arouse in me forebodings and fear, when I am struck as if by lightning by the thought, is your heart in accord with your head, your talents? Has it room for the earthly but gentler sentiments which in this vale of sorrow are so essentially consoling for a man of feeling? And since that heart is obviously animated and governed by a Demon not granted to all men, is that Demon heavenly or Faustian? Will you ever, and that is not the least painful doubt of my heart, will you ever be capable of truly human domestic happiness? Will you ever be capable of imparting happiness to those immediately around you?

Heinrich saw that Jenny, too, 'felt a fear laden with foreboding'.

During the following four and half years, while Karl studied in Berlin, his father watched and worried and Jenny shared his concern; she had confided in Heinrich, although it was a year before she dared tell her own parents. And he was fond of her; 'The bewitching girl', he wrote to Karl, 'has turned my old head too and I wish above all to see her calm and happy.' He was overwhelmed that Jenny, who could have married a prince, should have chosen Karl. 'Jenny is making a priceless sacrifice for you, she is showing a self-denial which can only be fully appreciated in the light of cold reason. Woe to you if ever in your life you forget this!'

Both Heinrich and Jenny were aware of the complicated nature of the man they loved, seeing in him the Marx that a fellow student described in a satirical poem:

But who advances here full of impetuosity?
It is a dark form from Trier,
An unleashed monster,
With self assured step he hammers the ground with his heels
And raises his arms in full fury to Heaven
As though he wished to seize the celestial vault
And lower it to earth.
In rage he continually deals with his redoutable fist
As if a thousand devils were gripping his hair.

Yet with his family, and especially with Jenny, he was usually calm, gentle and humorous. These contradictions in Karl Marx would all his life puzzle his friends and enemies alike.

His mother was also worried that during his years at Berlin University he would neglect his health. 'Have a weekly scrub with sponge and soap', was advice obviously much needed: Marx was remembered as a grubby student. 'Your amiable muse will not be offended by your mother's prose', she shrewdly observed. 'Tell her that the higher and better is achieved through the lower.' Later in life his doctors would echo her warnings.

To Henrietta and his sisters Karl was still the *Glückskind*, the child of fortune. His sisters adored him. As children they had eaten the cakes he had made with his grubby hands; they had allowed him to drive them like horses down the streets of Trier, and they had forgiven him because of the magical stories he could tell them.

Sophie in particular was a close friend of Jenny's and during the years when Karl was at Berlin University she acted as their go-between, delivering his letters to her and loyally supporting both. The Westphalens at this time had moved some distance from the Marxes' house, and Jenny had to make a special effort to visit them. The girls were obviously conscious of a difference in their social status and were flattered when Jenny came. 'Our parents and your brothers and sisters loved her very much,' Sophie wrote to Karl in Berlin, 'the latter beyond all measure. She is *never* allowed to leave us before ten o'clock. How do you like that?.' When Jenny failed to write to Berlin, Sophie assured the worried Karl that 'Jenny loves you; if the difference in age worries her that is because of her parents.' There was a difference not only in age, but in class and race. In fact Jenny was silent because, until she had told her parents of her secret engagement, she was reluctant to deceive them.

Often the intensity of his passion reduced her to despair. 'How frightful would my fate be if your ardent love were to cease,' she wrote to him, and often she had to remind him of the importance of 'external matters, of life and reality'. When he was jealous and she felt he no longer trusted her, she was afraid that she would not be able to keep his love 'fresh and young, and in that thought', she told him, 'lies death'. 'If only', she complained, 'you could be a girl for a little while and be such a peculiar one as I am.'

She assured him that, though she still enjoyed a full social life in Trier, she remained faithful. 'I have never, never been wanting in any way towards you, yet all the same you do not trust me.' She had, she told him, been often seen in

lively and cheerful conversation in society with all kinds of men . . . I can often joke and carry on a lively conversation with absolute strangers . . . things I cannot do with you. You see, Karl, I could chat and converse with anyone, but as soon as you merely look at me I cannot say a word for nervousness, the blood stops flowing in my veins and my soul trembles.

When Sophie brought Karl's poems to her, Jenny was moved to tears, and although in later life she and Karl would laugh at their youthful romanticism, she was deeply touched.

At the beginning of his university career the chief outlet for his explosive energy was poetry. 'There were moments', he wrote, 'when suddenly as if by a magic touch I caught sight of the glittering realm of true poetry like a distant fairy palace.' In this realm, Jenny was Queen, and his inspiration. In November 1837 he confided to his father, 'When I left you, a new world had just begun to exist for me, the world of love, that was at first drunk with its own desire and hopeless . . . no work of art was as beautiful as Jenny.' To her he dedicated his *Book of Love* and his *Book of Poems*, written in the autumn of 1836, which were, as he admitted, 'diffuse and inchoate expressions of feeling . . . built out of moonshine'.

> See! I could a thousand volumes fill,
> Writing only 'Jenny' in each line.
> Still they would a world of thought conceal,
> Deed eternal and unchanging will,
> Verses sweet that yearning gently still,
> All the glow and all the Aether's shine,
> Anguished sorrow's pain and joy divine,
> All of Life and Knowledge that is mine.
> From the Zephyr it comes back to me,
> From the being of the wild waves' thunder.
> Truly, I would write it down as a refrain,
> For the coming centuries to see –
> LOVE IS JENNY, JENNY IS LOVE'S NAME.

His poetry was sentimental and derivative, but it delighted Jenny.

> Look into those eyes of yours so bright,
> Deeper than the floor of Heaven,
> Clearer than the sun's own beaming light,
> And the answer shall be given.
>
> Dare to joy in life and being fair,
> Only press your own white hand;
> You yourself shall find the answer there,
> Know my distant Heaven-land.

Ah! When your lips only breathe to me,
Only one warm word to say,
Then I dived into mad ectasy,
Helpless I was swept away.

It was not only love that was racking Karl. In a long, frank letter to his father he described his emotional and intellectual development during his first year in Berlin, from his passion for Jenny and poetry to his study of law and the urge to wrestle with philosophy. Obviously at this time his powerful mind was driving him through the mists of abstract thought to the edge of insanity.

He described to his father his nervous breakdown and his escape to Stralow, a quiet village outside Berlin. Here, he 'got to know Hegel from beginning to end', and struggled to find his own philosophy. He had now 'arrived at the point of seeking the idea in reality itself. If previously the Gods had dwelt above the earth, now they became its centre'. He finished with a detailed explanation of his aims for future study and an appeal for forgiveness and understanding from his 'dear, ever loving father'. 'Often', he confessed, 'my heart seems to have erred, overwhelmed by my militant spirit.'

But Heinrich's patience had snapped. He replied in an equally long letter complaining of such self-probing self-indulgence. His father had watched Karl's development with alarm and anger, anger that his brilliant son was again deep in debt. 'As if we were men of wealth, my Herr Son disposed in one year of almost seven hundred talers', he complained on 9 December 1837,

> whereas the richest spend less than five hundred and why? . . . His is no rake, no squanderer. But how can a man who every week or two discovers a new system and has to tear up old works . . . worry about trifles? How can he submit to the pettiness of order? Everyone dips a hand in his pocket and everyone cheats him so long as he doesn't disturb him in his studies.

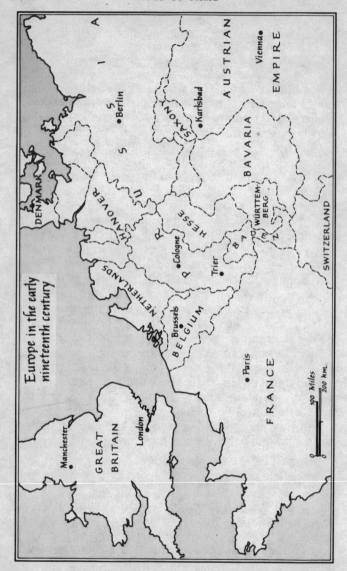

Europe in the early
nineteenth century

Heinrich was worried for Jenny's sake. Karl should, he believed, bear in mind

> that he has undertaken a duty . . . to sacrifice himself for the benefit of a girl who has made a great sacrifice, in view of her outstanding merits and her social position, in abandoning her brilliant situation and prospects for an uncertain and duller future and chaining herself to the fate of a younger man. The simple and practical solution is to provide her a future worthy of her in the real world, not in a smoke-filled room with a reeking oil-lamp at the side of a scholar grown wild.

Not only that, Karl had grown thoughtless about his family. His brother Edward was dying. Heinrich himself was ill and cholera was raging in Berlin. But 'your next letter', Heinrich complained, 'contained not a single word about it, but merely some badly written lines . . . a crazy botchwork which merely testifies how you squander your talents and spend your nights giving birth to monsters'. His illness made him bad-tempered, and, aware of his impending death, he worried about the future. Jenny visited him often, cheering him in his last days.

In May 1838 Heinrich Marx died. He never had the satisfaction of seeing Karl receive his Doctorate of Philosophy, but neither did he suffer the disappointment of seeing Karl fail to become a university professor or a lawyer. In spite of his thoughtlessness, Karl loved his father deeply and all his life carried Heinrich's portrait with him. Throughout the coming years his prophetic words must have echoed again and again.

Meanwhile, in Trier, Jenny too had been following Karl's career with the same anxiety. She must have heard with relief of his rejection for military service because of his weak lungs. She knew she was taking on a difficult man, but an ailing genius would be even more of a problem. She certainly was not happy about his growing interest in politics, 'the riskiest thing there is', as she wrote. For Jenny throughout her life was torn between a bourgeois desire for comfort and security and a romantic readiness to flout convention. His outspoken attack on what he called 'The Lord in Heaven and the Lords on Earth' must have alarmed her family. At this time Jenny frequently remembered Karl in her prayers.

Desperate to keep up with him intellectually because she worried that his genius would take him out of her reach, she studied Greek and Latin and read history and philosophy. In a singularly revealing dream she thought that Karl had been embroiled in a quarrel for her sake, and had subsequently fought a duel.

> Day and night I saw you wounded, bleeding and ill and, Karl, to tell you the whole truth I was not altogether unhappy in this thought; for I vividly imagined that you had lost your right hand, and Karl, I was in a state of rapture, of bliss, because of that. You see, sweetheart, I thought that in that case I could really become quite indispensable to you, you would then always keep me with you and love me. I also thought that then I could write down all your dear, heavenly ideas and be really useful to you.

But those ideas seemed anything but 'heavenly' to Henrietta Marx. Now a widow with numerous daughters to provide for, she would have expected the eldest son to get a steady job and shoulder the family responsibilities. But instead of becoming a professor or lawyer, he was becoming involved in journalism, and writing inflammatory articles against Church and State. And with no income he was about to take a wife and expected her to provide for them. It is not surprising that Henrietta was incensed, and her relationship with Jenny was never to be comfortable. When Marx left university and returned to Trier, he became estranged from his family and spent most of his time with Jenny's dying father.

Jenny now saw a gentler Marx, who lightened the Baron's last days – unlike her neglectful brother Edgar. In March 1843 Jenny was to write that when Karl left her she saw 'only the true image of you in all angelic mildness and goodness, sublimity of love and brilliance of mind'.

With both sympathetic fathers dead, the Westphalen and Marx families now argued against the marriage until Jenny was on the edge of a nervous breakdown. But she was resilient and her mother was supportive. A cure in a nearby spa town revived her.

Ferdinand and Louise were now established in Trier. Undoubtedly, as the new head of the family, he now led the campaign against the marriage. And if the stepsisters had been against Jenny's former engagement they were even more hostile to a man whose revolutionary and atheistic ideas were causing them all some embarrassment.

Karl left Berlin University in April 1841 and, having failed to get a professorship at Bonn, turned to full-time journalism. In October 1842 he moved to Cologne to become editor of the *Rheinische Zeitung*. This paper was backed by rich liberals and dedicated to the principles of freedom of speech, equality before the law, and the ultimate unification of Germany. Although Marx's early articles dealt with the plight of wine growers and wood gatherers, the main drive for his political interests at this stage came from theory. He had little first-hand experience of workers and was more worried about censorship and injustice than the human condition.

It was in his office at the *Rheinische Zeitung* that Karl first met the man who was to play such an important part in his life. Friedrich Engels was two years his junior, tall, fair, blue-eyed and handsome, brimming with energy and self-confidence. The son of a wealthy cotton manufacturer in the textile town of Barmen, like Marx he had been brought up in comfortable circumstances. His parents were Protestants, and pillars of the local church. Engel's father was strict and puritanical, while his mother doted on her brilliant son and often formed a buffer between him and his father. Friedrich, then and always, needed the affection of women, and his relationship with his sisters, particularly with Marie, was close and affectionate.

Like Marx, Engels had received a thorough classical education at the local *Gymnasium*. Unlike Marx he had left school to go straight to work in his father's factory, and was then sent to work in a trading house in Bremen. He was now doing his compulsory military training in Berlin and at the same time attending lectures there, studying Hegel. He and his fellow young Hegelians enjoyed shocking the town with their wild revels. Like Marx, he had a passion for poetry – he translated Shelley – and was influenced by 'Prometheus Unbound'. Engels was inspired by David Strauss's provocative *Life of Jesus*, as were many young men of his time, he challenged his strict, pious parents and Protestant friends to religious argument, enjoying the cut and thrust of debate just as he revelled in his skill in fencing.

All this did not endear him to Marx, who had to cope with his increasingly worried liberal backers. The growing spirit of rebellion all over Europe was causing the Prussian government to clamp down on any newspaper which was too critical of Church or State. Since the *Rheinische Zeitung* spoke openly against the censorship laws, it was in danger of being closed down. So this first meeting was frosty, and it would be some years before their friendship was established.

Engels was on his way to Manchester to work in the cotton mill that his father owned in partnership with the brothers Ermen. In the two years that he worked there Engels was able to experience at first hand the conditions of the British working class. His understanding of their problems was deepened by his relationship with an Irish mill girl, Mary Burns, who became his mistress.

Marx on the other hand, was preparing for his wedding. Jenny's mother had moved from Trier to Bad Kreuznach, presumably in order to escape her domineering stepson, Ferdinand. Marx visited Jenny there, and she wrote:

> I think that you have never been as dear, as sweet, as charming. Every time we parted before I was certainly enraptured with you and would have had you back to tell you once more how dear, how completely dear, you were to me . . . If you were back here again, my dear little Karl, what a capacity for happiness you would find in your brave little girl; and even if you showed a still worse tendency and even nastier intentions, I would still not take reactionary measures; I would patiently lay down my head, sacrificing it to my naughty boy . . . do you still remember our twilight conversation, our beckoning games, our hours of slumber. Dear Heart, how good, how loving, how attentive, how joyful you were!

A modern reader might well misinterpret their relationship from this letter, but Karl, as he showed many years later in his advice to his future son-in-law, was in these matters strict and slightly prudish.

But his marriage prospects were dimmed when in April 1843 the newspaper of which he was editor was closed by censorship. Fortunately, he had already come to the conclusion that his future lay in the free air of France, so he seized with delight an offer to co-edit a Franco-German review at a comfortable salary. Now he could get married.

The wedding was to be quiet, but Jenny was not to be done out of her wedding finery. She wrote to Karl giving him instructions:

> Now I come to a matter of dress. I went out this morning and I saw many new pieces of lace at Wolf's shop. If you

cannot get them cheap . . . then I ask you, sweetheart, to leave the matter in my hands . . . That applies also to the wreath of flowers. I am afraid you would have to pay too much and to look for it together would indeed be very nice. If you won't give up the flowers, let them be rose-coloured. That goes best with my green dress.

. . . And doubtless with her clear green eyes.

After the honeymoon they enjoyed the comfort of the Baroness's house at Bad Kreuznach for a few months. In the evenings they strolled on the green lawns among the roses and listened to the nightingales in the woods across the clear river.

Throughout the summer and early autumn of 1843 Karl was working on two pamphlets, the *Critique of Hegel's Philosophy of Right* and *The Jewish Question*. The anti-Jewish theme of this latter article has been much criticised. Indeed throughout his life Marx writes of Jews in terms abhorrent to modern readers appalled by the horrors of the Holocaust. His attitude may not be forgivable – it is, however, in the light of his childhood experience, understandable. He had been cut off from his roots by the father he loved, and in Catholic Trier, as a Jewish Protestant, he was doubly alienated. The hostility of Jenny's family in the period leading up to his marriage must have left him bruised and, in a typical mood of self-torture, he lashed out, rationalising his fury.

In the months he spent in his study in his mother-in-law's house in Trier he realised his talent for vituperative and provocative writing. Words would be his bullets in the journal which he and Arnold Ruge proposed to start, but it was clear that there would be no chance for such a journal to succeed in Germany. Paris, the home of revolution, offered a better base, and in late October he and Jenny left Bad Kreuznach. The days of birdsong and roses were over; there would not be many such in their life to come.

For the next seven years, from 1843 to 1850, as Karl became more and more involved in politics, they were to move to and fro across a disturbed Europe, now drawn by the hope of revolution, now expelled as the counter-revolution caught up with them. Paris would be the pivot of their wandering, from there to Brussels, to Cologne and back again before their final exile to England.

So happy a marriage in which joy and suffering . . . were shared

Karl and Jenny's first home in Paris was a house in the Rue Vanneau shared with the poet Herwegh and his wife and other German refugees. It was a large, solid building in a respectable neighbourhood. They intended to live as a commune, sharing the kitchen and taking turns with the cooking, but this did not last long. Jenny, older and more intelligent than the other women, did not fit in, and Marx was by inclination a solitary individual. A few days of communal life were enough, and they moved to another house in the same street. There would be many times in their lives when theory and practice did not go hand in hand.

Jenny found Paris exhilarating, enjoyed the vitality and the life in the open-air cafés, admired the shops and bought new clothes. She was much admired for her beauty and intelligence; their friends were poets and intellectuals who respected her mind. Heine, who was in Paris at this time, came to read his poems to her.

But some illusions quickly faded. Marx had intended his journal to be written by Germans and Frenchmen and to deal with 'political systems of the day'. But they found it difficult to get contributions for a magazine whose declared aims were 'to castigate base and servile newspapers', and 'to deal with men and systems which have acquired a useful or dangerous influence'. After one edition it folded. From now on they had to live on occasional fees from freelance journalism and Jenny's money.

In Paris she soon learned of the disintegrating effect of émigré life. Paris at this time was bristling with theorists of all kinds, and the German exiles were divided. There were those who expected to march back to Prussia immediately and defeat the government with their bare hands. There were those who advocated general destruction, with no plans for life after chaos. There were utopians who dreamed of ideal communes. And there was a gulf between them and the genuine workers. Marx and his friends often spoke slightingly of the exiled workers who followed the German tailor Wilhelm Weitling.

Jenny, as she later wrote, was depressed by the 'gossip and quarrels over trifles' and by the 'pettiness of so-called great men'. On 1 May 1844 their first daughter was born. The baby, Jenny – or Jennychen as she was called – was delicate and the inexperienced young mother was often desperately worried. Once, when the baby almost died during an alarming seizure, help came unexpectedly from Heine, who recommended a warm bath and saved the child. It was with some relief that Jenny left Paris and went back with her sick Jennychen to Trier and the family doctor.

There, under his care, the baby recovered and Jenny relaxed in the warmth and comfort of her mother's affection. Trier was at that time bustling with excitement over what she called the 'humbug of the Holy Coat'. Her letters, however, show that she secretly enjoyed the festivities. Certainly she enjoyed queening it among her friends, holding court in her mother's house while visitors and relations and even Marx's mother and sisters came to admire the new baby. Jenny was not going to reveal the fact that they were living in some poverty and that her husband was no longer an editor. She wrote to Karl:

Indidentally I behave towards everyone in a lordly fashion and my external appearance fully justifies this. For once I am more elegant than any of them and never in my life have I looked better and more blooming than I do now. Everyone is unanimous about that and people constantly repeat Herwegh's compliment asking me 'when my confirmation has taken place'. I think to myself too, what would be the good of behaving humbly . . . and people are so happy if they can express their regret . . .

In August she wrote to her 'high priest and bishop of my heart':

In Trier there is such a stir and bustle as I have never seen . . . all the shops have been newly smartened up, everyone is arranging rooms for lodging. We, too, have got a room ready. The whole of Koblenz is coming here and the cream of society is joining in the procession. All the hotels are already full up . . . Everyone has to join a procession . . . Frau Stein has already sold four hundred talers worth of tiny copies of the sacred linen cloth, made out of old strips of ribbon . . . I too have brought a little medallion for my little one and yesterday she herself obtained a small rosary.

In the bath she splashes with her little hands so much, that the whole room is flooded and then she dips her tiny fingers in the water and afterwards licks it hastily . . . when she cries we quickly draw her attention to the flowers in the wallpaper and then she becomes quiet as a mouse and gazes so long that tears come in her eyes.

While Jenny was away in Trier Marx met Engels again, and though they had only ten days together before Engels returned home to Barmen, a friendship was forged which would last a lifetime. Engel's two years in Manchester had matured him, though he was as ebullient and optimistic as ever, still convinced that the revolution that would transform Europe was just round the corner. But his practical experience in his father's cotton mill had given him an insight into workers' lives that Marx, the theorist, never had. And that experience was deepened by his mistress, Mary Burns, though she, an Irish émigré, was not a typical English working girl. Engels studied newspaper articles and the parliamentary reports on working conditions in mines and factories, and saw at first hand conditions in the slums and in industry. This gave his abstract doctrinaire socialism a new dimension. Now he realised that in all the welter of socialist theories of the time there was neither a coherent study of social history nor a practical plan for the future. In those ten days he saw clearly what their future tasks must be. Marx would produce what Engels called a 'fat book' and would be both their historian and their prophet.

Back in Barmen, in his efficient way Engels settled down and wrote his *Conditions of the Working Class in England*. It was, and still is in its way, a minor classic, a vivid picture of the England of that time. Marx, on the other hand, began his massive research into social, political and economic history from classical times onwards. It would be fifteen years before even the outline of the first part would be published, and twenty-four years before *Das Kapital* was finally printed. From this time onwards Engel's letters to Marx sing the constant refrain: 'Get on with the book.' But he saw from the beginning that Marx was the one man who could create some design from the political chaos. He was the great maestro to whom for the rest of his life he would willingly, as he said, play second fiddle.

Early in their friendship they began to formulate the theories that would form the basis of their life work. In his introduction to Marx's *The 18th Brumaire of Louis Bonaparte*, Engels, with customary generosity, gave his colleague the credit for being the first to discover

the great law which governs the march of history. According to this law, all historical struggles, although

they seem to take place on the political, religious, philosophical or any other ideal plane, are, in reality, nothing else than the more or less clear expression of
struggles between social classes. The existence of these
classes and their collisions are themselves determined
by the degree of development in the economic situation,
by the prevailing mode of production, and by the
methods of exchange which result. This law bears the
same relationship to history as the law of conservation
of energy bears towards the physical sciences.

For the rest of his life Marx would painstakingly amass
a mountain of evidence to support this theory. Now
that they had understood the nature of history, as they
believed, their aim was to change it.

When Jenny went back to Paris she found that during
her absence the activities of Marx and his revolutionary
friends had drawn the attention of the police. Louis
Philippe's government was becoming worried by the
secret societies which honeycombed Paris. Guizot, his
Minister, recognising that Marx was a dangerous ring-
leader, moved into action: encouraged by the Prussian
government, he decided to exile troublemakers.

Jenny had returned accompanied by her mother's
own trusted maid, Helene Demuth, who was to play
such an important role in their lives. Helene, or
Lenchen as she was known, was an even-tempered
baker's daughter who had come to the Westphalen
family as a young maid. She had left home at the age of
eight to be a nurserymaid with a Trier family where she
was grossly overworked – she never forgot the size and
weight of the baby she had to lug around all day. It was
a relief to move to the Westphalen household, where
she was treated as a friend. She attached herself to
Jenny in particular.

Hardly had Jenny settled in with Jennychen, Lenchen
and the nurse, Gretchen, than a police commissioner
knocked at their door with a government summons.
Karl Marx must leave Paris. 'I was given a longer delay,'

Jenny wrote in her autobiography, 'which I made use of to sell my furniture and some of my linen. I got ridiculously little for it but I had to find money for our journey.' Marx moved to Brussels, and in the bitter spring of 1845 Jenny followed with her baby. She was sick and ill and in the first months of her second pregnancy.

When Marx was banished from Paris he advised Lenchen to go back to Germany since they were at this time unable to pay her salary. But she could not bring herself to leave them. When they departed she packed her trunk and left Paris; her battered belongings, however, she sent not to Germany but to Brussels. Later she herself joined them there. Lenchen became the linchpin of the Marx household, cheerfully uprooting herself from Germany for a life of wandering. Her portrait shows a firm, pleasant face and a neat, though sturdy, figure. She was intelligent: she often played chess with Marx and she frequently won. Years later Engels paid tribute to her shrewd judgement of people and politics. Lenchen was never reluctant to speak her mind.

Citoyenne et Vagabonde

Brussels was to be their home for the three years 1845–8. For a few weeks they lived in a small hotel, Le Bois Sauvage; then, in May, they rented a small house in the Rue de L'Alliance, Faubourg St Louvain. Jenny's brother Edgar came to join them there. He was feckless but amusing, and at this time he was still her 'dear brother'. Edgar, though not by nature a political animal, tended to take on the protective colouring of his surroundings, and in Brussels he became, at least in name, a Communist.

The 'Villette' of Charlotte Brontë was a pleasant town – there were broad streets and seats under the linden trees, elegant shops and gaiety on the *jours de fête*. Jenny remembered in her journal how pleasant it was sitting with their German friends in the pretty cafés on warm spring evenings. It was, she later remembered, one of the happiest periods of her life, and here they made lifelong friendships. Wilhelm Wolff, nicknamed Lupus, joined them there, and the poets Freiligrath and Weerth lived nearby. Josef Weydemeyer, another friend, remembered a hilarious day when they took a train to the suburbs and had lunch in a little café. Stephen Born remembered meeting them in 1847: 'I have seldom known so happy a marriage in which joy and suffering . . . were shared and all sorrow overcome in the consciousness of full and mutual dependency. Moreover I have seldom known a woman who in outward appearances as well as in spirit was so well-balanced and so immediately captivating as Mrs Marx.' They must have been an impressive pair at this time, Jenny in full beauty with shining chestnut curls and clear green eyes, and Marx a powerful figure with a mane of black hair and piercing black eyes.

During the years in Brussels when Marx and Engels were working at theories that they hoped would change the world, Jenny too was, in her own way, making a contribution. For the first time she had been meeting genuine workers among the German émigrés and, realising the intellectual gulf between them, trusted in education to form a bridge. So she delivered lectures on poetry and literature to the exiled German workers and gave dramatic readings of Shakespeare with considerable success. Undoubtedly there was some jealousy among the other wives; an aside in one of her letters suggests that they called her Lady Macbeth.

She also took part in the political plotting that occupied Marx and Engels at this time. They were establishing a Communist Correspondence League which aimed to keep German, French and English socialists in touch with each other. On a visit to Manchester Marx met the leaders of the English Chartist movement, Ernest Jones and Julian Harney, who were campaigning for a people's charter which would grant universal male suffrage, annual parliaments, vote by ballot, payment of MPs and equal electoral districts. Julian Harney proved a disappointment to them: he was a practical, sensible realist, who foresaw that the British would never take to the barricades. He was right: in 1848 a monster Chartist demonstration fizzled out. As David Livingstone realised, 'While foreigners imagine that we want the spirit only to overturn capitalists and aristocracy, we are content to respect our laws until we change them, and hate those stupid revolutions which might sweep away time-honoured institutions, dear alike to rich and poor.' But at this time Engels was fired by a naïve optimism. Like so many European revolutionaries the Brussels comrades were convinced that the day was dawning when the armies of the reactionaries would be swept away. So they sat up all night, scheming and writing. Years later Lenchen recalled how they were all disturbed by their guffaws and gales of laughter. Some of the wives were affronted by their husbands' desertion. Mrs Harney, a formidable Scotswoman whom the Marxes disliked, wrote that the wives should form their own league and protest at their husbands' desertion.

Certainly Jenny was again beginning to feel irritated by petty quarrels among the émigrés; undoubtedly she was also feeling some jealousy that Engels was taking Karl away from her. From the beginning there was a coolness between her and Engels which was never totally dissipated. At the end of her life, after long years of close friendship, she would still write, 'Dear Mr Engels'. Like Marx, Jenny was conventional and even somewhat prudish, while Engels was a cheerful, unrepentant womaniser. He had brought Mary Burns with him. She was a sharp, lively woman whom Jenny obviously disliked, for there was neither then nor at any time room in Jenny's idealistic philosophy for the free love that Engels so enthusiastically practised.

Undoubtedly, for the first time, Jenny felt something of an outsider. It was with relief that, accompanied by Lenchen, she went back to her home in Trier for six weeks' holiday.

Jenny was glad to be in Germany again, though she wrote to Marx, 'to say so in the face of you arch anti-Germans calls for a deal of courage, does it not?' The squabbles of Brussels were far away. 'It was in glorious France and Belgium that I first made acquaintance with the pettiest and meanest of conditions. People are petty here, infinitely so, life as a whole is a pocket edition, but there heroes are not giants either, nor is the individual one jot better off.' Jenny, the romantic, was learning fast.

Now, soon to give birth to her second child, she was aggressively honest:

> For men it may be different, but for a woman, whose destiny is to have children, to sew, to cook and to mend, I commend miserable Germany. There, it still does one credit to have a child, the needle and the kitchen spoon still lend one a modicum of grace and, on top of that, and by way of reward for the days spent washing, sewing and child-minding, one had the comfort of knowing in one's heart of hearts that one has done one's duty. But now that old-fashioned things such as duty, honour and the like no longer mean anything, now that we are so advanced as to consider even old watchwords such as these outmoded . . .

Jenny went on to give Karl instructions for the arrangement of the house in preparation for her baby.

> Having concluded my important business on the upper floor I shall remove downstairs again. Then you could sleep in what is now your study and pitch your tent in the *salon immense*. The children's noise downstairs would then be completely shut off . . . I could join you when things were quiet and the living room could, after all,

always be kept reasonably tidy . . . At all events we
must install a good, warm stove.

She found it difficult to tear herself away – her mother
would be lonely without her, she wrote – and she
enjoyed the visitors who came to see her and her little
Jennychen. 'Everyone is quite besotted with the child
who has become the talk of the town . . . her favourite
is the chimney sweep by whom she insists on being
picked up.' It was a comforting small community that
Jenny most needed at this time. Nevertheless she
returned to Brussels, and on 26 September 1845 her
second daughter, Laura, was born. Two years later their
third child was born, named Edgar after her brother.

Money was, as ever, a problem. Harassed by creditors, Jenny and Karl pawned their belongings and
finally Marx wrote to his mother asking for a loan.
Henrietta, struggling as a widow to support the family,
grudingly sent six thousand francs as an advance on his
inheritance. That money quickly disappeared.

Henrietta would have been horrified had she known
that her money was used not only to pay the landlord
but also to buy arms for the German workers in Brussels. 'Daggers, revolvers, etc. were procured,' Jenny
wrote in her memoirs, and 'in all this the government
saw conspiracy and criminal plans: Marx receives
money and buys weapons. He must therefore be got rid
of.'

It was not surprising that the Belgian government
was alarmed. Marx had been allowed into Belgium on
condition that he did not engage in political activity, yet
for three years he and his friends had been doing
nothing else. At the end of 1847 the authorities must
have been perfectly aware that Marx and Engels were
preparing for publication that textbook of revolution,
the *Communist Manifesto*, which ended with the inflammatory words, 'Workers of the world, unite. You have
nothing to lose but your chains.' But even before it was

published in London in 1848 the year of revolutions had begun.

Paris had given the signal. In February Louis Philippe's monarchy was overthrown and he was exiled to Britain. In Paris a provisional government was set up composed of radicals, democrats and reformers of all kinds. There was even a worker in the government for the first time. In Brussels the news was greeted with general wild excitement and the exiles prepared themselves for action. It was time for the Belgian government to act.

Marx was arrested on 3 March 1848 and Jenny, beside herself with anxiety, ran through the streets trying to get help. 'Suddenly I was seized by a guard,' she wrote in her autobiography,

> arrested and thrown into a dark prison. It was where beggars without a home, vagabonds and wretched fallen women were detained. I was thrust into a dark cell. As I entered, sobbing, an unhappy companion in misery offered to share her place with me: it was a hard plank bed. I lay down on it. When morning broke I saw at the window opposite mine, behind iron bars, a cadaverous, mournful face. I went to the window and recognized our good old friend Gigot. When he saw me he beckoned to me, pointing downwards. I looked in that direction and saw Karl being led away under military escort. An hour later I was taken into the interrogating magistrate. After a two hours' questioning, during which they got little out of me, I was led to a carriage by gendarmes and towards evening I got back to my three poor little children.

Jenny had a taste for the dramatic and her account reads like a scene from grand opera. Certainly the arrest of Jenny von Westphalen caused a great stir in Brussels. The newspapers reported the lurid story of the Baron's daughter thrown into jail with common prostitutes and vagrants, and the authorities were forced to dismiss the police officers concerned.

The ordeal changed Jenny. She had now had first-hand experience of suffering; she had seen poverty and the inside of a prison, and all her humanitarian emotions were aroused. Now she was blooded, she had proved her worth as a fighting partner. Increasingly she adopted Marx's aggressive language and signed her letters, with a flourish, '*Citoyenne et Vagabonde*'.

Some of Marx's old friends were now in the French provisional government and Flocon sent an effusive letter to Marx inviting him to Paris. So they set off for what Jenny called 'the Rising Sun of the New Revolution'. '[I] hastily packed my belongings and sold what I could but left my boxes with all my silver plate and best linen in Brussels in charge of the bookseller . . . it was a cold, dull day and we had difficulty in keeping the children warm, the youngest of them was just a year old.' That silver and damask was to follow them throughout their lives. It was the crested silver from the Argyll inheritance, and Scottish damask tablecloths and napkins.

The cradle of the new Europe

They were received enthusiastically in Paris by the provisional government, and for a while they could observe with amusement their French comrades in power occupying the royal palaces. Engels lunched at the Tuileries, in the Prince de Joinville's suite. 'In Louis-Philippe's apartments now', he wrote, 'the wounded lie on the carpets, smoking stubby pipes.' The city was, in the words of Arnold Ruge, 'the cradle of the new Europe'.

Marx did not stay long in Paris; he saw his place in Germany, directing the revolution there. In April once again Jenny packed the trunks and, while Marx set up their base in Cologne, she took the children to Trier. Later she joined Marx and for a year Cologne was their home. Marx, realising that his contribution to revolution must be with the pen and not with the sword, started a new daily paper, the *Neue Rheinische Zeitung*, which was intended to spur all radicals to action. But when on 25 September revolution broke out in Cologne, Marx's journal was suspended under martial law. Defying the court ruling, the paper reappeared in October, and Marx was tried on charges of incitement to rebellion.

Meanwhile in Barmen Engels was terrifying his parents. He had leaped into the fray with relish, sword in hand, and his mother must have watched with anguish while her bright son manned the barricades in Barmen and later fought in Baden with the rebels. This was, he believed, the triumphant revolution that he had so eagerly awaited.

But in fact in the summer and autumn of 1848 all over Europe the revolutions had been failing. For the most part untrained, and often divided, the rebels were losing the struggle against the disciplined counter-revolutionary forces. 'The Hungarian Revolution, the Baden insurrection, the Italian uprising, all collapsed,' as Jenny described later in her memoirs. In April, in England, the great Chartist demonstration had been a failure. Engels had been so confident of the Chartists' ability to overturn the government that he had wagered that in one month Julian Harney would replace Palmerston as Prime Minister. When the Baden rebellion failed, Engels went to fight a rearguard action to protect the retreat of the rebel troops. He showed great courage but to no avail; finally he escaped to Switzerland.

Marx's trial for sedition dragged on all winter until finally, in February 1849, the jury acquitted him. However on 16 May that year he was expelled from Prussia. He produced one final inflammatory edition – printed in red – and in June left Cologne and headed for Paris again.

Once more Jenny pawned the silver to pay for her

journey to Trier with Lenchen and the three children. But her beloved home town was no longer comfortable. She herself had changed and was irritated by the complacency of her friends who could not see that their world was crumbling beneath their feet. Above all, as far as her Westphalen stepbrother Ferdinand was concerned, she was now irrevocably on the other side of the barricades. And she was involved now no longer in the battle of words and ideas, but in that of guns and bullets. Ferdinand was hoping to become a minister in the Prussian government, and it was he who ordered the censorship and closure of Marx's journal.

In France too the splendid vision had faded. The provisional government, a coalition of disparate idealists, had disintegrated. The long-sought manhood suffrage, granted by the government, brought in an assembly which was afraid of experiment and violent change. The socialist Louis Blanc's pet remedy – national workshops for the unemployed – had not been given a chance to succeed. When, on 22 June, they were closed, the workers were dismissed and hundreds of angry unemployed roamed the streets, alarming the government. Once again the barricades went up in the narrow streets of Paris. There followed four days of ferocious fighting until General Cavaignac restored order. Turgenev, who was at this time living in the same house as Jenny's friend Herwegh, wrote of the workers' sense of hopelessness after that bitter fight. He heard an old worker tell Herwegh, 'The provisional government deceived us. It made many promises, but kept none. It did nothing for the workers. We'd spent all our money on food, and there was no work, nothing to do. Some republic! Well, so we made up our minds to fight. We were done for, anyway.'

The radicals, liberals and socialists were disillusioned, the workers exhausted. When the assembly voted to become a republic with an elected President, the way was opened for a man whose name gave hope. Louis

Napoleon, the nephew of the great general, had scarcely been taken seriously; he was a sparrow to an eagle. But his name and assiduity won him support. He became a candidate for the presidency and swiftly moved to power. In December 1848 he assumed the title of President, declaring: 'I shall regard as enemies of our country all those who attempt by illegal means to change what France has established.'

It was into this sour city, where cholera had followed despair, that Marx returned in the summer of 1849. No longer a welcome visitor, he went into hiding. Yet in spite of this Jenny and Lenchen brought the three children to join Marx. By this time they were penniless – Jenny had pawned her last piece of jewellery and to Marx's humiliation they were now dependent on public collection among his Rhineland friends. They were in hiding at this time, and Jenny acted as a courier, bearing messages. And though they had hoped to escape discovery, they now knew that the secret police had tracked them down. Daily they expected the dread knock on the door.

Nevertheless Jenny was in high spirits. In Trier she had 'an intense nostalgia' for Paris, and like many wives of exiles was unhappiest when separated. Her letter to Edgar's fiancée, Lina Schöler, on 14 July 1849 was brimming with optimism. She wrote of 'pretty convenient lodgings in a salubrious district'. Lenchen was a 'pillar of strength – *toujours la même*'. Her cheerful letter, which contrasts so strongly with Marx's letters of that period, was no doubt partly inspired by the need to put on a good face for those in Trier who were always waiting to say 'We told you so'; so she did not mention cholera, or poverty, or the police.

My dear Lina,

At this moment Paris is splendid and luxurious in the extreme. The aristocracy and bourgeoisie suppose themselves safe since the ill-starred 13 June and the fresh

victories their party has won. On the 14th all the gran-
dees, together with their carriages and their liveried
retainers, were already creeping out of the holes in
which they had been hiding and thus the marvellous
streets are awash with magnificence and splendour of
every description. Paris is a gorgeous city. How often
during the past few days have I not wished you were
beside me as, filled with admiration and amazement, I
walked along streets that were alive with people.

She was not allowed to enjoy the delights of Paris for
long. On 19 July once again the police sergeant
knocked, bringing an order exiling them to Morbihan in
Brittany. Marx chose to consider that banishment to
those marshy, mosquito-infested regions would be a
death sentence, and on 24 August he left for England,
leaving Jenny to arange yet another move. Ill and seven
months pregnant, she had to sell up their furniture yet
again and, with Lenchen's help, she packed their
trunks. Later she remembered how, 'sick and exhausted
with my three poor persecuted small children', she
faced the rough crossing to England.

Loud-mouthed, muddle-headed, impotent émigré rabble

For the rest of Marx and Jenny's lives England was their
home. There would be times when they considered
moving on to America or returning to Germany. But the
former was too expensive and, as for the latter, Marx
had given up his Prussian citizenship and, though he
tried from time to time to get it back, he never
succeeded.

During the next seven years, from September 1849,
Jenny had to bring up a family in appalling conditions.
The great revolutionary wave had receded, leaving
thousands stranded. London at this time was the haven
for all the displaced persons of Europe. Accommodation

Mary Livingstone

David Livingstone

Top: The Livingstone children in Scotland

Left: Anna Mary Livingstone, aged about twenty

Above: Robert Livingstone

David Livingstone's funeral in Westminster Abbey

Mary's grave at Shupanga on the Zambesi

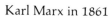
Karl Marx in 1861

Jenny Marx
in 1850

Jennychen in 1850

Eleanor Marx about 1874

Laura Marx

Mr Charles Darwin
On the part of his sincere
admirer

Karl Marx
London 16 June 1873
1, Modena Villas
Maitland Park

Das Kapital.

Kritik der politischen Oekonomie.

Von

Karl Marx.

Erster Band.

Buch I: Der Produktionsprocess des Kapitals.

Zweite verbesserte Auflage.

Das Recht der Uebersetzung wird vorbehalten.

Hamburg

Verlag von Otto Meissner.

1872.

Title page of the copy of *Das Kapital* presented by Marx to Charles Darwin, and inscribed in Marx's hand

Darwin with his son William

Emma with her son Leonard about 1853

was difficult to find and expensive. For a penniless refugee with three children and another expected it was almost impossible. Mary Livingstone faced the same problem. As Jenny soon discovered, you could rent a large house in Germany for the price of two rooms in London. She was met by their old friend from Paris days, the poet George Weerth, now a wholesale trader in London, who found them lodgings in a boarding house in Leicester Square belonging to a master tailor. But it was too expensive, and they were soon turned out and moved to a little house in Chelsea, then still a small village. Here, on 5 November 1849, Jenny gave birth to a son: 'While the people outside were shouting Guy Fawkes for Ever! small masked boys were riding the streets on cleverly made donkeys and all was in an uproar . . . my poor little Heinrich was born. We called him little Fawkes in honour of the great conspirator.' Old Heinrich Marx would not have been pleased to be united with such an incendiary character.

They were evicted from Chelsea for non-payment of rent. Finally they found two rooms in the German hotel in Leicester Street, Leicester Square, where 'for five pounds a week we were given a human reception'. It was from this temporary refuge that she poured out her woes to Josef Weydemeyer. For once the buoyant Jenny was near hysteria.

> As wet-nurses here are too expensive I decided to feed my child myself in spite of continual terrible pains in the breast and back.

The baby had screamed constantly.

> In his pain he sucked so hard that my breast was chafed and the skin cracked and the blood often poured into his trembling little mouth.

When the baliffs came,

They threatened to take everything away in two hours. I would then have had to lie on the bare floor with my freezing children and my bad breast . . . Forgive me, dear friend, for being so long and wordy . . . but my heart is bursting this evening, and I must at least once unload it to my oldest, best and truest friend. Do not suppose that I am bowed down by these petty sufferings, for I know only too well that our struggle is not an isolated one and that, furthermore, I am among the happiest and most favoured few in that my beloved husband, the mainstay of my life, is still at my side.

But what tortured her was the thought that Karl, 'who so willingly and gladly helped so many others', was so helpless himself. Yet in spite of all, she wrote, he remained confident in the future, 'being perfectly content to see me cheerful and our dear children affectionately caressing their dear Mama'. She appealed to Weydemeyer to send them money that was owed Karl for his articles.

Then she finished in her usual cheerful style:

The girls are pretty, blooming, cheerful and in good spirits and our fat boy is a paragon of comical humour and full of the drollest ideas. All day the little imp sings funny songs with tremendous feeling and at the top of his voice and when he sings the verse from Freiligrath's *Marseillaise*

Come O June and bring us deeds
Fresh deeds for which our hearts do yearn

in a deafening voice, the whole house reverberates.

Once again she was the enthusiastic *citoyenne* of old: 'Perhaps it is the historic destiny of that month, like its two unfortunate precursors, to open the gigantic struggle during which we shall all clasp one another's hands again.'

There was, however, to be no political comfort in

June – Paris remained obstinately quiet. Neither was there domestic comfort. After one week their host, weary no doubt of a screaming baby and the house-shaking little Edgar, and with no prospect of rent, turned them out. 'One morning our worthy host refused to serve us breakfast,' she wrote in her memoirs. They finally found two rooms at No. 64 Dean Street, Soho, in the house of a Jewish lace dealer. Later they would move to No. 48, which was to be their home for the next six years.

In the eighteenth century Soho had been a pleasant, flourishing neighbourhood, and even ten years before the Marxes' arrival Soho Square had almost a rural air. But at this time it was swarming with foreign refugees, French, Italian and German, all babbling in a multitude of tongues and all desperately poor. In the summer the stench from the ancient sewers was suffocating: for Jenny and Karl, brought up in the clean air of Trier, the streets were unbearable. When in 1852 sewers were constructed for the area, the open trenches were found to be built over the old plague pits. In the cloacal imagery of Marx's letters of this period one smells the streets of Soho: 'I am stuck in *petit bourgeois* muck up to my skull.' Cholera was rife here, as it had been in Paris. One in three in their area 'croaked', Marx reported to Engels. For the whole of this period their letters are filled with sickness, death and complaints of grinding poverty.

It was Jenny who bore the heaviest burden. Apart from anything else, Marx spoke little English, and although he soon learned to read it fluently it was years before he could speak it without embarrassment, and even then it was always with a guttural Rhenish accent. In September 1856, he was reluctant to dine with an American publisher because 'my poor spoken English might put me to shame'. So it was Jenny who dealt with the creditors and the pawn shop.

And in August 1850 it was Jenny who, realising that

yet another child was on its way and desperate for
money, made the uncomfortable journey to Holland to
beg from Karl's uncle. Lion Philips, brother-in-law of
Marx's mother Henrietta, was a generous man but his
business had been nearly ruined by Marx's revolutionary friends and he refused to help. 'However', wrote
Jenny, 'as I was going he pressed into my hand a
present for my youngest child and I saw that it hurt him
not to be able to give me more.' Jenny returned home
in despair to the house in Dean street above which, far
in the future, the name Philips would arc in neon lights,
advertising the great enterprise which his family would
found. In November, tragedy followed disappointment.
The one-year-old Heinrich, whose constant wailing had
irritated the other tenants in Chelsea, now contracted
meningitis. In the suffocating little room the agonised
crying finally ceased. After the baby's death Jenny could
bear the lodgings no longer, and they moved to another
house in Dean Street. Here, with Lenchen and the
children, they lived in two rooms, though later they
rented an extra small room as a study for Marx.

Somewhere in the suffocating chaos of the apartment
Lenchen found a corner for herself. She was attractive
and competent and could have found other more comfortable employment. But, devoted to them both, she
chose to stay; cleaned, cooked and mended for them
and frequently trudged to the pawn shop. For during
their years in Soho not only the Marxes' remaining
valuables, silver, linen and watches, were left at
'uncle's, but Jenny's shawls and even her skirts and
shoes. And when the family were reduced to living on
bread and potatoes, Lenchen starved with them.

Poverty was not the only problem. Most of the
émigrés were penniless but the committees set up to
help them were constantly disrupted by dissension.
Jenny recalled how the German democrats on the one
hand officially separated from the socialists, and 'there

was a clear rift even among the communist working men'.

With the failure of revolution all over Europe, London was at this time filled with disillusioned and squabbling refugees. Italians argued among themselves, some eager to follow Mazzini back into the fray while others listened to the more cautious advice of Garibaldi, the practical soldier. The French exiles were split between the utopian followers of Proudhon and the revolutionaries who saw in little Louis Blanc the hero who could oust Louis Napoleon. But the Germans rows were particularly sulphurous. According to the Russian émigré Alexander Herzen, 'The German emigrants were distinguished from the others by their ponderous, prosy and cantankerous nature. . . . They had no common plan: their unity was supported by mutual hatred . . . except for a few of the leaders they were tearing each other to pieces with indefatigable frenzy.'

Marx and his followers saw more clearly than the other Germans how unprepared uprisings were doomed to failure when faced with the trained troops of the counter-revolution. But men like August Willich, a swashbuckling ex-Prussian officer, were straining at the leash, longing to be back on the barricades. He accused Marx of cowardice. The fact that Willich was an experienced officer who had fought with skill and courage in the Baden uprising did not endear him to Marx, who was no man of action.

A committee, of which Marx was chairman and Engels secretary, had been set up to raise funds for German refugees. Now at committee meetings the comrades hurled insults and accusations at each other, and Jenny remembered that 'Karl above all was persecuted beyond measure, calumniated and defamed.' Finally the committee split. Then there were arguments over who should have the funds, and Marx was accused of misappropriating some of the refugee money. He had, in fact, when in dire straits, borrowed twenty pounds from the committee which he pledged to pay back in instalments. This, as Engels later confirmed, he did, but the gossip rumbled on for a long time, wounding Marx's pride.

Jenny was particularly distressed by the absurd accusation that, because her stepbrother Ferdinand was a minister in the Prussian government, Marx was a spy. As he was quick to point out, it was Ferdinand who had closed down his journal in Cologne.

There were personal grievances too. Jenny remembered in her memoirs how Willich had tried to seduce her.

> Early one morning he made his appearance in our bedroom, dressed like a real Don Quixote in a grey woollen doublet and a scarlet cloth wound round his waist instead of a belt, roaring with Prussian horse-laughs, perfectly ready to begin a long theoretical debate on 'natural' communism. Karl put a quick end to these attempts. From time to time he would come to visit me, because he wanted to pursue the worm which lives in every marriage and draw it out.

In September 1850 the feuding culminated in a duel. Willich challenged Marx – who did not deign to pick up the glove. Instead, one of his militant young supporters, the Hotspur of their group, Conrad Schramm, accepted the challenge on Marx's behalf. Marx attempted to prevent the duel, but to avoid English law Schramm and Willich crossed over to Ostend with their seconds and fought. Jenny waited the outcome with intense anxiety. Their friend Wilhelm Liebknecht described how Barthelemy, Willich's second, brought the news back to London:

> In the evening of the following day the door of Marx's house was opened – he was not at home, only Mrs Marx and Lenchen – and Barthelemy entered bowing stiffly and replying with a sepulchral voice to the anxious

question 'What news?' *'Schramm a une balle dans la tête!'* Schramm has a bullet in his head – whereupon bowing stiffly once more he turned and withdrew. You may imagine the fright of the half insensible lady; she knew now that her instinctive dislike had not deceived her.

One hour later she related the sad news to us. Of course, we gave up Schramm for lost. The next day, while we were just talking about him sadly, the door was opened and in he came with a bandaged head but gaily laughing, the sadly mourned one, and related that he had received a glancing shot which had stunned him. When he recovered consciousness, he was alone on the sea coast with his second and his physician.

Throughout the year the rows continued between the factions, leading to brawls in the pubs where German émigrés congregated and even fist-fighting at a public meeting for the refugees of all countries.

But Marx and Engels held themselves aloof. As Jenny wrote, they 'broke off completely from the doings of the bulk of the emigrants and never took part in a single demonstration'. Engels, according to Jenny, 'after trying in vain to earn his living by writing in London went to Manchester and worked as a clerk in his father's textile business on very bad terms'. When Marx and Engels retreated, their opponents whispered that 'whatever the outcome of the revolution, Marx is *perdu*'. Engels, however, claimed that they were 'glad to get rid of the entire loud-mouthed, muddle-headed, impotent émigré rabble', who were 'dastardly swine, rooting about in the cesspits of the press'. He and Marx, Engels declared, would 'never be loved by the democratic, the red, or even the communist mob'.

A man of genius and energy

Gradually some of the émigrés found work and settled down; the poet Freiligrath, surprisingly, became a banker – assistant manager at the Swiss Crédit Mobilier in London. A very gentle man, whose 'felicitous poetry' Jenny greatly admired, he was one of the few who remained loyal to Marx and of whom Marx spoke – at least at first – with unusual kindness. But he too would later encounter Marx's wrath as he dared to associate with bourgeois democrats, and Jenny would call him 'the fat philistine'.

But many of the old friends were now dispersed. The poet Herwegh had escaped to Switzerland and settled there. Heine was desperately ill in Paris. Georg Weerth, whom Engels called 'the first and most important poet of the German proletariat', was dying of boredom in Bradford – 'a beastly hole'. Later he was to break out and roam around Europe and South America, finally to die of fever in Cuba. Wilhelm Pieper, a clever young philologist, first worked as a tutor in the Rothschild family, then wandered, a shabby, somewhat seedy and pathetic figure, into the Marx circle. He acted as Marx's secretary for a while, and taught the Marx children. The transition to the slums of Soho must have caused him considerable cultural shock.

There were some friends, like Liebknecht, who remained faithful and were laughed at for their pains. Karl Bauer wrote scornfully: 'On the top throne its the all-knowing, the all-wise, the Dalai Lama Marx, then a long gap, then Engels and . . . last the sentimental ass Liebknecht.' But Liebknecht's warm heart and kindness endeared him to the Marx children – they called him their 'Dear Library'; he lived nearby, saw them every day and joined in their expeditions. When he took them to watch the Duke of Wellington's funeral he panicked when he lost them in the crowd.

The greatest support to the whole family was Engels. Without him, as Marx later admitted, *Des Kapital* would never have been written and Marx would probably have remained an obscure émigré scribbler. At this time Engels was learning his father's textile business in

Manchester, which he did quickly and thoroughly and eventually became a partner. Finally, in 1869, he sold his share for a considerable sum and gave Marx an annual allowance of three hunded and fifty pounds. Engels was perfectly prepared all his life not only, as he said, to play second fiddle, but also to support Marx and his family financially. Over the years Engels gave generously to Marx – almost two thousand pounds between 1866 and 1869 alone. Sometimes he posted five pound notes cut in half to deter thieves, sometimes much larger sums.

Meanwhile, although he hated the business world, he made the best of the social life in Manchester. He enjoyed good food and wine, and rode to hounds with the Cheshire Hunt – he loved galloping across the countryside, training himself, he claimed, for the revolution. He sent for textbooks on military training, read Napier on Wellington and the Peninsular War; after buying up the library of an ex-officer in the Prussian army he became, theoretically, a military expert. Engels was now keenly aware of the amateur nature of their uprisings of 1848 and hoped that the next revolution would not come until he had mastered the art of war. Marx's children gave him the nickname 'General', and little Edgar became his adoring 'Colonel Musch'.

The Marx family were fond of nicknames. Eleanor was always Tussy, elegant Laura was Cacadou, the name of a smart tailor, while Jenny was usually Möhme or Möhmchen, a German version of Mummy. Marx himself was usually Moor, a reference either to his dark countenance, or a comparison with Othello. But he was also sometimes Chaley, a children's corruption of Charlie.

Engels ran two establishments in Manchester. In one he entertained his business acquaintances and his father when he paid his rare visits; in the other he lived his private life with his mistress, Mary Burns, and her sister Lizzie. Little appears to be known of the two girls who were so important in Engel's life. They were both illiterate but Mary Burns was intelligent and witty, while Lizzie was practical and wise. Engels was devoted to them both.

During the following years, when the Marxes were increasingly isolated from their old comrades, Karl had the consolation of the intellectual companionship of Engels. When they were separated they wrote long, frank letters to each other, and after Engels finally moved to London in 1870 they met daily. Marx could unburden himself in his letters to Engels with total freedom. He could describe his ill health – his piles and his carbuncles. To Engels he could release his pent-up irritation and frustration and write with malicious freedom about their mutual friends. Above all he could discuss politics. No one else could understand exactly what it was he was trying to achieve.

Not only did he have the relief of writing to Engels, he also had the refuge of the British Museum. He took out a reader's ticket there in June 1850, and when home life became unbearably uncomfortable he could escape. Under the great silent dome he could sit in warmth and comfort and bury himself in research. There he could retreat into the intricacies of medieval land rent and agriculture, and struggle with the works of other economists. Hopeless though he was with his own finances, he could master the abstractions of economics even when the mechanics of simple addition and subtraction eluded him.

Marx had his avenues of escape, but in the difficult years Jenny had no Engels and no British Museum; as Marx himself admitted, 'She had no such refuges.' She had always enjoyed the intellectual stimulus of their literary friends but now gradually all, except Freiligrath, had become scattered. When they quarrelled with the rest of the Germans they also withdrew from the German Workers' Educational Society, so cutting Jenny off from their pleasant outings to Richmond and Hampton Court and the literary meetings at their Soho headquarters.

Nor did they enjoy the social life of the other émigrés. Marx, conscious that he spoke English badly, was also ashamed of their poverty, and in any case he regarded most of the émigrés from other countries with disdain. So not for Jenny were the pleasant drawing room discussions that Mazzini enjoyed. The Italian exile could bask in the admiration of Thomas and Jane Carlyle, and Emma Darwin's sister-in-law Fanny Hensleigh held fund-raising evenings for him in her pleasant London house. But Marx poured scorn on all those who co-operated with such bourgeois politicians. Though they did attend the scientific lectures given in London by people such as Huxley, they appear to have made no effort to meet the brilliant men and women who shone in London in the 1850s. The remarkable fact was that Marx, a man of deep and wide cultural interests, seems to have been totally insulated from the intellectual life of his adopted city.

Yet Charles Dickens, wandering through Soho, finding his inspiration for *A Tale of Two Cities* among the French refugees, might well have met them at this time. What, one wonders, would he have made of the proud, beautiful German lady who walked so swiftly alone through the streets? He would have been as intrigued as one of her German friends, nicknamed Red Wolf to distinguish him from 'Lupus' Wolff, who, it is said, accosted a lady in the street and raised her veil, only to find to his horror that it was Jenny Marx. Appalled, he rushed away and did not come near them for months.

A vivid picture of their life in Soho in 1852 is given in this report sent back to Prussia by a police spy. At this time the police in Cologne were tracking down and putting into prison their old friends, and had spies working in London and Manchester:

The leader of this party is Karl Marx; his lieutenants are Engels in Manchester, where there are thousands of

German workmen; Freiligrath and Wolff (known as Lupus) in London; Heine in Paris; Weydemeyer and Cluss in America; Bürgers and Daniels were his lieutenants in Cologne, and Weerth in Hamburg. All the rest are merely Party members. The shaping and moving spirit, the real soul of the Party, is Marx; therefore I will go on to acquaint you with his personality.

Marx is of medium height, thirty-four years old. Although in the prime of life, his hair is already turning grey. He is powerfully built . . . and his hair and beard quite black. The latter he does not shave at all. His large piercing fiery eyes have something demonically sinister about them. The first impression one receives is of a man of genius and energy. His intellectual superiority exercises an irresistible power on his surroundings.

In private life he is an extremely disorderly, cynical human being, and a bad host. He leads the existence of a real bohemian intellectual. Washing, grooming and changing his linen are things he does rarely, and he likes to get drunk. Though he is often idle for days on end, he will work night and day with tireless endurance when he has a great deal of work to do. He has no fixed times for going to sleep and waking up. He often stays up all night, and then lies down fully clothed on the sofa at midday and sleeps till evening, untroubled by the comings and goings of the whole world.

His wife is the sister of the Prussian Minister von Westphalen, a cultured and charming woman, who out of love for her husband has accustomed herself to his bohemian existence, and now feels perfectly at home in this poverty. She has two daughters and one son, and all three children are truly handsome.

As husband and father, Marx, in spite of his wild and restless character, is the gentlest and mildest of men. Marx lives in one of the worst, therefore one of the cheapest quarters of London. He occupies two rooms. The one looking out on the street is the *salon*, and the bedroom is at the back. In the whole apartment there is not one clean and solid piece of furniture. Everything is broken, tattered and torn, with a half inch of dust over everything and the greatest disorder everywhere. In the middle of the *salon* there is a large old-fashioned table covered with an oilcloth, and on it there lie manuscripts, books, and newspapers, as well as the children's toys, the rags and tatters of his wife's sewing basket, several cups with broken rims, knives, forks, lamps, an inkpot, tumblers, dutch clay pipes, tobacco ash – in a word, everything topsy-turvy, and all on the same table. A seller of second-hand goods would be ashamed to give away such a remarkable collection of odds and ends.

When you enter Marx's room smoke and tobacco fumes make your eyes water so much that for a moment you seem to be groping about in a cavern, but gradually, as you grow accustomed to the fog, you can make out certain objects which distinguish themselves from the surrounding haze. Everything is dirty, and covered with dust, so that to sit down becomes a thoroughly danger-ous business. Here is a chair with only three legs, on another chair the children are playing at cooking – this chair happens to have four legs. This is the one which is offered to the visitor but the children's cooking has not been wiped away; and if you sit down, you risk a pair of trousers.

It was in this chaotic setting that on 28 March 1851 Jenny's daughter Franziska was born. 'We gave the poor little thing to a nurse for we could not rear her with the others in three small rooms.' They were at this time hungry, ill, harassed by creditors and shunned by other émigrés. But there was worse to come.

Père Marx . . . is adding amazingly to his knowledge but also to his family

On 31 March 1851, at the end of a letter bewailing all these troubles, Marx wrote to Engels, 'Finally, to cap the climax in a tragi-comic way, there comes a secret . . . in which you play a role.'

There is not much comedy in the following story. The mystery of which he dared not write was revealed to

Engels when Marx made a special journey to Manchester, and a secret it remained until the end of the century. While Jenny was in Holland, Lenchen had become pregnant and by March her condition could no longer be concealed. In Manchester, Marx confessed to Engels that he was responsible but that on no account could the truth be told. The part that Engels was to play, and did successfully until just before he died, was to take the blame. When Lenchen's baby was born on 23rd June he was named Frederick and given to a foster mother. Marx's son disappeared into the mists of history, only to reappear after Marx's death as Frederick Demuth, a workman in Hackney.

It is extraordinary that the free-thinking Marx should have been unable to reveal the truth. The fact is that his pride was so great that he would not expose himself and Jenny to the mockery of the German émigré community. It was probably true too, as was later claimed, that he was afraid that Jenny might leave him.

One cannot be totally sure that Jenny knew the truth. But they all lived too close for concealment, and Marx, with all his faults, was no good at lying. His friend Liebknecht said of him that 'he was incapable as a child of pretending – his face was the mirror of his heart'. In her autobiography Jenny wrote simply of 'the event in the early summer of 1851 . . . which I do not wish to relate here in detail, although it greatly contributed to increase our worries, both personal and others'.

Marx's letters to Engels suggest that Jenny knew the truth and was distraught. 'At home everything is always in a state of siege. For nights on end I am set on edge and infuriated by floods of tears . . . I feel sorry for my wife. The main burden falls on her and *au fond* she is right. Industry should be more productive than marriage', and he added honestly, 'I am *très peu endurant* and even *quelque peu dur*.'

Lenchen is scarcely mentioned, and her story is never

told; but it cannot have been easy for a warm-hearted girl to give away her baby. A year later Marx reported that Lenchen was ill with 'a sort of nervous fever'. One is not surprised. All her maternal affection was afterwards lavished on the Marx children, and they in turn returned her love. She was their confidante, their friend, their dear old 'Nym' who must never be forgotten. It says much for the character of both Jenny and Lenchen that they were apparently able to live together in friendship for the rest of their lives.

The full story of Karl Marx and Lenchen can never be known. One can only guess that, given Marx's character, this was no more than a lapse. Marx was a hard-drinking Rhinelander – and so was Lenchen – and in that close apartment there was little privacy. One thing is certain: whoever won at chess, at least one time it was Lenchen who lost the match.

Marx retreated to the British Museum, where he lost himself, as he told Engels, from nine in the morning to seven in the evening. 'Père Marx', Engels wrote to a friend, 'goes daily to the library and is adding amazingly to his knowledge, but also to his family.'

For Lenchen the summer must have been a nightmare, and Jenny too was on the edge of a nervous breakdown. 'She would', Marx wrote to Josef Weydemeyer, 'go under if things continue much longer, the constant worries, the slightest everyday struggle wears her out.' Apart from anything else the baby, Franziska, was constantly ailing and Lenchen was unable to help.

But the hardest burden to bear was the constant criticism from the other German émigrés. Jenny, who always cared for the good opinion of others, who needed affection, had to listen to their carping. Marx was now genuinely worried. 'Her nervous system is impaired,' he continued in his letter to Weydemeyer, 'and is not revived by the exhalations from the pestiferous democratic cloaca daily administered to her by stupid tell-tales.' These rumours were mostly concerned with Marx's financial situation, and he must have been desperately afraid that if his enemies, too, knew the truth about Lenchen, Jenny would finally go under.

Gradually the miserable year of 1851 wore on and Jenny, always resilient, began to find her own kind of escape. They had now acquired a tiny room as Karl's study and here she gradually took over the work that Wilhelm Pieper had been doing. Intellectual exercise, Jenny found, was the best of all remedies for her distress. For the next few years she was Marx's personal assistant and secretary. She answered his letters, arranged his business affairs, copied out his work – and doubtless improved his style. Marx would often work all night and then dictate to her for hours on end in the morning. This must have reminded Jenny of those days when, as a girl, she had worked as her father's secretary; certainly she later remembered the days 'spent in his little study copying his scrawly articles' as the happiest of her life. Marx's handwriting was notoriously illegible; Jenny was one of the few who could decipher it, and even she made mistakes.

She always followed with passionate interest the events in Paris. When in December 1851 Louis Napoleon made himself Emperor after a *coup d'état*, she shared Marx's fury that such an insignificant little man should be aping his heroic uncle. That Marx should be unrecognised while 'Krapulinsky' triumphed was for Jenny an unbearable tragedy. She took particular pleasure in copying Marx's brilliant articles written after the *coup d'état*, and posted them to Josef Weydemeyer who was now trying to establish a journal in New York. Marx's articles were published under the title *The 18th Brumaire of Louise Bonaparte*, a title suggested by a phrase in a letter from Engels. Like most of the other journals that Marx and his friends established, this one too was short-lived, but the articles were reprinted as a pamphlet and it remains one of the most brilliant that Marx ever wrote.

Their only income at this time came from occasional articles written for progressive journals, and from presents from Jenny's mother. Consequently Marx had very little time to continue with the great unwritten work, and his frustration produced both real and imagined illnesses. Jenny was particularly irritated when he and Engels went on what they called a 'colossal binge' at Christmas-time, which made Marx seriously ill for a fortnight. Marx's health was not improved by his way of life – until his death he was to suffer from myriad complaints. At this stage it was piles, headaches and liver disorder.

My head is disintegrating . . . and now I can no more

The following year brought more tragedy. 'At Easter 1852', Jenny wrote in her memoirs,

> our poor little Franziska fell ill with severe bronchitis. For three days the poor child wrestled with death. She suffered much. Her little lifeless body rested in the small back room; we all wandered out into the front room and when night fell we made our beds on the floor, and the three living children lay with us and we wept for the little angel who lay cold and lifeless nearby. The death of our beloved child took place at the time of our bitterest poverty.

None of their friends was able to help. Finally Jenny ran to a French émigré who lived near and begged him for help. 'He at once gave me £2 with the friendliest sympathy and with the money the small coffin was bought and there my poor child now slumbers peacefully. She had no cradle when she came into the world and for a long time she was refused a last resting place.

How we suffered when the coffin was carried away to the graveyard.'

It was not until the summer that Jenny pulled herself out of this new crisis. Marx, as was his custom, spent some time in June with Engels in Manchester, leaving Jenny to cope with the bills and the children's problems. As always he felt guilty. 'You don't have to feel embarrassed reporting everything to me,' he wrote with unaccustomed gentleness. 'When you, poor little devil, live through bitter reality, it is only fair that I share with you the distress at least in my mind. I know, moreover, how endlessly elastic you are and how the slightest favourable thing revivifies you. Hopefully you will receive this week or at the latest next Monday another five pounds . . .'

But in 1853 their desperate financial situation improved. Charles Anderson Dana, editor of the *New York Daily Tribune*, commissioned two articles a week which more often than not were written by Engels. With supreme confidence Marx would ask Engels to produce an article for him at short notice. As he later boasted to a friend, Engels, drunk or sober, day or night, could write brilliantly. For once, Christmas 1853 was celebrated in good Trier fashion with a Christmas tree and presents and good wine sent by Engels.

Life in Soho was not all agony. They were great walkers and Hampstead Heath was not far away. Liebknecht never forgot their Sunday expeditions:

> I generally led the way with the two girls, entertaining them with stories or acrobatics or picking wild flowers, which were more abundant then than now. Behind us came a few friends and then the main body: Marx with his wife and one of the Sunday visitors who was deserving of special consideration. In the rear came Lenchen and the hungriest of our party, who helped her to carry the hamper . . .

Once they had eaten and slept there were 'races, wrestling, heaving stones and other forms of sport'. But the greatest treat was when they all went for donkey rides. Marx 'had fun himself and gave us plenty . . . his horsemanship was so primitive and he exerted such fantasy to assure us of his skill! And his skill boiled down to having taken riding lessons once when he was a student – Engels maintained that he had never got further than the third lesson'.

On these Sundays Marx was released from the incubus of work and became a boy again, shouting old German folksongs on the heights of Hampstead, while Jenny and Lenchen were back in the hills around Trier. The topographical writer William Howitt remembered the Heath at this time. Down in the Vale of Health, 'in front of a row of cottages and under the shade of willows were set out long tables for tea, where many hundreds at a trifling cost partook of a homely and exhilarating refreshment'. Families could take their own tea and bread and butter and have water boiled and table accommodation found for them for a few pence.

Nor was Soho all squalor. Now that Jenny had a little more money she could enjoy the shops in nearby Oxford Street, and in those years there were a number of exciting museums nearby. The Royal Panopticon of Science and Art was opened in Leicester Square in 1852-3; with its domes and minarets it was one of the most elegant buildings in London. Then there was Wyld's Great Globe, a circular building in which the world was represented. During the Crimean War thousands flocked there to see the spectacular models of troops in action. North-west of Soho Square was the fashionable Soho Bazaar. Jenny and the children must have wandered with great pleasure among the stalls, where there was a rustic aviary and a stream of running water. Dean Street itself had a small theatre, the new Opera House, and a drama school. Nearby in Greek Street were the showrooms of Josiah Wedgewood, where their famous dinner services were displayed. Looking back on this period, Jenny remembered with nostalgia 'my long walks in the crowded West End streets after my meetings, our clubs, and the familiar public house with the cosy conversation, which have so often helped me to forget for a while my worries'. In 1854 there was enough money to send Jenny for a holiday to rural Edmonton and even to rig her out for a visit to Trier.

But there were never many months without sickness. In the summer of 1854 all three children had measles and Edgar became seriously ill, so there were heavy doctor's bills. Dr Freund himself was in financial trouble and dunned them for his fees – Jenny, expecting her sixth child, needed him. Eleanor was born in January 1855, and scarcely had Jenny recovered when Edgar became ill again.

Marx was in bed with bronchitis, but he hastily threw off his own illness to take care of the little boy. Gastric fever was followed by abdominal consumption. Marx was distraught, for he adored Edgar with his huge head, large round eyes and impish humour. Forgetting his own ills for once, he nursed him night after night with unaccustomed patience. The day Edgar died he wrote brokenly to Engels, 'My heart is bleeding, the poor child was never once untrue to his nature.' Lieb-knecht never forgot the stricken family on the day of the funeral:

> The mother was weeping in silence, bending over her dead child, Lenchen standing by and sobbing, and Marx, a prey to a terrible agitation answering violently and almost wrathfully any attempt to console him, the two girls weeping silently and pressing close to their mother who clung feverishly to them as if to defend them against death which had robbed her of her boys . . . I went in the coach with Marx. He sat there without a word with his head in his hands.

Marx, made gentle by tragedy, and knowing how much Jenny was suffering, took her for a rare visit to Engels. 'She must', he wrote to Engels, 'have a change of scene . . . I must help her over the next few days.' The death of this child shattered him as nothing else had done. Months later, he wrote, the memory of the 'poor dear child torments us', and Jenny was still 'completely broken down'. The following letter is undated but Jenny might well have written it after the death of Edgar: 'Meanwhile I sit here and go to pieces. Karl, it is now at its worst pitch . . . I sit here and almost weep my eyes out and can find no help. My head is disintegrating. For a week I have kept my strength up and now I can no more.'

My love for you . . . is a giant, in which are crowded together all the energy of my spirit and all the character of my heart

Jenny could not face Dean Street again. When their German friend Imandt offered them his cottage in rural Camberwell she and Lenchen and the children gratefully retreated there. Although in July her daughter Laura wrote that 'Möhmchen is as thin as a halfpenny candle', the country air of Camberwell suited them all and gradually she recovered. There was another good reason for staying out of London. Dr Freund was now suing Marx, and to avoid him Marx went into hiding in Manchester. Once again Engels rescued them.

By March Jenny was almost herself again and making a spirited claim for her grandfather's papers, which her brother-in-law as head of the family was proposing to give to the Prussian government. 'He imagines that I, like the rest of my submissive sisters, will leave everything . . . to the mighty chief of the family. There he is mistaken.'

Jenny was anxious to visit Trier again, since her

mother was seriously ill. Fortunately, a long-awaited small inheritance from a Scottish uncle enabled her to pay their debts 'and once again silver, linen and clothes were withdrawn from their exile at the pawnbroker's'. Now she could enjoy the forgotten luxury of new clothes and, with the three girls smartly fitted out, she could face the sharp eyes of Trier. She returned 'in my new clothes to the dear old house'. Soon after her arrival her mother grew worse. Caroline spent her eighty-first birthday with her beloved family, but it was her last.

Meanwhile Marx was frantically searching for some way of getting out of Soho. With the rest of the money from the inheritance they could afford to move. Now, in Jenny's absence, Marx realised how desperately he needed her. Perhaps, too, he was afraid that at home in Trier she might be tempted to escape permanently from the squalor of Soho – and from him. Certainly the letter he wrote to her from Manchester on 21 June 1856 was as intensely passionate as those he had written in his student days.

My heart's beloved

I am writing you again, because I am alone and because it troubles me always to have a dialogue with you in my head, without your knowing anything about it or hearing it or being able to answer. Poor as your photograph is, it does perform a service for me, and I now understand how even the 'Black Madonna' [ikon], the most disgraceful portrait of the Mother of God, could find indestructible admirers, indeed even more admirers than the good portraits. In any case, those Black Madonna pictures have never been more kissed, looked at, and adored than your photograph, which, although not black, is morose, and absolutely does not reflect your darling, sweet, kissable *dolce* face. But I improve upon the sun's rays, which have painted falsely, and find that my eyes, so spoiled by lamplight and tobacco, can still paint, not only in dream but also while awake. I have you vivaciously before me, and I carry you in my hands, and I kiss you from head to foot, and I fall on my knees before you, and I groan 'Madame, I love you'. And I truly love you more than the Moor of Venice ever loved. The false and worthless world views virtually all characters falsely and worthlessly. Who of my many slanderers and snake-tongued enemies has ever reproached me that I am destined to play the role of chief lover in a second-class theatre? And yet it is true. If the scoundrels had had wit, they would have painted 'the production and direction' on one side, and me lying at your feet on the other. *Look to this picture and to that* they would have written underneath. But dumb scoundrels they are and dumb they will remain, in *seculum seculorum*.

Momentary absence is good, for in constant presence things seem too much alike to be differentiated. Proximity dwarfs even towers, while the petty and commonplace, at close view, grow too big. Small habits, which may physically irritate and take on emotional form, disappear when the immediate object is removed from the eye. Great passions, which through proximity assume the form of petty routine, grow and again take on their natural dimension on account of the magic of distance. So it is with you my love. You have only to be snatched away from me even in a mere dream, and I know immediately that the time has only served, as do sun and rain for plants, for growth. The moment you are absent, my love for you shows itself to be what it is, a giant, in which are crowded together all the energy of my spirit and all the character of my heart. It makes me feel like a man again, because I feel a great passion; and the multifariousness, in which study and modern education entangle us, and the scepticism which necessarily makes us find fault with all subjective and objective impressions, all of these are entirely designed to make us all small and weak and whining. But love – not love for the Feuerbach-type of man, not for the metabolism, not for the proletariat – but for the beloved and particularly for you, makes a man again a man.

You will smile, my sweet heart, and ask, how did I come to all this rhetoric? If I could press your sweet,

white heart to my heart, I would keep silent and not say
a word. Since I cannot kiss with my lips, I must kiss with
language and make words. I could really even make
verses and rhymes like Ovid's *Libri Tristium*, which in
German means *Bücher des Jammers* [Books of Laments].
But I am exiled from you, which is something Ovid did
not conceive.

There are actually many females in the world, and
some among them are beautiful. But where could I find
again a face, whose every feature, even every wrinkle, is
a reminder of the greatest and sweetest memories of my
life? Even my endless pains, my irreplaceable losses I
read in your sweet countenance, and I kiss away the
pain when I kiss your sweet face. 'Buried in her arms,
awakened by her kisses' – namely, in your arms and by
your kisses, and I grant the Brahmins and Pythagoras
their doctrine of regeneration and Christianity its doctrine of resurrection . . . Goodbye, my sweet heart. I
kiss you and the children many thousand times.

Yours,
Karl

On 23 July Caroline von Westphalen died. In her
lonely last years she had become querulous and
demanding, but Jenny had always been deeply attached
to her. At least she had the comfort of being with her
mother at the end, and Caroline had the pleasure of
seeing her three pretty grandchildren. Jenny was, Marx
wrote to Engels in August 1856,

greatly affected by the old lady's death. She will have to
spend a week or ten days in Trier in order to put up for
auction what little in the way of effects her mother has
left and to share the proceeds with Edgar. She has
proposed the following scheme: After spending a few
days more in the vicinity of Trier with a woman friend
of hers, she will travel to Paris and thence direct to
Jersey, having decided that we ought to spend September and October there. First, so that she herself can
recuperate; secondly because it's cheaper and pleasanter

than London and, finally, so that the children should
learn French, etc. . . .

But Jenny was drawn back to London by the hope of
a new home, though she did spend some time in Paris,
where she heard from her old friends the full, sad story
of the death in poverty there of the poet Heine.

In the first week of September she was back in Dean
Street. Wilheim Pieper was pushed out, but after two
days he had returned to help them with the move. For
two weeks they spent 'the whole day from morning to
night . . . in search of lodgings', as Marx wrote to
Engels. 'At last', he wrote in triumph on 22 September,
'we found a place, a whole house which we have to
furnish ourselves. It is 9, Grafton Terrace, Maitland Park,
Haverstock Hill, Hampstead Road. Rent £36. We are to
move in on 29 September; this week we have to furnish
it.' Jenny was in her element. She went to auctions,
bought carpets and curtains and rickety furniture in
junk shops. And before long they were short of money
again. 'We are in something of a quandary', Marx
confessed to Engels, 'as we have about £26 to pay out
in town and a great deal more for the new set-up.' Once
more Engels came to the rescue, this time as a loan.
Jenny's inheritance, so her stepbrother Ferdinand told
them, had been invested in Lower Silesian Railway
Bonds and it was a bad moment to sell. At last, after
what Marx called much hurly-burly, they were settled
in their new home and 'more or less straight'. It was the
close of a chapter and the beginning of a new life.

Into the land of the Philistines

'*La Vie de Bohème* came to an end,' wrote Jenny,

and where previously we had fought the battle of
poverty in exile freely and openly, now we had the

appearance of respectability and held up our heads
again. We sailed with all sails flying into the land of the
Philistines. There were still the same little hardships, the
same struggles and the same wretchedness, the same
intimate relationship with the three balls – but the
humour had gone. I first came to know the real oppres-
sion of exile during this first phase of our truly bourgeois
life as Philistines.

Yet this break with the past was, Jenny considered,
absolutely essential for the sake of the children.

Haverstock Hill at this time was still rural. Engels
looked it up on the map and noted with surprise that
they were really out in the country at the foot of the
Hampstead hills. But the busy Victorian builders and
the march of progress were changing all that. Houses
were now mushrooming all along the northern routes
out of London, and it was a comfortable new house
they came to in Grafton Terrace.

In October Jenny wrote lyrically to Louise von Westphalen's brother, Wilhelm von Florencourt, in Germany
of their 'exceptionally pretty house', and of the beauty
of the site near Hampstead Heath. 'It is surrounded by
fresh green meadows and pastureland . . . Before us
stretches the misty silhouette of the great giant city of
London . . . with its view on clear days of the dome of
St Paul's.' The back room looked out over a hilly
landscape to 'delightful Highgate with its church
throned high on a hill'. She luxuriated in the unaccustomed space – the three floors of large rooms, the loft,
the basement and the garden, where she built a 'palace'
for chickens out of old packing cases. 'I really felt
magnificent at first in our snug parlour,' she wrote to
Louise Weydemeyer. 'All the linen and other small
remains of past grandeur were redeemed from "Uncle"
and I again had the pleasure of counting old Scottish
damask napkins.' The children were enchanted. The
girls had pretty rooms of their own and Eleanor, the

baby, was 'forever kissing the new carpets', while 'the little dog crouched on the felt hearth rug'.

As always Jenny turned the bright side towards Germany, but her autobiography tells a different story. In fact their first winter was not so idyllic. Building was going on all round.

> We had to pick our way over accumulations of rubbish, and when it was raining the red clay clung to the soles of our boots, so that it became a tiresome struggle to lift our hundredweight boots into the house. And when darkness fell over this barbaric district, rather than spending the evening in a struggle with the dark, the rubbish, the clay and the heaps of stones, we preferred to gather round the warm fireside.

Grafton Terrace was not easy to reach and the few friends who remained were reluctant to brave the journey. It was months before Jenny got used to the isolation and there were even times when she hankered after the lights and vitality of Soho.

With Marx buried in work, or in the British Museum, she desperately needed intellectual companionship and could not find it among her neighbours. 'Fortunately,' she wrote, 'I still had the article for *Tribune* to copy out and that kept me in touch with world events.'

But gradually the income from *Tribune* dried up. Marx, who had been earning two pounds an article twice a week, was reduced to writing one article a week, thus halving their income. The world economic crisis of this year not only affected the New York *Tribune*, it meant that those to whom Marx was in debt were themselves hard-pressed and dunned him. Luckily in April Dana, his American editor, asked him to contribute to the *New American Cyclopaedia* at two dollars a page. It was a godsend at this time, for Jenny had spent the winter, she said, 'surrounded by a battery of medicines'. She was in fact once again pregnant – approaching the 'catastrophe', as Marx called it. This time the word was justified. The baby – Jenny's seventh – expected in May or June was born in the first week of July. But, as Marx wrote to Engels, 'The child was not viable; it died immediately.'

The mystery surrounding this baby's death probably will never be solved, but Marx could not bring himself to write about it, even to Engels. 'The death in itself was no misfortune,' he wrote, 'but partly because of the circumstances directly connected with it, it has made a frightful impresssion on my imagination; partly because the circumstances that led to this result were such that the memory is distressing.' If it 'unnerved' him 'for some days', what must it have been like for Jenny? Engels was quick to point out that Marx had not mentioned his wife. 'You yourself maybe are taking the child's death stoically but hardly your wife. How *she* is you don't say.'

Not surprisingly Jenny was depressed and ill for some months. She was also, Marx told Engels, 'extraordinarily out of temper, for which I don't blame her though I find it wearisome'. But once again she put on a brave face for the benefit of her stepfamily in Trier. When, in January 1858, she wrote her annual letter to Louise von Westphalen she passed over the baby's death in a few words. 'On the 6th of July our family was once more enriched by the advent of a tiny being, who unhappily only survived for a few moments and another quiet hope was laid in the grave, calling to mind anew the old pain and longing for the dear departed . . .' She described with enthusiasm how she and the girls had spent 'the lovely, hot summer days' in the open air and had wandered around in the woods and meadows.

With maternal pride she wrote of her three girls who gave her 'much happiness with their friendly, loving, modest characters'. Little Jenny was almost as tall as she was, and, she added, 'I was always a right long Lala as they say in Trier.' Eleanor – Tussy as they called her – was thoroughly spoilt by the older girls, as if they had transferred

> all the love . . . for their dear brother [Edgar] to the tiny creature . . . who came as a Godsend when our house was a place of desolation and suffering . . . On her third birthday, under the direction of our chief court dressmaker, Lenchen, Jennychen and Laura made Tussy an outfit in light silver grey material, trimmed with pink blush.

So, to Louise, Jenny presented their family life in the best light, now and then transforming their real life into one that Louise – the minister's wife – could recognise and admire. London, she reported, was very colourful, with surging crowds gathering for the marriage celebrations of Prince Friedrich Wilhelm of Prussia to Princess Victoria, Queen Victoria's eldest daughter. Jenny confessed that they had not yet braved the rough English crowds to visit the Royal Chapel and state apartments, now open to the public. She knew that Louise, and Jenny's stepsister Lisette, who was a lady-in-waiting at the Prussian Court, would undoubtedly be involved in the excitement. Their good English, Jenny considered, would come into its own, for there certainly would be a lot of English spoken at the Prussian Court. Was there perhaps a sign of envy as she sent her good wishes to Louise's young daughter, who was undoubtedly 'looking forward to the many entertainments'? This was the glittering world in which she and her pretty daughters could have shone. And though she had few regrets for herself, she was determined not to sacrifice their education on the altar of her political beliefs. 'We have devoted all our energies to their upbringing,' she wrote to a friend.

So in spite of the fact that, once again, they were penniless, the girls were sent to an exclusive seminary for young ladies – South Hampstead College for Ladies,

Clarence House, 18 Haverstock Hill, ran by Miss Boynell and Miss Rentsch. Jennychen and Laura had
attended a little school in Soho, and Wilhelm Pieper
had given them some lessons, but now they shone in
their new school, winning prizes. As Marx wrote with
pride to Engels, 'Jenny was first in class and Laura
second.'

In addition, they had extra art, music and dancing
lessons. The last Jennychen needed, for Jenny told
Louise that at fourteen she was 'angular and clumsy'
and that when 'in charge of the tea table all the tea cups
were constantly at risk'. A piano was hired, and Marx
and Jenny listened with some pride and nostalgia to
their German duets.

Jennychen and Laura continued their music and language lessons even after they left school. Jennychen's
special talent, Jenny wrote to a friend, 'is in elocution
and the child has a very beautiful speaking voice, "a
voice low and sweet", and has studied Shakespeare
since childhood with fanaticism. She has a deep strong
bent to dramatic representation and in fact she would
long ago have gone on the stage if consideration for her
family' had not held her back. Jennychen was 'strikingly
dark, hair, eyes and skin and looks really sparkling with
her childish, round, rosy cheeks and her deep sweet
eyes. Laura, somewhat slighter and fairer, is really
prettier than the oldest sister because she has more
regular features and her greenish eyes with dark brows
and long lashes gleam with fiery lights . . .' Nevertheless even the fond mother had to admit that there was
something wanting in the set of Laura's mouth. Laura
was sharper and wittier than her sister, but her letters
revealed a colder, more selfish nature. Later she became
something of a beauty – Laura, in her elegant riding
habit, was quite a sensation on Haverstock Hill.

As for Tussy, she was growing up with her gang – a
tomboy on the unmade streets. But even at that early
age she showed the passion for politics that endured all

her life. At six she was writing long letters of advice to President Lincoln which Marx gravely pretended to post. She too shared the family passion for Shakespeare – old Baron von Westphalen's cultural legacy lasted as long as his Scottish silver.

But the cost of living in the 'land of the bourgeoisie' was crippling and their few valuables were often pawned to pay for it. Once a suspicious pawnbroker challenged Marx's right to possess the crested silver. By the summer of 1858 Marx was desperate. In July he sent Engels a detailed account of their desperate financial state, showing that Jenny 'hasn't spent a farthing on clothes etc for herself, while the situation as regards the children's summer dress is sub proletarian'. Even should he take the 'children away from school, get rid of the maids, live on potatoes . . . auction my household goods,' he claimed, 'the creditors would still not be paid'. He would not mind living in Whitechapel, but, for his wife, 'such a metamorphosis might entail dangerous consequences, and it would hardly be suitable for young girls'.

This time Engels, who was ill himself, could only offer his surety for a loan to pay for Jenny to have a holiday in Ramsgate. She had a week as a 'parlour boarder' and enjoyed the company of what Marx called 'refined and "*horribile dictu*" clever Englishwomen. After years during which she has enjoyed only inferior company, if any at all, intercourse with people of her own kind seems to agree with her'. She sent for Lenchen and the children and they spent blissful days sunning themselves on the 'magnificent beach'. 'After breakfast,' she told Louise von Westphalen, 'we went into the sea in a bathing cabin and I had a lot of trouble getting my three water sprites out of the waves and often had to get a rather frightful looking woman wrapped in blue flannel to catch them for me.' After the short commons at home, her landlady's roasts and puddings were ambrosial.

The holiday, Marx told Engels, left her 'mentally much more refreshed, but physically (save that her nerves are stronger) she is not yet all that she might be'. And though Jenny herself, at the end of 1858, wrote to Louise von Westphalen with her usual buoyancy of their happy summer and their walks on the Heath in the magnificent autumn weather, it was a different picture that Marx presented to Engels:

> In this house things look more dreary and desolute than ever since my wife cannot even arrange Christmas festivities for the children – instead she is beset on all sides by dunning letters, on top of which she has to copy my manuscript and, in between whiles, to run errands to the pawnshop in town – The atmosphere is gloomy in the extreme.

According to Marx, not even the thought of the impending revolution cheered her. 'After all the *misère* she had to go through, the Revolution will only make things worse and afford her the gratification of seeing all the humbugs from here celebrating their victories over there.'

If only Karl had made capital instead of writing about it

The manuscript that Jenny was so painfully copying was the *Critique of Political Economy*, the first part at least of the monumental work he had planned as far back as 1844. Originally he had intended it to be a massive, six-volume scientific study of the history and practice of economics. But in 1857–8 he was still working on the rough draft of the first volume, on capital. The other five were to deal with landed property, wage labour, the state, international trade and the world market. So meticulous was his research, so voluminous his notes, that Volume I was rapidly growing into a three-volume work, and even the first part of that was monstrously increasing.

And now it became urgent to publish at least something. In 1857 an international monetary crisis was rocking the world and Marx and his friends were convinced that revolution would follow a collapse of currencies. As he had done since the beginning of their friendship, Engels begged him to finish the book. But just as Marx had, as a student, found great difficulty in finishing any work, so now it was the greatest labour for him to produce for the printers his *Critique of Political Economy*. It was not until years later, in 1867, that what was intended to be the third chapter of Part I of Volume I was published as *Das Kapital*.

So, labouring up the foothills of an ever-receding mountain, Marx was visibly relieved when the expected revolution did not happen. While he was struggling with his *Critique of Political Economy*, Jenny was dealing with the problems of their domestic economy. But at last, in January, the *Critique of Political Economy* was ready to be sent to the printers in Germany, finally to be published in June. He had to borrow the money for postage from Engels. 'I don't believe', he reflected wryly, 'that anybody has ever written about money whilst suffering such a lack of money.' Later Marx was to recall his mother's shrewd words: 'If only Karl had made capital instead of writing about it!'

Whether it was his difficult style, or the density of thought, or the erudition that weighed it down, or, as Marx himself thought, the hostility of his enemies, the long-awaited *Critique*, launched with such hope, dropped into a well of silence. 'I expected to be attacked and criticised but not to be utterly ignored,' he wrote. Even the faithful Liebknecht almost wept. 'Never has a book disappointed me so much.' For Jenny, who had sacrificed so much, the disappointment was unbearable. 'The secret hopes we had long nourished in regard to Karl's book,' she complained to Engels, 'were all set at nought by the Germans' conspiration of silence.' Nevertheless she still hoped that the second instalment might startle the slugabeds out of their lethargy.

Fiercely loyal, Jenny was furious when a German émigré scientist, Karl Vogt, wrote what she called 'a defamatory attack on Karl . . . in which he told the most infamous lies'. As for Marx, instead of continuing with the work on Volume II he spent months collecting material to refute the calumny. Jenny worked through the autumn, copying his pamphlet, a vicious reply to Herr Vogt, in which all the bile and frustration of the past years were released.

Jenny was herself now at breaking point. Marx had worried all year about her health and in the summer of 1960 he had, with Engel's help, sent her for a summer holiday to Hastings. As Marx wrote, 'She had all sorts of nervous complaints.' In fact she was mentally and physically exhausted. It had been a decade not only of poverty and illness but of great tragedy. The deaths of her children left scars which would never heal. But in November 1860 there was a sickening blow which left scars of a different kind.

I did not know whether I would remain enveloped in eternal night

In November Jenny contracted smallpox, though according to Marx she had been twice vaccinated. If it had not been smallpox, her doctor claimed, she was so exhausted that she might have had typhoid and would not have survived. Marx and Lenchen were both innoculated again and nursed her, but the children were immediately sent to the accommodating Liebknecht. 'That very noon the girls, carrying their few belongings, went into exile,' Jenny wrote to Louise Weydemeyer. Once again to these old friends she unburdened herself. The Weydemeyers were two friends to whom she could

write honestly of the terrible times when she thought
she was dying. The agony was intense, and the burning
pains in her face made her lose

> all use of my outward senses though I was fully con-
> scious all the time. I lay constantly by the open window
> so that the cold November air would blow over me,
> while there was a raging fire in the stove and ice on my
> burning lips and I was given drops of claret from time to
> time. I could hardly swallow, my hearing was getting
> weaker and finally my eyes closed so that I did not know
> whether I would remain enveloped in eternal night.

By 28 November the 'tenderest and truest care' of
Marx and Lenchen had restored her, but the doctor
warned that she must go away immediately for at least
four weeks. Marx, again, was in dire straits – Jenny
could not this time be sent to the pawnbroker's. He
appealed once more to Engels – describing in detail his
own appalling toothache. Always interested in the
relation between physical pain and creative thought, he
added, 'This physical pressure furthers very much the
ability to think and hence of the power of abstraction,
for, as Hegel says, pure thought or pure being or
nonbeing are identical.'

Hegel had no such consoling words for Jenny. She
had always been proud of her youthful good looks.
'Five weeks before', she wrote ruefully to Louise
Weydemeyer,

> I had looked quite respectable beside my healthy girls.
> Surprisingly I had no grey hair and my teeth and figure
> were good and therefore people used to class me among
> the well-preserved women . . . But now I seemed to
> myself a kind of cross between a rhinoceros and a
> hippopotamus whose place was in the zoo rather than
> among the Caucasian race.

Even in March 1861, as she told Engels, her face was
still 'disfigured by pockmarks and of a red which is just

the "magenta" that is now in fashion'. However lightly she might write, this disfigurement was a sickening blow for Jenny who was proud of her beauty and always cared desperately for the good opinion of others. Her self-respect, so battered in the last years, had been maintained by her knowledge that at least she had kept her looks.

There is no doubt that she was beginning to feel that she was no longer the partner of old. Her beautiful, intelligent daughters were taking over from her as Karl's assistants. 'Today my Jennychen is copying the articles in my place,' she had written to Engels in December 1859. 'I believe my daughters will soon put me out of business and I shall then come on the register of those entitled to assistance. A pity there is no prospect of getting a pension after my long years of secretarial duties.' If, as has been said, there was a time when their marriage nearly foundered, it was in these years. Certainly Marx often complained to Engels that she was querulous and crotchety and in a nervous state, and, as he admitted, he did not blame her.

The bourgeoisie will have cause to remember my carbuncles

Her temper could not have been improved by Marx's prolonged visit to the continent in 1861. Once more, desperate for money, he decied to ask Uncle Philips in Holland for a loan. In the comfort of his uncle's home he relaxed and enjoyed a mild flirtation with his 'sweet little cousin', Nanette.

He also took advantage of the Prussian amnesty on the death of Friedrich Wilhelm IV to visit Berlin, where he stayed, again in great comfort, with Ferdinand Lassalle, a successful social democrat lawyer. Though Lassalle was generous and helpful to Marx, there was always some tension between them. For Marx was irritated beyond measure that Lassalle had managed to have his cake and eat it. In Lassalle's fine house, on a pleasant street in Berlin, he must have been haunted by the thought of what might have been and stricken by guilt.

Lassalle, an active socialist, had managed to stay in Germany and run a flourishing legal practice. And he had kept his Jewishness, something which touched a sensitive place in Marx's heart, provoking him to the most malicious of his anti-semitic remarks. Jenny, Engels and Marx always privately sneered at Lassalle, referring to him as 'Ikey', 'Flashy', and 'a slimy Jew'. Then Lassalle had successfully acted on behalf of the Countess Ratzfeldt in her divorce case. She had given him a pension, set him up in his handsome house and visited him daily. Though Lassalle's brand of socialism drew fire from Marx and Engels, he managed on the whole to keep the respect of the German workers, though some complained of his lifestyle.

But what made Marx most furious was that Lassalle not only had the temerity to invade with his books Marx's own political and economic territory, but also found time to write plays and a long study of Heraclitus. Nevertheless Marx had a grudging respect for him and needed his friendship. Lassalle exerted himself mightily, if unsuccessfully, to get Marx back his German citizenship and offered him joint editorship of a journal he was founding. Marx refused the offer, but for a while seems to have been quite tempted by the idea of returning to Germany. Meanwhile he basked in the admiration of the Countess and accompanied her to the theatre, where they sat in a box next to King Wilhelm, who was no doubt aware of the identity of the courtly, bearded gentleman who quizzed him with his monocle. Marx visited Parliament and dined out with distinguished Berlin citizens, among them a general, a Privy Councillor, a painter and a historian.

In a long and gossipy letter to Nanette Philips, he revealed his admiration for the blue-eyed, blonde

Countess. Even if she found her complexion in her make-up box and reminded him of a Grecian statue with a wonderful bust but whose head had been battered by the vicissitudes of time, she was a 'quite outstanding lady, no blue-stocking, has great natural intelligence, more than usual vivacity, a deep interest in the revolutionary movement and an aristocratic ease of manner'. He returned via Holland, and at Salzbommel Uncle Philips welcomed him and gave him a loan of a hundred and fifty pounds. And Nanette, who had written long letters to him in Berlin, signing herself 'the girl who loves you', gave him adoration that rejuvenated him.

Meanwhile Jenny had had weeks of misery. She had no idea where Marx was; for a long time he did not write and then, as she complained to Engels, his letter was obscure, giving only the scantiest information. She was also hounded by the butcher and baker. Then Lenchen, normally phlegmatic, had given way and Jenny had to nurse her through what seems to have been a complete physical and mental breakdown. In despair she wrote to Engels, and his swift response enabled her to 'provide every comfort, a constantly warm room, wine and even such luxury as eau de cologne. So useful when there is frequent fainting'.

At last, she reported with relief to Engels, the 'inflammation had passed, though there was still danger of loss of blood or recurrence of the fever'. Jenny had found the hysteria particularly frightening, but finally the 'delirium, singing, crying and agitated conduct' ceased too, and Lenchen was her former sturdy self again, sunning herself by the front door.

The news from Marx that he was considering editing a journal with Lassalle in Berlin, and that he had been visiting the Countess, infuriated Jenny. The thought of returning to Berlin and living in the shadow of 'that Babylonian woman' appalled her. When she heard of the Countess's invitation to send Jennychen and Laura to act as her companions, she exploded with rage. As for returning to Berlin, she and the girls were now rooted 'in the land of Shakespeare'. Besides, she could not bear the idea of being bankrupt in Berlin. As she later wrote to a friend,

A move just now would bring us no advantages . . . London is so colossal that here one disappears into nothingness. Here the individual does not count, and just because of that one stops being important to oneself or others . . . no-one takes any notice of one, whereas in Germany everyone knows the next day what was on the table and what the income of 'Herr Gemahl' [the husband] is.

By November Marx was reporting to Engels that his wife was suffering from 'a dangerous nervous condition . . . but from her natural buoyancy I do not doubt she will recover'. But for the next two years she had little chance to recover. They were in worse trouble financially than they had ever been. Marx's only income was from journalism; his great work occupied most of his time, and it would be years before it was finished.

Their constant indebtedness to Engels must have been particularly galling for Jenny, whose relationship with him was always courteous but cool. In January 1863 they nearly lost his friendship for ever. Mary Burns, his mistress for many years, died and Engels was heartbroken. Marx sent him, instead of a warm letter of condolence, a long wail about his own troubles with a short reference to Mary's death. Engels was cut to the quick. All his friends had shown him sympathy and friendship, but 'You found this moment appropriate to display the superiority of your cool intellect.' Marx apologised and managed to throw the blame on Jenny. Engels – generous as always – forgave him, for Marx had proposed the unthinkable. Jenny had apparently agreed to Marx's suggestion that: 'I will declare myself bankrupt . . . my two oldest daughters would take positions as governesses . . . Lenchen would enter another service and my wife and I with Tussy would go to live in the City model lodging house.' Marx had even applied for a job as a railway clerk – and to his relief was refused because of his appalling handwriting. As he must have known, Engels could not let all this happen.

In fact the Marxes did not seriously consider crossing the Victorian gulf between classes and becoming proletarian. It would not, Marx thought, have been 'appropriate' for their daughters – though, he said, he might have considered it had they been boys. In fact both Jenny and Marx were bourgeois to the core and, however difficult it was, they remained so for the rest of their lives. When in July 1862 Lassalle came to stay, for pride's sake they concealed their poverty. Jenny's irritation at the unwelcome visitor, who squandered money on cigars and cabs, is not concealed under the light tone. 'Lassalle', she remembered in her autobiography,

> was almost crushed under the weight of fame he had achieved as a scholar, thinker, poet and politician. The laurel wreath was fresh on his Olympian brow . . . or rather on his stiff bristling negro hair. As on the wings of the wind he swept through our rooms perorating so loudly . . . that our neighbours were scared by the terrible shouts.

They were glad to see him go – but equally prepared to accept a loan from him. Though they mocked him, nevertheless they expressed genuine sorrow for the old comrade when he was later killed in a duel.

Jenny had come through extreme poverty in the past, but with three growing girls and the struggle to keep up appearances she was now, in 1862, more desperate than ever. For the first time she wrote for help to her stepbrother, Ferdinand von Westphalen – something she had never done before, she told Engels, 'not in the darkest days'. This she did without telling Marx. Equally he did not know that she had successfully appealed for money to an old friend in Germany, Bertha Markheim. But the culmination of a black year came when just before Christmas Jenny went over to Paris to try to get a loan from an old banker friend. Unfortunately he had just had a heart attack, was paralysed and unable to help. In a letter to Engels Marx described the 'series of mishaps' that befell Jenny as 'tragi-comic'.

> On the way over, her ship had been battered by a great storm and there was trouble with the locomotive so that the train was delayed for two hours. Later the omnibus on which she travelled turned over. And yesterday the London cab in which she sat got tangled in the wheels of another one. She got out and came home on foot with two boys carrying her trunk. But this was not all. Two hours before her return Lenchen's sister Marianne had died of a heart attack . . . I will have to pay the undertaker £7½ cash. This has to be procured. It is a fine Christmas spectacle for the poor children.

It is not surprising that in this year Jenny lost her good humour, and, as Marx told Engels in June 1862, 'My wife says to me every day she wishes she and the children were dead and I can't blame her.' Poverty, sickness, the birth of seven children and the death of four, and finally the loss of her beauty – all this Jenny had suffered for the sake of a genius who still had little to show except articles, pamphlets, an immense mountain of illegible notes, and the first instalments of the Great Work.

Now often ill herself, she was increasingly worried about Marx. Since boyhood his chest had been weak and he had long complained of his disordered liver. Jenny told her stepsisters: 'Karl often suffers from his liver, an illness due to his very sedentary life, fatiguing

study and overwork'. It was also because he drank and
smoked too much and often worked all through the
night. Jenny's patience frequently snapped. All that
year she had been ill herself and nevertheless acted as
Marx's secretary. 'One invalid is writing for another,'
she wrote to Engels. 'Chaley's head hurts him almost
everywhere, terrible toothache, pains in the ears, head,
eyes, throat and God knows where else. Neither opium
pills or creosote do any good.' In fact the real problem
was the combination of many things, both physical and
mental. Overhanging everything was the shadow of the
great unfinished book.

Now there were times when he vomited daily, weeks
when his eyes were inflamed and Jenny had to write
his letters for him. In 1863 he began to be plagued by
what Jenny called the 'carbuncle disease', which tor-
mented him for the rest of his life. In the following
years he reported on the progress of his carbuncles from
his cheek to his penis in all their grisly detail. Sometimes
the doctor operated, sometimes in desperation Marx
himself slashed them with a razor. As he struggled with
Das Kapital, often unable to sit or stand, he reflected
grimly. 'The bourgeoisie will have cause to remember
my carbuncles.' 'On November 10th,' Jenny recalled, 'a
terrible abscess was opened, and for a fairly long time
he remained in danger. The illness lasted a good four
weeks and caused severe physical suffering. The physical pain was accompanied by nagging cares and spiritual tortures of all kinds.'

But just when they were 'on the edge of the abyss',
there came the news of the death of Marx's mother.
Although only half recovered, Marx set out for Trier to
arrange 'the question of the legacy'. From Trier he
wrote on 15 December with the old passion for Jenny.

I have made daily pilgrimages to the old Westphalen
house that interested me more than the whole Roman

antiquity because it reminded me of my happiest youth and had once harboured my dearest treasure. I am asked daily on all sides about the former 'most beautiful girl in Trier' and the 'Queen of the Ball'. It is damn pleasant for a man when his wife lives in the imagination of a whole city as an 'enchanted princess'.

He went to Salzbommel to his uncle Lion Philips – the executor of his mother's estate. Here once again he was afflicted with furuncles and carbuncles so that he could 'neither walk nor stand nor sit and even lying down is damned hard'. In the comfort of the Philips home he remained until late February, nursed by his uncle, 'a splendid old boy who puts on my plasters and poultices and by my amiable, witty and dangerously dark-eyed cousin who tends me and takes good care of me'. He was clearly not displeased that the doctor forbade him to travel to London.

Meanwhile Trier's 'enchanted princess' spent a lonely, desolate Christmas. But thanks to Marx's mother's legacy, in March 1864 they were able to move to a comfortable new house, 1 Medina Villas, in nearby Maitland Park. Jenny took great pleasure in buying the new furniture and in this villa they lived until 1875 when they moved to another in the same Park. At Easter they moved in, and Jenny's spirits lifted in this 'new, sunlit, friendly house with the bright airy rooms'. Marx had a light, pleasant study overlooking the Park.

Now they were able to afford the annual seaside holidays which Marx needed as his health grew worse. Hastings, Margate, Ramsgate were all tried in the following years in the search for health. He took the waters at Harrogate and Malvern and later went every year to the elegant surroundings of the Hotel Germania in Karlsbad, signing himself in as 'Gentleman of Independent Means'. He took Tussy with him on two occasions; her unhappy love life was wrecking her health, reducing her to the edge of a nervous break-down. Together they walked through the mountain woods, drinking the bitter water at the spring, listen-ing to the music and talking of art and literature and philosophy with the intelligent guests. Sometimes his treatment must have been more dangerous than the disease – he took arsenic, which made him fuddled, as well as opium and laudanum like other famous Victorians. He even took Spanish fly. Later he was to try blistering and tattooing. It is a nightmarish catalogue.

But at least at this time he could afford to be ill. A new legacy surprised them. Their old friend Wilhelm Wolff – Lupus – died and left them the considerable sum of seven hundred pounds. This was the turning point in their fortunes, and in the autumn Jenny 'gave the first small Ball in our new house and several small parties afterwards'. The invitation cards went out from the 'Baroness'. Guests came to stay: Marx's sister Sophie, who had been their go-between in the old days, came for a month, as did Jenny's old friend Lina Schöler, who was now a governess in England. A less welcome guest to Marx was Jenny's brother Edgar, whom she had not seen for sixteen years. He had fought for the South in the American Civil War and was now on his way back to Germany. Edgar was an invalid and self-centred, and though the children found him great fun, Marx became increasingly irritated by his presence.

This was a year when for the first time in their lives money poured into their laps. When Engel's father died, his son became a partner in the Manchester firm and was able to contribute even more generously to the Marx family finances. Nevertheless in an alarmingly brief time the money slipped easily through their fin-gers, and though, as Jenny wrote, 'We sailed along for a time happily', it was always 'between rocks and sand-banks, drifting between Charybdis and Scylla'.

If I had to start my life again . . . I would not marry

Now both Marx and Jenny were concerned to get their daughters settled. Jennychen and Laura were intelligent girls, anxious to earn their own living. Jenny was sympathetic; no one, she told Tussy, understood better than she their need for independence; but Marx, typical of his class and period, was reluctant to let them go. So, though Jennychen did finally escape and become a governess, she never became the actress she longed to be, and Laura continued to act as his secretary and research assistant in the British Museum.

Marx complained to Engels about Jenny's irritability and the friction in the home at this time, but he admitted that the girls took it with good humour. They certainly always wrote of Jenny with great affection, and were tolerantly amused at Mama's repeated, 'I have known better times.'

Laura soon attracted suitors. A striking blonde, she was talented and as much at home in the British Museum as in the drawing room and kitchen. Jenny was delighted when Laura became engaged to Paul Lafargue, a medical student from a well-to-do French Creole family. At least, she hoped, Laura would be spared a life of penury and politics – which, as she had said in her girlhood, was 'the riskiest thing there is'. As for Marx, he wrote a fierce Victorian letter to Paul: 'Before your relations with Laura are definitely settled, I must be completely clear about your economic circumstances.' He was determined that Laura's life must not be wrecked, as Jenny's had been. 'You know that I have sacrificed my whole fortune to the revolutionary struggle. I do not regret it. Quite the contrary. If I had to start my life again, I would do the same. But I would not marry.' So Darwin and many other great men have thought at this period in life, when wife and family distract them from their work.

Marx and Jenny may have been worried about Paul's

mixed blood but they joked about it freely and affectionately. Paul was descended from a mixture of Indian,
mulatto, Jewish and Irish ancestors. He became 'our
negro', and Jenny looked forward to 'one, two, three
little nigger boys'. What concerned Marx was that Paul's
courtship was excessively passionate. Again the Victorian father, he wrote sternly, 'In my opinion, true love is
expressed in reserve, modesty, and even shyness of the
lover towards his idol, and never in temperamental
excesses or too premature intimacy.' It was no use Paul
invoking his 'Creole temperament'. 'If you are unable
to show your love for her in the form consonant with
the London latitude, then it is advisable that you love
her from a distance.' Jenny must have smiled, remembering Marx's own passionate wooing.

The marriage took place on 2 April 1868, at St Pancras
Register Office, of 'Paul Lafargue, 26, medical student,
to Laura Marx, 22, spinster and daughter of Charles
Marx, gentleman'. The father of the bride wore band-
ages – he was still suffering agonies from his carbuncles.
Jenny, typically, had worried about what the neighbours would make of a register office wedding. The
solution offered by a Chartist friend – that she should
explain that Paul was a Catholic and Laura a Protestant
– was not wholly satisfactory; they were in fact both
atheists. Jenny seems to have kept some nostalgia not
only for the outward forms of religion, but for the
comfort and stability they brought. Paul qualified as a
surgeon at St Bartholomew's Hospital, and then they
returned to France where, as Jenny regretfully told a
friend, Paul 'forsook Father Asclepius and became
deeply involved in revolutionary politics'.

Jennychen and Tussy too were drawn into the political whirlpool – both were becoming passionately
involved in Irish affairs. Tussy, particularly – who was,
Jenny reported, 'a politician from top to toe' – was much
influenced by Lizzie Burns, who after her sister's death
became Engels's mistress. A long holiday with Engels

in Manchester turned her into what her parents called a complete Fenian. Lizzie Burns was a passionate supporter of the Irish revolutionary movement, and Manchester was buzzing at this time with the news of the Fenian attacks in Chester. Engels wrote of her: 'She was of genuine Irish proletarian stock and her passionate, innate feeling for her class was of far greater value to me and stood me in better stead at moments of crisis than all the refinement and culture of your educated and aesthetic young ladies.'

Although she had disliked Mary Burns, in later years Jenny became very fond of simple, illiterate Lizzie. Tussy, the democrat, had broken down the class barrier that had always existed between Jenny and the Burns sisters. During Marx's periods in Karlsbad Jenny often took her holidays with Engels and Lizzie at Shanklin in the Isle of Wight, and at Ramsgate. While Karl was taking the waters, Jenny and Engels and Lizzie would stroll to the station bar at Ramsgate for their morning glass of port. When Lizzie died she was genuinely mourned; Engels had been devoted to her, and to please her had married her on her deathbed. Jenny, too, grieved for one of the few members of the working class whom she could genuinely call a friend.

Marx was now closely concentrating on *Das Kapital*, which he had originally hoped to have finished in a year. In fact, the work dragged on for eight years and was not published until 1867. Engels considered that 'the accursed book, the everlasting unfinished thing, was an incubus at the root of all Marx's physical ills'. He could not bring himself to publish until he had rooted out every relevant historic detail.

But also there was a psychological block, which his old co-editor, Arnold Ruge, had noticed in 1844. 'He has a peculiar personality – perfect as a scholar or an author but completely ruinous as a journalist. He reads a lot; he works with unusual intensity and has a critical talent – But he finishes nothing, breaks off everything

and plunges himself ever afresh into an endless sea of
books.'

Perhaps it was to avoid conclusion that in 1864,
instead of finishing the book, he had thrown himself
into organising the first Communist International –
which for the next six years occupied much of his time.
As usual, as Ruge had noticed, when he was overworked he became 'irritable and hot-tempered, particularly when he has worked himself sick and not gone to
bed for three or four nights on end'. If Jenny was
irritable too during these years, she surely had good
reason.

Yet he claimed to Engels that, during the period of
his worst physical affliction, his brain 'box' had never
worked better, and though by 1867 he was, he wrote,
'ready for the knacker's yard', in April the last page was
written. Engels rejoiced and sent him his fare to Hamburg. Last time there had been delays. This time Marx
was determined that he would keep an eye on the
printing himself.

While waiting for the proofs, he went to Hanover to
stay with Dr Kugelmann, a long-standing admirer. The
doctor was a courageous and distinguished gynaecolo-
gist, at a time when such specialisation was considered
rather indecent. Frau Kugelmann was charming, intelligent and adoring, and in their comfortable home Marx
relaxed, enjoying the library, where there was a larger
collection of his and Engel's works than he had himself,
and the music room with its collection of marble classical busts. Here he was once again the gallant, courtly
doctor of philosophy, flirting with the ladies and with a
certain clever, pretty Frau Tenge. Tactlessly, he sent his
daughters a photograph of the lady. Laura replied:
'There is a certain lady occupies a large part of your
letters . . . is she pretty . . . do you flirt with her? If I
were Möhme I should be jealous.' And Jenny of the
ravaged face undoubtedly was.

For Marx the weeks in Hanover were 'among the

most beautiful and delightful oases in the desert of life'. He did not hurry back to London. He had been away for over a month, yet even when he reached London he wasted the day escorting a petty girl – Bismarck's niece – to her train. He stayed for two days with Jenny, then went straight to Engels in Manchester. And he was there when on 14 September 1867 *Das Kapital* was published. It was dedicated to Wilhelm Wolff (Lupus). Marx sent a copy of the second edition to Darwin in June 1873, but it now seems improbable that, as was once thought, he intended to dedicate Part II to him. Jenny expected that honour.

For this book Marx had sacrificed wife, family and his own health. But once again his work fell flat, even though Engels had organised reviews in various journals. There was hardly a ripple of interest in Germany, and there was to be no English translation until after his death. Only in Russia was there any serious interest, and the first translation was into Russian.

The failure of *Das Kapital* depressed Jenny. She wrote to thank Dr Kugelmann, who had tried to whip up interest in the book without success. 'It seems that the Germans prefer to express their appreciation by silence and complete dumbness.' For once Jenny had lost her buoyancy. 'I was not at all well last year,' she wrote to Dr Kugelmann, 'and sadly I have lost a good deal of my faith and of my courage recently.' That the book should be ignored was unbearable. 'Seldom,' she wrote,

> has a book been written in more difficult circumstances and I could easily write a confidential history which would bring to light endless silent cares and anxieties and worries. If the workers had any idea of the sacrifice necessary to complete this work, which was written only for them and in their interests, they would perhaps show more interest.

She prepared for Christmas 1868 as usual, but once again, as so often, it was a sad time. Marx had two carbuncles, one 'in a painful spot so that he must lie on his side'. Laura was ill in Paris, expecting her first baby. But Dr Kugelmann sent them a present which brightened the house. 'Yesterday evening', she wrote in her letter of thanks,

> we were all sitting together in the downstairs rooms of the house, the kitchen quarters in the English arrangements from which all creature comforts flow to the upper regions, busy preparing the Christmas pudding with conscientious thoroughness, raisins were stoned (a very disgusting, sticky business), almonds, orange and lemon peel and suet finely chopped and the whole mish-mash mixed with eggs and flour into a strange pot pourri; then suddenly, a ring at the bell, a carriage stops at the door, unknown steps go back and forth, whispering and rustling echoed through the house; at last comes the call from upstairs, a big statue has arrived. If there had been the cry 'Fire! Fire! The Fenians are here', we could not have rushed up with more perplexed confusion and there it stood in its colossal splendour, in its ideal purity, old Father Jupiter, intact, undamaged (a little corner somewhat broken) before our staring delighted eyes.

The statue, which had stood among others in the music room of the Kugelmanns' Hanover house, had been thought to bear a strong resemblance to Marx. Jenny was not sure whether it was Father Zeus or Father Jupiter, but, even after all she had gone through, to her Marx was still heroic.

If Mother Nature is kind to us we shall still live to see that triumph

Now that he had finished the first part of *Das Kapital*, Marx turned his attention to what turned out to be the closing stages of the International. He had founded the First International Working Men's Association in 1864 in order to co-ordinate all the divergent socialist movements of the day. It had been difficult enough for Marx and his followers to remain on good terms with the various kinds of socialists in London. Now their rallying cry of 1848, 'Workers of the world, unite', was proving even more ironical. But Marx soldiered on. As chief of the International he visited his comrades in France, travelling incognito as 'A. Williams'. Laura and Paul had now settled in Paris, and he took this chance to take Jenny there to see their first grandson. Jenny had enjoyed Paris, marvelled at the new city of the Second Empire. Laura and Paul took her to the theatre and opera, though they saw with some concern that she was looking ill and becoming deaf.

Then in 1870 war broke out. Louis Napoleon, in trouble at home, needed a foreign triumph and declared war on Prussia; he was defeated at the battle of Sedan, imprisoned and exiled. The workers of Paris, refusing to accept the armistice drawn up by a provisional government which permitted the entry of Prussian troops into Paris, rioted. They took over the capital and established a central committee which called itself the Commune, after the assembly of 1793. Jenny and Marx heard the news with excitement and alarm. Once more Paris was raising the standard for what they hoped would be a European revolution that would change the world. But this time neither felt the same youthful certainty, and Laura and her baby were in danger. In fact, backed by the Prussian forces, French troops fought their way back into Paris. This time the workers of Paris had no chance. New wide streets had been built since 1848 to make barricading difficult, and after the bloodiest of battles the Commune was over. Those days in May were more terrible than any that had gone before, and Jenny and Marx heard with anguish of the bitter fighting and the deaths of old friends. By 28 May 1871 the revolution was over. For Marx it was almost the final disillusion.

Meanwhile their anxiety over Laura and Paul and the baby grew. The Lafargues had escaped to Bordeaux and then over the border to Spain. Paul was a marked man and Laura, as Marx's daughter, was in danger too. Their anxiety was doubled when Jennychen and six-teen-year-old Tussy decided to go to their sister's aid. Jennychen, though delicate, was courageous and acted as a courier carrying secret messages from Marx – just as her mother had done in the old days. They reached Laura at Luchon in Spain; then, on their return into France, they were captured and interrogated for many hours. Once again the pattern of Jenny's own life was repeated and when her first grandchild – the adored little 'Schappy' – died in Spain all the old wounds were reopened. But at last they all returned to London, and for a while the family was united again. Paul worked in London, for until an amnesty was declared in 1880 he could not return to France.

In March 1872 Jennychen married Charles Longuet, in spite of Laura's warning that 'Frenchmen do not make good husbands'. Jenny thought him a 'fine and proper man', and was glad when, after a brief trial at teaching in Oxford, they returned and settled nearby in north London – he to teach French at King's College School, and Jennychen to teach at Clement Dane's School.

Tussy, however, was a problem. At seventeen she had fallen deeply in love with Prosper Lissagray, who was both a Basque count and a courageous Communard – doubly romantic in Jenny's eyes. Lissagray was twice Tussy's age, and Marx and Lafargue for some reason disapproved of him, but, with Jenny's backing, they became secretly engaged. Jenny, remembering her own youth, remained supportive; but Marx, once again in his role of Victorian father, absolutely forbade Tussy to meet or write to him. When Tussy escaped to Brighton and found a post in a school, Jenny wrote long, affec-tionate letters. 'I alone understand how dearly you long for work and independence, the only two things that can help one over the sorrows and cares of present-day society.'

In spite of Jenny's support, and Tussy's pathetic letters of appeal, Marx was adamant. Tussy's anguish lasted for years and clouded her relationship with her parents. However unsuitable the match, it could not have been worse than the alliance she was later to make. Marx, in trying to save Tussy from her mother's fate, did in fact help to destroy her. Some time during the 1870s Jenny, Marx and Tussy were present at the annual prizegiving at the Orphan Working School at the end of their road in Maitland Park. Here they heard a compelling young lecturer and enthusiastic Darwinian, Dr Edward Aveling, give an address entitled 'Insects and Flowers'. This was the first and last time that he was to meet Marx and Jenny; but he was to play a disastrous role in Tussy's life. It was as well that they could not see the future and the misery he would bring their beloved Tussy.

Meanwhile, Jenny tried to console her, sent her little luxuries – jam and potted meat. She fussed about her clothes and, though she knew 'how little store you set by these things and how lacking in variety and love of finery', she sent 'outfits'. With a touch of the old Baroness, she packed up a 'light modern costume for church and promenade'. She visited Tussy in Brighton and never told Marx that their daughter was secretly meeting Lissagaray there.

From now on ill health dogged the family. During the 1870s Marx worked away at Parts II and III of *Das Kapital*, but when Engels looked at his notes after Marx's death he found incoherence and confusion. There seemed to be little to show for a lifetime of study. In 1872 the Communist International, on which he had spent so much time since 1864, foundered at the Congress of The Hague. Its headquarters was transferred to New York where it was finally dissolved in 1876. Marx and Jenny attended the last Congress at The Hague and celebrated the end in a farewell dinner and concert at the Grand Hotel. Marx was glad to see the end of an organisation which was in any case slipping out of his control.

Much of Jenny's time in the early 1870s was spent in organising relief for the refugees from the Paris Commune, distressing work which was the more painful because the exiled Communards were regarded with general hostility in England, even by the working class. So it was a great relief to turn to literary pursuits.

A frustrated actress herself, Jenny now took a lively interest in her daughters' theatrical friends and she became a regular theatre-goer. Keen Shakespearean that she always was, when Jenny played the Victorian game of Confession she made Coriolanus her favourite hero. Perhaps she saw some likeness to Marx: both were men defiant of public opinion, guilty of *hubris* but redeemed by love of wife and family. She became a passionate admirer of Henry Irving, whose interpretations of Macbeth and Richard III were causing controversy. Critics complained that Irving was overturning all the old traditions.

Now that the girls had taken her place as Marx's assistants she needed another outlet for her talents. Perhaps it was the feeling that she had come to the end of a chapter that had led her, some time in the summer or autumn of 1865, to begin writing her autobiography. Her manuscript has survived, although eight of the original thirty-seven sheets of paper have been torn out. Were they critical of Marx? Were they too personal? We shall probably never know; for after the death of their parents the daughters carefully expurgated passages not only from Jenny's work but also from their own letters. So the autobiographical sketch is indeed brief – the last date mentioned being 16 May 1865.

Now, encouraged by Tussy, she began writing again, producing theatrical reviews which in October 1875

Tussy sent to Karl Girsch, the Paris correspondent of the *Frankfurter Zeitung*:

> Mother would like you if you can, to publish this letter in the *Frankfurter Zeitung*. If father had the time, he himself would have written an article about Mr Irving, in whom we are very interested (although we do not know him personally). Firstly because he is a man of rare talent, and also because the entire English press, as a result of the most scurrilous intrigues have taken up arms and launched a veritable campaign against him . . .

The first article was published anonymously, and probably without Marx's knowledge, under the title 'The London Theatre World'. Her style is lighter than that of Marx, but throughout her theatre criticism there runs a similar vein of irony and that sense of superiority which they both showed towards English intellectuals. 'John Bull', she wrote,

> boasts of his renowned constitution, his Milton with whom he is not acquainted, his port and pâté with which he is very well acquainted and lastly, his William Shakespeare. But they are empty boasts. He takes only the pâté seriously. There is more than enough national arrogance and sanctimoniousness when it comes to putting up a monument to the 'Swan of Avon', the greatest of all poets, but the contributions of the lower classes bring it about. Only actors who love their Shakespeare, and workers who know his work thoroughly from cheap one shilling editions and who carry their 'William' deep in their hearts, gathered around the small oak planted on Primrose Hill eleven years ago during the third centenary of the playwright's birth. Over twenty years ago Phelps, an actor at a small theatre in London's eastern outskirts, succeeded in awakening and maintaining over a long period the workers' interest in Shakespeare.

She complained of the neglect of Shakespeare among London theatre-goers, described how the old Drury

Lane Theatre was compelled to give up playing Shake-speare since 'Shakespeare meant bankruptcy'. Then she moved on to the rise of Henry Irving, a young actor who until a 'year ago . . . with a reputation only in the Provinces . . . ventured to present *Hamlet* again. He had resolved to spurn the old tradition and indepen-dently to create the true and original Shakespearean role'. Irving's more natural style had puzzled audiences accustomed to the ranting of Victorian actors. Jenny was as angry with the press which attacked him as with the fashionable Londoners who flocked to his plays. It was now, she wrote, 'considered *bon ton* to go into raptures over Shakespeare!' When Irving played Mac-beth, only *The Times* 'supported the young, questing actor with fair and encouraging words'. The rest of the dailies were full of petty criticisms, some complaining about his gait, some finding him affected. 'The popular Press lowered themselves to mediocre, utterly false attacks which bear witness only to powerless spite, intrigue and envy.' What puzzled Jenny was that, although the theatre was packed, 'there are no ovations to inspire the young artist. Every one sits stock still frozen in their seats.' She suspected that high society really wanted to turn back to 'melodrama with blazing ships, crumbling cliffs, real carriages, horses, camels and goats'.

Years of copying out Marx's articles gave a class edge to her criticism; the bourgeois

> is too lazy to think: each morning beside the obligatory eggs and bacon his newspaper hack does his thinking for him . . . he boards the omnibus, travels to the City or his club and takes his place in a theatre box in the evening with newspaper phrases ready in his pocket . . .

But a working-class audience has a

> huge advantage. The Press cannot cloud their thinking. When they go to the theatre they trust only to their eyes

and their ears, clap and whistle as they please and see fit, and, moreover, always in the right places.

The *Frankfurter Zeitung* published five articles: 'The London Theatre World', November 1875; 'A London Season', March 1876; 'The Study of Shakespeare in England', December 1876; 'Shakespeare's *Richard II* at the London Lyceum', February 1877; and 'From a London Theatre', May 1877.

Jenny's success as a literary critic encouraged her to take up more serious journalism. In September 1878 she published three articles in the *Frankfurter Zeitung*, on 17, 19 and 30 September, in which she dealt with the rising tide of revolution in Russia. She was at this time recuperating in Malvern and Marx kept her supplied with all the relevant newspapers and telegraphed despatches. Jenny gleaned most of her information for her articles from these newspapers, and from articles published in the *Pall Mall Gazette* by the English journalist Grenville-Murray. Although Grenville-Murray was, as Jenny stressed, 'a bourgeois English diplomat and journalist' and she did not agree with his political conclusions, she found his scenes of Russian life at first hand vivid and moving. In a style that is as scathing as Marx's own she attacked the military, the police and officialdom in Russia for their corruption and tyranny, and concluded by strongly attacking the despotic regime of the tsarist government and its spies within Russia and on the European continent. Like Marx, Jenny foresaw a great revolutionary upheaval ahead. 'It will be a great storm,' wrote Marx, 'and if Mother Nature is kind to us we shall still live to see that triumph.'

Jenny was involved not only in the literary and political worlds; throughout her life in London she frequently attended public lectures on philosophy and science. Generally both she and Marx were dismissive of the Chartists as philosophers, but she praised the oratory of Ernest Jones. 'Yesterday evening we went to

Ernest Jones's first lecture on the history of the Papacy. His lecture was very good, simply outstanding for the English; it was not quite as excellent for us Germans who have experienced the rigorous discipline of Hegel and Feuerbach.'

She was also interested in the free-thinking movement developing 'in stuffy old England'. 'The most prominent scientists, led by Huxley . . . are now giving educational free-thinking and bold lectures for the people in St Martin's Hall which still echoes to waltz tunes. This moreover takes place on a Sunday evening, at that very time when God's lambs usually flock to the Lord's pastures.' She took her three daughters to these lectures, which were packed: 'Two thousand people were unable to get into the . . . airless room.' In spite of the disapproval of the clergy these lectures remained popular and were followed by concerts. 'Handel, Mozart, Beethoven, Mendelssohn and Gounod, got an enthusiastic reception from the English, who until now on Sundays had been permitted only to bawl out the hymn "Jesus, Meek and Gentle", or get drunk in a tavern.'

I should so like to live a little longer

In the last years of their lives, Jenny and Marx sailed into calmer waters. After the dissolution of the International, Marx was less actively involved in politics. He must have accepted that he would never finish the last volumes of *Das Kapital*, though he continued to make voluminous notes. Now their chief pleasure was to be with their daughters and grandchildren.

Their relationship too grew easier in the last years. Tussy remembered their immense sense of humour:

Assuredly two people never enjoyed a joke more than these two. Again and again – especially if the occasion

were demanding decorum and sedateness – have I seen
them laugh till the tears ran down their cheeks, and
even those inclined to be shocked at such awful levity
could not choose but laugh with them. And how often
have I seen them not daring to look at one another, each
knowing that once a glance was exchanged uncontrollable laughter would result. To see these two with eyes
fixed on anything but one another, for all the world like
two schoolchildren suffocating with suppressed laughter
. . . is a memory I would not barter for all the millions I
am sometimes accredited with having inherited.

One of Tussy's theatrical friends remembered the
relaxed, good-humoured atmosphere of the Marxes'
home in these later years. Tussy was a leading member
of a Shakespeare reading club, the Dogberry, whose
fortnightly meetings were often held at Maitland Park.
Marx and Jenny in these later years rarely went out at
night, so they delighted in the readings. Jenny must
have taken part, though Marx never did. According to
Marian Skinner, a friend, 'He had a guttural voice and
decided German accent' – and he was very self-
conscious. Jenny herself was remembered as a lovable,
charming woman, obviously beautiful in her youth –
'but ill health and perhaps turbulent times, had taken
their toll. Her skin had faded to a waxen pallor, there
were purple brown stains under her eyes, yet there was
still an air of breeding about her and a certain distinction
of manner'.

There was no sign on these evenings of the bitter,
venomous Marx; the play readings often finished with
games and charades, with Marx laughing and joining in
the fun. Marian Skinner said he was 'the oldest in years,
but in spirit as young as any of us'. In fact Jenny was
the oldest, but Marx's grey beard aged him. Visitors
remembered how tender and considerate Marx was to
his wife. Materially, these were the most comfortable
years of their lives. Callers were surprised to find the
dreaded revolutionary living, as a reporter from New

York found, 'in very comfortable quarters, such as might have been those of a thriving stockbroker'. He had expected to smell explosives – instead there was a handsome volume of Rhine views on a side table and the scent of roses filled the room.

Jenny had survived, though her looks and her buoyancy had gone. But gradually the old good temper came back and it is significant that Tussy remembered only the laughter of those last years – or was it that, in the later misery of her own life, she desperately wished to preserve this last illusion?

Though they were no longer haunted by debt, the old wounds were still there. In 1877, when she was sixty-three, she wrote to an old friend, Sorge, in America, apologising for her silence when she had heard of the death of two of his children.

> I didn't write because I didn't want to approach your grief with all the commonplaces of condolence and phrases of consolation. I know only too well to what degree these things are painful and how much it needs time to regain one's equilibrium after such losses. However, it is life that comes to our rescue with its little joys and its great troubles . . . and the great grief is softened by the little troubles of the moment, and almost without knowing the violent grief grows less. Not that the wound ever heals, above all in a mother's heart, but little by little there awakes in the heart a new awareness, even a new sensibility, to a new trouble and new joy. And thus it is that one still goes on living still with a wounded heart but always hoping that at last all will be calm and that it will be eternal peace.

In 1877, knowing that she needed treatment, Jenny insisted on accompanying Marx for a spa treatment. They took Tussy, who was still ill, and spent some weeks in Neuenahr, a quiet resort in the Rhineland. In the balmy air of the whitewashed little town and later in the Black Forest Jenny regained her strength. But in

1878 Marx took her to consult specialists and realised that her disease was incurable. It was in fact cancer of the liver.

Now Marx's letters were more concerned with Jenny's health than his own. He would have taken Jenny to Karlsbad in the summer of 1878 – but was afraid he would be extradited since the authorities at this time were clamping down on suspected revolutionaries. So she went for the cure to Malvern with Jennychen and a little grandson. But in November 1879 he wrote to Sorge, 'My wife is still dangerously ill.' In the summer of 1880 he took her to their favourite Ramsgate for a holiday and then to Manchester to consult Engel's friend, Dr Edward Gumpert. Marx thought he had concealed from her the truth about her condition. But Jenny knew. She put on a brave face, and went out to the theatre in Manchester. Here she was cosseted as never before. She stayed in comfort with Sam Moore, Engels's lawyer, and, though she was sometimes bored and irritated by the smugness and intellectual inferiority of his well-off friends, she enjoyed the chance to shine at their dinner parties. There were many interesting fellow refugees from Germany in Manchester at this time, among them Charles Hallé, whose success Jenny observed with interest, regretting that she was not well enough to attend his Wagnerian concert. She went to the Catholic church – as she said, 'for the music' – and knelt. Marx wrote to Dr Fleckles, his doctor in Karlsbad, for advice and Jenny – unknown to Marx – wrote too:

> Dear good Doctor,
> I should so like to live a little longer. How strange it is that the nearer the whole thing draws to an end, the more one clings to this 'vale of tears'.

During 1880–1 Jenny was often in great pain, but as Tussy wrote to Jennychen Longuet, 'She has her ups and downs.' On good days she went to the theatre. But it was a 'down-day' when Jennychen finally left to join her husband in Argenteuil near Paris. Had she been well, her mother wrote, she would have 'quickly packed up my little bundle as in the old days and galloped after the dear grandchildren'. That summer, they persuaded her to spend three weeks at Eastbourne. 'I have actually sunk to a bath-chair,' she wrote. 'I who was always a pedestrian par excellence.'

But most of all she hankered after a last sight of Jennychen and the children. And to Jenny's delight Dr Donkin, her new young doctor, encouraged her. 'I never knew how dear you are to me till now,' Jennychen wrote, and she could hardly sleep for excitement. Typically, Jenny sent money to buy beds and bedding, knowing how short of funds the Longuets were. The crossing was fortunately smooth, but she was ill with diarrhoea and needed Lenchen's sturdy support. It was not until late at night that they reached Jennychen's home at Argenteuil.

When they were together they were young again, she a loving girl and he a loving youth

Her pain alleviated by morphine injections, Jenny made one last expedition to Paris, driving round their old haunts with Marx, resting from time to time in the cafés she had loved. But this visit was cut short, for Marx was called back to London by Tussy's serious illness.

'Naturally,' Marx wrote, 'it was painful for me,' but he trusted Lenchen to bring Jenny safely back. They took the journey slowly and travelled first class, stopping at Amiens and Boulogne. Back in London and game to the last, she insisted on going herself in a cab to Maple's to buy more blankets for Jennychen and the children.

But by November Tussy, now recovered, was reporting to Jennychen, 'Mama is very ill.' At this critical time, when they all knew that the end was approaching, Marx himself became ill with pleurisy. He was a 'terrible patient', needing day and night nursing. Jenny, on the other hand, remained amazingly cheerful – even joking with her visitors and rejecting offers of night nursing. In great pain she wrote a last long letter to Jennychen. 'How could she,' Tussy wrote, 'she is so thin and weak now it's a miracle.' Tussy, herself nervously over-stretched, nursed them both with Lenchen's help.

Our mother lay in the large front room – Moor in the little room behind and next to it. And they who were so used to each other, whose lives had come to form part of each other, could not be in the same room any longer. Never shall I forget the morning when he felt strong enough to go into mother's room. When they were together they were young again, she a loving girl and he a loving youth, on the threshold of life, not an old man devastated by illness and an old woman parting from each other for life . . . She remained fully conscious almost to the last moment and when she could no longer speak she pressed our hands and tried to smile . . . but the last word she spoke to Papa was 'good'.

Jennychen had been unable to make the journey to London. She herself was severely ill and knew she had not long to live. But on 4 December Tussy sent her

some of her dear hair, it is as soft and beautiful as a girl's. If you could have seen her face at the last – the look in her eyes was simply indescribable. Not only that they were so clear – clear as one only sees in children's eyes, but the sweet expression as she saw and recognised us as she did to the end . . . Oh Jenny she looks so beautiful now – her face was quite transfigured, her brow absolutely smooth – just as if some gentle hand had smoothed away every line and furrow, while the lovely hair seems to form a glory round her head.

Marx, too, wrote to console Jennychen, who had been so close to her mother in the last years. 'The characteristically unbearable pains', he told her, 'began only in the very last days (and even then still controlled with injections of morphine), which the doctor deliberately reserved for the "catastrophe".' The word Marx had always used for birth now meant death. He was relieved that her energy collapsed in time, so that even in the last hours, 'there was no death struggle, but a gradual passing away, her eyes were fuller, more beautiful, more radiant than ever'. Later, to cheer Jennychen, he told her how in her last days Jenny had relived every moment of her visit to Argenteuil, laughing gaily 'when she told Laura how you and I went to Paris with Johnny and there chose for him a suit that made him look like a little *bourgeois gentilhomme*'. His daughter replied, mourning one 'who could so intensely enjoy life. Mama's heart was large enough for us all'.

She was buried near her baby grandson, Charles Longuet, in Highgate Cemetery, with little ceremony, as she had wished. 'We are no such external people,' she had replied a few days before her death, when a nurse asked her 'if anything ceremonial had been neglected'. Engels spoke briefly at the graveside. 'If ever there was a woman whose greatest happiness lay in making others happy, this was she.'

Marx was too ill to attend the ceremony. Letters of condolence flooded in from all kinds of people from many countries. Liebknecht wrote to Marx, 'The news of the death of your wife shook me deeply . . . You know what this gallant woman meant to me – it is thanks to her that the misery of London exile didn't destroy me.' 'Everyone,' Marx wrote to Jennychen, 'expressed appreciation of Möhmchen's spirit of truthfulness and deep sensitivity, rarely found in such conventional communications. I explain it on the ground that everything about her was natural and genuine, artless and unaffected; hence the impression she made on third persons as vital and luminous.' Even the old comrades now estranged sent condolences. 'In her,' one of them wrote, 'nature has destroyed its own master-piece, for in my whole life I have never encountered another such spirited and amiable woman.'

When his 'vital and luminous' wife died the light went out for Karl Marx too. 'Moor is dead,' Engels said on the day of her death. He was right. For the fifteen months that remained, Marx moved to one resort to another in search of health, submitting with resignation or even relief to a veritable torture of the flesh. Again he was blistered and tattooed, underwent noxious sul-phur treatment, took opium and arsenic. 'The only effective antidote for sorrows of the spirit', he told Engles, 'is bodily pain.' In spite of the treatment he still suffered the old eruption of the skin, liver disorder and bronchitis.

In December he took a cure in the Isle of Wight, and in February he looked for sun in North Africa. But Algiers could not warm him, and the lime-dusty wind brought on his bronchitis. Yet the view from his hotel room, he told Engels, was splendid. 'You see the Mediterranean Bay, the port of Algiers, villas rising on the *colline* like an amphitheatre. In the morning, at eight o'clock, nothing is more magical than this panorama, air, vegetation, the wonderful European Africa melange. Yet', he added, and the words had a double meaning, 'with all that, one lives only in dust.' For he was haunted by the memory of Jenny. He confessed to Engels that few people were more averse to demonstra-tive pathos than he, 'still it would be a lie not to confess that my thoughts to a great part are absorbed by reminiscences of my wife, such a part of my best part of life'.

Now he turned to his daughters for comfort. 'Tell my daughters,' he begged Engels, 'to write to old Nick.' To Laura he wrote, 'How often I think of you, at East-bourne; of the sick bed of my Jenny and the daily

devoted visits so cheering to cantankerous old Nick.'
He decided to go for peace and quiet to Jennychen at
Argenteuil; by quiet he meant 'family life, the noise of
children, this microscopic world that is much more
interesting than the macroscopic one'.

But there was trouble in the 'microscopic' world.
Jennychen was ill, in pain from the cancer of the bladder
that, in a few months, would kill her. She was expecting
her sixth child and getting little help from her husband,
who in Marx's eyes was selfish and uncaring. So he
took Laura for a long holiday to Switzerland, to Lau-
sanne and Vevey. Here they heard of the birth of
Jennychen's sixth baby – a daughter they named Jenny.
In October he went alone to the Isle of Wight, where,
in January, Tussy brought him news of Jennychen's
death. Tussy had needed no words – her stricken face
told him what he had long feared.

It was the final blow. He returned to London and in
March had no heart for the last battle with bronchitis.
When, on 13 March, Engels paid his daily visit he found
the house in tears. 'A sudden deterioration had set in,
our good Lenchen, who cared for him as no mother
ever did for her child, went up and came down again:
he was half asleep, would I come with her? When we
entered, he sat there sleeping, but never to wake up
any more.' Engels and Lenchen, the two who had in
their different ways loved him deeply, watched as 'in
two minutes he quietly and painlessly passed away'.

On Saturday, 17 March, Marx was buried beside his
wife and grandson in Highgate Cemetery. Seven years
later, by his daughters' express wish, Lenchen joined
them. Engels spoke the funeral oration, comparing
Marx with Darwin: 'Just as Darwin discovered the law
of development of organic nature, so Marx discovered
the law of development of human nature.' He was,
claimed Engels, 'the best hated and most calumniated
man of his time . . . yet he died beloved, revered and
mourned by millions of revolutionary fellow workers,

from the mines of Siberia to California, in all parts of Europe and America. His name will endure through the ages, and so also will his work.'

Engels's enthusiasm carried him away. In fact, Marx died without knowing what a force he would become in the world. He had seen the collapse of much that he fought for and for which he had sacrificed his wife and children. The Communist League and the International had disintegrated. The 1848 Revolutions and the 1870 Paris Commune had ended in failure. And although he had innumerable pamphlets and articles to his credit, his 'fat book', the great labour of his life, was only one-third finished. But he had been grateful for a friendly article by Ernest Bax, praising him as one of the leaders of modern thought. According to Marx, Bax was the first English critic to be genuinely interested in social-ism. His praise had greatly cheered Jenny in the days before her death.

Jenny, at the end, accepted the fate of those who live with demon-heroes, and no one understood better than the brilliant and doomed Tussy what this had meant to Marx.

It is no exaggeration to say that Karl Marx could never have been what he was without Jenny von Westphalen, Never were the lives of two people, both remarkable, so at one, so complementary of each other. Of extraordi-nary beauty – a beauty in which he took pleasure and pride to the end, and that wrung admiration from men like Heine . . . of intellect and wit as brilliant as her beauty, Jenny von Westphalen was a woman in a million . . . Truly he could say of her in Browning's words –

> Therefore she is immortally my bride
> Chance cannot change my love
> Nor time impair.

Emma
DARWIN

Very like a marriage of Miss Austen's

On 29 January 1839 the lane below the litle village church at Maer rang with unaccustomed noise – the clatter and jingle of horses and carriages, voices calling and laughter. It was supposed to be a quiet family wedding, conducted by the bride's uncle, and certainly the event caused scarcely a ripple in the outside world. But in Staffordshire and Shropshire the marriage of a Darwin to a Wedgwood filled the church. After all, the Wedgwoods had been part of the history of Staffordshire from as far back as the fourteenth century, long before the elegant pottery of Emma's grandfather had brought royal patronage and international fame. Emma's father, Josiah II, had tried to move south, but in Surrey and Dorset he was ill at ease, feeling that 'a Wedgwood living out of Staffordshire must lose something of his proper importance'. He came back and settled at Maer Hall, a rambling Elizabethan manor house set among gently undulating hills.

In nearby Shrewsbury also the wedding was the subject of great interest. Here Charles Darwin's father, Robert, was a doctor of distinction; and his grandfather, Erasmus Darwin, had an even greater reputation which stretched far beyond the bounds of the county. Charles himself had recently caused quite a stir. In October 1836 he had returned from an epic voyage round the world on the *Beagle*. Though the full story of this journey was not yet known, Charles Darwin was already beginning to make a mark in the scientific world.

The wedding breakfast was brief and quiet. Emma's

The Allen Family

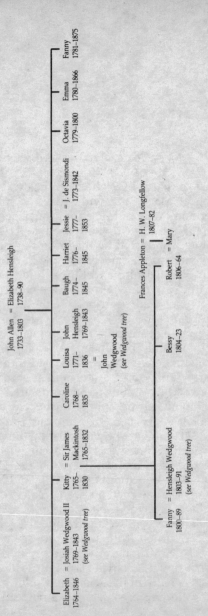

John Allen = Elizabeth Hensleigh
1733–1803   1738–90

Elizabeth = Josiah Wedgwood II
1764–1846   1769–1843
(see Wedgwood tree)

Kitty = Sir James Mackintosh
1765–   1765–1832
1830

Caroline
1768–
1835

Louisa
1771–
1836
=
John Wedgwood
(see Wedgwood tree)

John
Hensleigh
1769–1843

Baugh
1774–
1845

Harriet
1776–
1845

Jessie = J. de Sismondi
1777–   1773–1842
1853

Octavia
1779–1800

Emma
1780–1866

Fanny
1781–1875

Fanny = Hensleigh Wedgwood
1800–89   1803–91
(see Wedgwood tree)

Frances Appleton = H. W. Longfellow
1807–82

Bessy
1804–23

Robert = Mary
1806–64

The Wedgwood Family

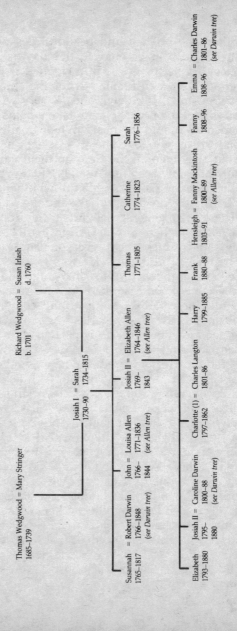

mother, the brilliant and beautiful Bessy of the past, who would so have enjoyed this day, lay upstairs, as she had done for years, in a clouded world. She had been awake when Emma left for the church, admired her grey-green silk gown and flowery white bonnet – glad that for once she had taken pains – and then slipped away into the mists. When Charles and Emma came to say goodbye she was asleep, and when she awoke they were in the train on their way to London. There had only been time for a brief farewell to Emma's father, a quiet minute by the fire with her sisters, a last look from the porch to the lake and the woods beyond.

There was general delight at this long hoped-for marriage, for here at Maer, from Josiah himself to the maids and gamekeepers, everyone considered Charles to be one of the family. He was Emma's first cousin, like her a grandchild of Josiah Wedgwood I, and since earliest childhood Maer had been his second home and his idea of paradise. Modest, and convinced that he was unprepossessing, Charles was sure that Emma was too good for him; in fact his portrait shows a pleasant, open face, and though he stooped somewhat, he was tall and broad-shouldered. Emma was not only sensible and balanced, but attractive too, with level, grey eyes, a firm, humorous mouth and rich chestnut hair.

'It is very like a marriage of Miss Austen's,' her friends, the Tollets, thought. And Ellen Tollet hoped that 'you will have a chimney that smokes or something of that sort to prevent you being quite intoxicated'. Emma Wedgwood would be 'an untold loss, you are the only girl of our own age in this country worth caring much for'. Emma's eldest sister Elizabeth, who had been like a mother to her, wrote sadly, 'That sunny face will leave a vacancy.' Even Darwin's doting and critical sisters conceded that Charles had done well. As for Dr Darwin, 'My father', Charles wrote, 'echoes and re-echoes Uncle Josh's words, "You have drawn a prize".'

The Darwin Family

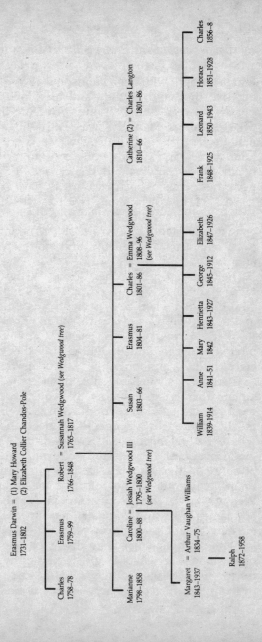

Erasmus Darwin = (1) Mary Howard
1731–1802   (2) Elizabeth Collier Chandos-Pole

Charles   Erasmus   Robert = Susannah Wedgwood *(see Wedgwood tree)*
1758–78   1759–99   1766–1848   1765–1817

Marianne   Caroline = Josiah Wedgwood III
1798–1858   1800–88   1795–1800
                         (see Wedgwood tree)

Susan   Erasmus   Charles = Emma Wedgwood   Catherine (2) = Charles Langton
1803–66   1804–81   1801–86   1808–96   1810–66   1801–86
                                        (see Wedgwood tree)

William   Anne   Mary   Henrietta   George   Elizabeth   Frank   Leonard   Horace   Charles
1839–1914 1841–51 1842   1843–1927   1845–1912 1847–1926 1848–1925 1850–1943 1851–1928 1856–8

Margaret = Arthur Vaughan Williams
1843–1937   1834–75

Ralph
1872–1958

No breeder doubts how strong is the tendency to inheritance

Emma brought with her a handsome dowry: Josiah gave her five thousand pounds and an allowance of four hundred a year. But she came with more than money. Charles, obsessed as he was with the problems of heredity and the origin of man, was very aware that Emma's rich and varied family background was exceptional. Since Darwins and Wedgwoods regularly married their cousins, Charles must have studied the records of his own family with a scientist's special attention. 'No breeder doubts how strong is the tendency to inheritance,' he wrote later. 'The inheritance of every character is the rule and non-inheritance the anomaly.'

Their mutual grandfather, Josiah Wedgwood I, had married another Wedgwood. Charles's mother Susan, who had died when he was eight, was Emma's aunt – and now Josiah was his 'uncle-father': Emma's brother Jos had married Charles's sister Caroline. And the interweaving continued; Emma was the youngest of eight children, and four of her family married cousins.

There were some formidable intellects in the Darwin strain. Charles's grandfather, Erasmus, was one of the most gifted men of his period. He was a brilliant doctor much admired by George III, a poet and zoologist, whose natural history in verse was to influence his grandson Charles in his study of evolution. The Lunar Society, or the Lunatics as Erasmus Darwin called them, grew out of the informal meetings of Josiah Wedgwood I with Erasmus Darwin, Matthew Boulton and James Watt, and gradually developed into a distinguished society, lasting forty years, where new mechanical and scientific ideas were discussed. Less is known of Erasmus's sad wife, Mary. The clever physician failed to cure his own wife of the violent headaches followed by delirium which made her a secret drinker and caused her to die, an alcoholic, at the age of thirty-one. The Darwin brilliance had its darker side.

Charles's brother, also called Erasmus, though something of a dilettante, had a fine, cultivated mind and was much admired in London literary circles. Their four sisters had few opportunities to show their talents beyond the home. Marianne, the eldest, left little mark in the family records, but the tall, handsome Caroline, who carried herself like a duchess, was highly intelligent and a dominant influence on Charles. After their mother's death she was mainly responsible for his earliest education. Susan and Catherine, who when young reminded Charles of Kitty and Lydia in Jane Austen's *Pride and Prejudice*, sobered into highly competent assistants to Dr Darwin, prescribing and making up his medicines for him.

Emma, with customary self-deprecation, often described herself and the Wedgwoods as stolid and lacking in imagination; and it was true that her elder brother Jos and her father were both taciturn by nature. But Charles described Josiah II as the wisest man he knew, and it was not the solid virtues but flair that had made Josiah Wedgwood I so successful a potter. Tom Wedgwood, Emma's uncle, was an unfulfilled genius; the friend and patron of the poet Coleridge, he discovered the process of photography, though he never completed his researches.

Emma's mother's family brought a sparkle to enliven the Wedgwood solidity. There can be few collections of family letters that radiate more vitality and bright intelligence than those of the Allen sisters. Their father, John Allen, was a Welsh country gentleman and they were brought up in a handsome house, Cresselly, in Pembrokeshire. Nearby, but tactfully screened from the house, was Mr Allen's coalmine. The girls were also screened from their father's second wife, a miner's daughter, who apparently never came to the big house.

Mr Allen, who was something of a tyrant, insisted

that his dinner table was animated by intelligent conversation, and thumped the table when he did not get it. He certainly produced a remarkable family. Elizabeth (Bessy), who married Josiah Wedgwood II, was much admired not only for her beauty and intelligence but also for a charm and kindness that shine through her letters. John Allen succeeded his father, and Baugh Allen became Master of Dulwich College. Emma hoped that Baugh would not come to her wedding – he would, she wrote to Charles, 'think it incumbent on him to be in a great state of liveliness'. Kitty Allen married James Mackintosh, MP, later Sir James; he was an eminent historian and one of the best conversationalists of the day. Jessie, affectionate and ebullient, married Jean-Charles Simonde de Sismondi, one of the great European scholars, a historian and economist whom even Karl Marx quoted with respect. Jane Allen was the beauty of the family, Harriet Allen the submissive one, and Emma Allen, though kind and intelligent, was exceptionally plain.

Charles Darwin, acutely conscious of the intellectual richness of Emma's background, was desperately worried, as he said, that she would find him 'a dull dog'. But Emma, surrounded from childhood by an affectionate family, brought a serenity to their marriage that needed no outside excitement. The youngest of eight children, she had a special place in the family. Her brothers, Jos, Harry, Frank and Hensleigh teased her affectionately. She was inseparable from Fanny, who, though two years older, was neither as pretty nor as intelligent. The older sisters, Elizabeth and Charlotte, adored 'the Dovelies', or 'Miss Pepper and Salt', as they called them. 'I always think of you as one person,' Charlotte wrote. As for Elizabeth, the oldest sister, she lavished on Emma all the frustrated love of an affectionate spinster. Sweet-natured but crookbacked, she would never marry. Emma was her child. 'Since from the time she could speak,' she told Charles, 'I have never had one moment's pain from her and a share of daily pleasures such as few people have it in their power to shed around.'

This childhood, spent lapped in love in a Staffordshire still rural, gave Emma a stability and tranquillity that marked her all her life. There was a period when, for the sake of economy, they moved from Maer Hall to Etruria Hall in sight of the Potteries. But they returned to Maer, and for Emma no flowers would ever bloom, no birds ever sing, more beautifully than they did at Maer. After morning lessons with her mother or Elizabeth she was free. She could rattle away on the old piano, or sit on the curving steps that swept down from the porch to the terrace and look out upon a landscape that even Capability Brown could not improve. Below the stone balustrade the still lake stretched, to a child's eye as wide as the sea. Beyond, sheep grazed the steep, green meadows between wooded slopes. From the stone boathouse below the terrace Fanny and Emma and her brothers rowed to the world's end at the far lake shore. And Emma never forgot the picnics at the Roman fort on the hills above Maer, or the pony rides across the heath.

There were visits to their friends the Tollets at nearby Betley Hall, and days when the older girls allowed her to ride with them to Handchurch through Swinnerton Park. 'A great honour', Emma later remembered, 'to a little girl . . . I remember Harry's high spirits and the short gallops we took up the little pitches of the pretty wood we were skirting.' At rowing, skating and archery Emma had an easy confidence and proficiency. When she was five years old, the eight children were taken for strawberries and cream at Trentham House, their neighbours' estate. The boys rode ponies, while the girls were crammed into the wagon, and Emma and Fanny spent the day in silent enjoyment, 'very grave, very demure all day, but very happy while running about the park', so Bessy told her sisters. Her childhood gave

Emma an abiding love of the open air, of birds and animals, of wild flowers and trees. When she was eleven, Aunt Emma Allen reported to Bessy:

> I have never seen [Emma's] expressive face take the shadow of an angry look and I do think her love for Fanny is the prettiest thing I ever saw . . . I ascribe much of Emma's joyous nature to her being secured, if not caused, by Fanny's yielding disposition. Had the other met with a cross or an opposing sister there was every chance that with her ardent feelings, her temper had become irritable. Now she is made the happiest being that ever was looked on.

Josiah and Bessy, influenced by Rousseau, gave their girls an exceptionally liberal education. All the same, as Josiah wrote to his wife, he found it singular 'that Rousseau, who has given so admirable a picture of domestic education, should have sent his childen to the *Enfants trouvés* [foundling hospital]'. Rousseau was not the only genius whose theory did not match his practice.

When Emma was ten she spent six months with the family in Paris. Then, while the rest of them proceeded on a grand tour of Switzerland and Italy, she and Fanny were left with their maid at a boarding school in Paris, and to the surprise of the older girls the Dovelies were delighted at the idea. Every Sunday they visited a relation who was a fishmonger. Emma never forgot the Sunday smell nor her odious little French cousin, who was her partner at the dancing school and 'bothers one very much', but she absorbed good French with the smell of the fish.

Four years later she went with Fanny for a year to a boarding school in Paddington Green, then a rural London suburb. She claimed that she learned very little there, but her talent for music was encouraged. She had always excelled as a pianist, and now, at Greville

House, she was produced as a star pupil to perform before Mrs Fitzherbert, George IV's morganatic wife. Emma had a crisp, fine touch, as her daughter Etty later remembered, and played with intelligence and clarity. The slow movements tended to be 'too allegro', for even then Emma hated sentimentality in music, as in life.

One year at Greville House was enough; the girls were homesick. They returned to Maer Hall to be taught by Elizabeth and visiting masters. Life at Maer was in itself a liberal education. Josiah Wedgwood had a comfortable, well-stocked library where the family read widely. Emma was famous in the family for having read the whole of 'Paradise Lost' as a little girl. The explorer Mungo Park caught her imagination, and years later she wrote to Charles Darwin, 'I remember being more interested in it when I was a child than in almost any book and admiring Mungo Park with all my heart.' Jane Austen was also a particular favourite, and Emma and her friends often identified with Miss Austen's characters. Emma Caldwell, the writer, remembeed that at Maer learning was absorbed with pleasure.

> They have freedom in their actions in this house as well as in their principles. Doors and windows stand open, you are nowhere in confinement; you may do as you like; you are surrounded by books that all look most tempting to read. You will find some pleasant topics of conversation or may start one as all things are talked of in the general family.

This freedom of speech on every subject and the openness and good sense that were evident in discussions at Maer made the house exceptionally delightful to visitors. For the Darwin cousins, Erasmus, Charles and their sisters, Maer was like heaven. Their own home was orderly, formal and somewhat oppressive. There was, as Emma later in life remembered, 'a want of liberty at Shrewsbury whenever Doctor Darwin was in the room; but then he was genial and sympathetic – only nobody must go on about their own talk'. The doctor made her nervous with his sharp 'What is Emma saying?' 'I find a week long enough at Shrewsbury', Emma wrote later, 'as one gets rather fatigued by the Dr's talk especially the 2 whole hours just before dinner. It is best to be there in the middle of summer as one has more sitting out with the girls.' Nevertheless, she added, 'The Dr has been as pleasant as possible.' As far as Charles was concerned, however, she observed, 'Everything his father did was absolutely true, right and wise.'

Charles never forgot the evenings at Maer – the music and the clear, pure voices of Elizabeth and Charlotte:

> in the evening there was much very agreeable conversation, not so personal as it generally is in larger family parties, together with music. In the summer, the whole family used often to sit on the steps of the old portico, with the flower-garden in front, and with the steep wooded bank opposite the house reflected in the lake, with here and there a fish rising or a water-bird paddling about. Nothing has left a more vivid picture on my mind than these evenings at Maer.

So on the summer lawns or in winter round the library fire, Emma even as a little girl absorbed a lasting interest in the world beyond Maer. Her mother was exceptionally well read, and when she and her sisters were together conversation sparkled. Josiah, her father, talked little but when he did it was with the sound judgement that made Dr Darwin describe him as the most sensible man he had ever met. He and his family had been active in the anti-slavery movement and, like the Allen sisters, he was a keen suppporter of the campaign for parliamentary reform. Emma's sister Elizabeth sat through the reform debates in Parliament, and one speech of Macaulay's 'almost made [her] cry with admiration'. Literature and politics were discussed with lively concern, but also with tolerance and good humour. Those same attitudes remained with Emma all her life.

Emma had ample opportunity to observe men and women of genius. Some of the great names of the period were their friends and discussed without awe. 'Flo' Nightingale was a frequent visitor, and Fanny Allen considered her 'a brave girl' even when young. Wordsworth often dined with Uncle Mackintosh, and Coleridge would have gone dinnerless had her father Josiah and her brother Tom not financed him. The Allen aunts and Emma thought him odious; in old age Emma thought it extraordinary that Josiah had been so duped by the impecunious poet – 'Dr Darwin', in her opinion, 'would have been more acute.' Byron could be surprisingly dull at Uncle Mac's dinners. They found Lady Byron cold and unattractive, but Aunt Jessie met her often in Geneva and was more sympathetic.

They were not easily shocked at the family gatherings at Maer Hall. The unconventional and outspoken writer Harriet Martineau was a welcome guest; it was a family joke that she was setting her cap at Charles Darwin's brother Erasmus. Certainly when she was in financial straits Erasmus offered help – and was refused. Aunt Jessie even confessed that she had a weakness for notorious ladies, and was particularly attached to Countess Guiccioli, Byron's mistress.

Remarkably, two of Emma's uncles were close friends of the brilliant but scandalous Madame de Staël, who dazzled many of the great men of Europe with her eloquence and wit. Even Karl Marx made careful notes of her famous work on the literature and philosophy of Germany, *In Germania*. Sismondi as a young man escorted her on a tour of Italy in company with the poet and dramatist Schiller. And when she was exiled from France for her opposition to Napoleon, Emma's uncle, Sir James Mackintosh, became her devoted admirer. She sent for him to be present at her dinners, it was

said, as though she were calling up the beans and
bacon. When she returned to Paris he followed her,
leaving his wife, Emma's Aunt Kitty. Kitty was the most
difficult of the Allen sisters – as Aunt Jessie once
observed, incapable of making herself or others happy.
But Sir James was not easy; an MP who never quite
fulfilled his promies, he had, as Coleridge said, 'a speck
of cold at the heart'. But he was a brilliant talker and
popular with the Whig great ladies. In the *New Whig
Guide* Thomas Moore wrote of Mackintosh:

> He frequents the assembly, the supper, the ball,
> The *philosophe beau* of unloved Staël,
> Affects to talk French in his hoarse Highland note,
> And gurgles Italian half down his throat.
> His gait is a shuffle, his smile is a leer,
> His converse is quaint, his civility queer.
> In short, to all grace and deportment a rebel
> At best he is but a half polished Scotch pebble.

So Emma was accustomed at an early age to the problems of living with great men and women. Her family
had great sympathy for the wife of the Rev. Sydney
Smith, whose wife was often snubbed by the great
ladies who adored the witty cleric. 'The wife of a wit',
his close friend Fanny Allen once wrote, 'is under
constant discipline of mortification.'

The laughter at Maer was often boisterous, and the
autumn of 1824 was particularly happy: 'Wicked times,'
wrote Emma in her diary. The house was full of cousins
and friends, there was dancing every night and Emma
was the girls' hairdresser, curling and gossiping in their
rooms. They formed themselves into the Tag Rag Company and produced *The Merry Wives of Windsor*. Sixteen-
year-old Emma was pronounced by Bessy as 'very good'
in the part of the decrepit old Justice Shallow. There
was 'a whirl of noise – we are very gay, very flirtish and
very foolish', wrote Bessy to her sister. Emma had in

the same month been confirmed, but it had not diminished her high spirits; it was done, as Bessy said, as a matter of form: 'It is better to conform to the ceremonies of our Church than to omit them. One does not know that in omitting them we are not liable to sin.' It was not until much later that Emma developed her deep religious sense.

The happiest time of my life

In 1825 Josiah and Bessy took all four girls on a Grand Tour to Paris and Geneva, then over Mont Cenis to Florence and Rome and back again to stay with Aunt Jessie in Geneva. On their way out Jessie delighted in showing them her elegant town house, and her villa, all coolness and space, at Chêne two miles away. Bessy, whose health was now delicate, stayed behind with Jessie in Geneva while Josiah and the girls went on to Italy. In spite of their enthusiasm for Rome and pleasure in Florence, it was on the whole a disappointing trip. The weather was poor, Josiah was uncomfortable and missed Bessy, and they were appalled at the beggars, the poverty and the dirt. It was with a mixture of amusement and embarrassment that they watched the fine ladies feeding the pilgrims at Rome. But the journey widened Emma's horizons. They spent a happy month reunited in Geneva, then returned with some relief to Maer. Josiah was still 'as good a John Bull as when he went out'.

In the following year the Simondis came to England and took Fanny and Emma back to Geneva with them for a nine months' visit. It was easy to be happy with the ebullient and affectionate Aunt Jessie, who did her best to give a little continental polish to the two fresh-faced country girls. But it was hard work making the Wedgwood girls take an interest in their appearance; at Maer no one had worried much. So the Thursday afternoons in the grand, red and gold drawing room under the critical eyes of Jessie's formal friends were heavy going.

Emma developed an affection for Sismondi in spite of his exceptional ugliness and his hand-kissing gallantry, though she never quite got over the flourish of his bows and the affected way he always greeted her with *'Ma petite Emma!'* Sismondi, who remembered the brilliant talk at Madame de Staël's table, tried to teach Emma and Fanny the art of conversation. But the two Staffordshire girls looked on through their spectacles and, as Jessie told their mother, tended to give way to 'a disposition of silence that casts almost imperceptibly a gloom around them'. And though their fresh complexions were much admired, they could never learn to be coquettes. Jessie confessed she loved them for their 'quiet qualities', though Sismondi 'wishes exceedingly to inspire them with some more showy ones'. Nevertheless, Jessie told Bessy, there was 'a pretty gaiety about Emma, always ready to answer to any liveliness and sometimes to throw it out herself, that will cheer anybody that lives with her or approaches her'.

Certainly Emma could not have had a better tutor than Sismondi, whose knowledge of European history and politics was unrivalled. Under his tuition Emma not merely learned to converse but gained a deeper understanding of politics which lasted all her life. And Sismondi was kind, if a little eccentric. When Florence Nightingale visited him in Geneva in 1838 she became his devoted admirer, reporting with amusement how he fed mice in his study and scores of beggars outside his door. Tactfully the Sismondis never compared Fanny with Emma; Fanny was plainer, less intelligent, methodical and painstaking. But Emma enchanted Sismondi. Watching her dancing so gracefully, he could not understand why the whole of Geneva was not in love with her. Yet Emma had no suitors in her nine months with the Sismondis and, although she and

Fanny enjoyed the balls, dancing till morning, and loved walking by the lake, entranced by the snowy mountain peaks, she was often violently homesick. Nevertheless on her return she wrote with gratitude to 'that naughty woman Aunt Jessie', telling her that it was 'the happiest time of my life' and 'that is saying a good deal'. And her Aunt Jessie desperately missed her 'dearest toad'.

Emma's father went to Geneva to bring the girls home, taking with him Caroline Darwin. Charles came too, but only as far as Paris; then he went back to England. Emma returned to Maer bronzed and more poised, self-confident and with fluent French, Italian and German, but her mother thought she was 'as unaffected as ever'.

Bessy was now becoming increasingly frail, so Emma helped Elizabeth to run the household. The two sisters took turns to nurse their mother. Emma also taught in Elizabeth's Sunday school, held in the laundry on the estate, and wrote for her rowdy pupils a little book of stories called *Plumb Pie*. Emma's spelling was not usually so erratic – perhaps she thought it more plummy that way. They are simple, engaging little tales – 'The Plumb Pie', 'The Little Foal', 'The Snowy Night' and 'Market'.

When Aunt Kitty Mackintosh came for a six months' visit, Emma was better able after Sismondi's tuition to cope with her pompous husband; she arranged a study for him where he could work, and set out his books on shelves. Sir James thought Bessie was 'a well-head of kindness and the gentlest of mistresses', but the rest of the Maer household was too boisterous for him.

By now Bessy was beginning to despair of seeing her daughters settled. In 1831 Elizabeth was, at forty-three, a confirmed spinster; the beautiful Charlotte was thirty-four and Fanny twenty-four, and no young man had asked for them; and Emma, the prize so much admired, had still not been won. She was now good-looking rather than pretty. Her manner was easy but she did not suffer fools, and the steady grey eyes behind their spectacles could be disconcerting. She and Fanny spent much of their time indulging in country pursuits, bazaars and fêtes, and the two girls were said to be 'dragonesses at archery'. Emma was, wrote Bessy, 'more popular than any of my girls, her manners with men are easy and undesigning without coquetry'. The truth was that Emma, perfectly happy at Maer and with her sister's companionship, felt no need to angle for a husband. And she was never lonely. Maer Hall was always full of lively friends and cousins.

It was a relief to relax with her Staffordshire friends after the constraints of Geneva, to ride over to neighbouring Betley Hall, up the long, tree-lined avenue to the comfortable Georgian house where the Tollet family greeted her with such warmth. Here, as at Maer, were extensive grounds and lakes. Here too was a good library where she could enjoy easy conversation with her clever friends, Ellen and Georgina. Their father, George Tollet, was described in his obituary, in 1855, as 'a Whig of the Old School . . . kind and frank and highly esteemed by all who knew him'. He was also keenly interested in the new agricultural methods, and some years later Charles Darwin was to value his advice. In 1839 he plied him with questions on the inheritance of characteristics such as timidity in cattle, and later still referred to George Tollet's experiments in cattle breeding in his *Variation of Animals and Plants under Domestication*.

Ellen Tollet was highly intelligent, the friend of Mrs Gaskell and Florence Nightingale, with whom in later years she was to work. Charles admired her judgement; in 1854 he asked his publisher, John Murray, to send the first pages of *The Origin of Species* to her so that she might advise on his style. Ellen remained, until her death in 1890, Emma's closest friend.

Though Charles Darwin had always been regarded

with affection at Maer he had shown little sign of intellectual brilliance, and on his visits there he was usually out from dawn to dusk with the gamekeepers, tramping, as he later wrote, 'through thick heath and young Scotch firs . . . and . . . totally devoted to shooting . . . My zeal was so great, that I used to place my shooting-boots open by my bedside when I went to bed, so as not to lose half a minute in putting them on in the morning'. Indeed his father once exploded with words that burned in his memory: 'You care for nothing but shooting, dogs and rat-catching and you will be a disgrace, to yourself and all your family.'

Certainly he himself admitted that he had not distinguished himself at school. After his mother's death, when he was eight, he was sent for a year to a Shrewsbury day school and thence to Shrewsbury Grammar School, which, he claimed in his autobiography, 'as a means of education was simply a blank'. He remembered enjoying Shakespeare and Byron, though Emma later frequently expressed surprise that he had read so little; and he never acquired her ability to learn languages. Because he appeared to be making no progress, his father sent him at sixteen to join his brother Erasmus studying medicine at Edinburgh University. But since he found the lectures tedious and the sight of operations sickened him, he gave up his medical studies after two years. Having decided that it would be pleasant to be a country clergyman he spent three years at Cambridge, and in 1831, attained an undistinguished BA in classics.

Yet during those years of apparent mediocrity he was developing a passion for natural history and a talent for careful observation that was to be the main ingredient in his particular genius. There were those who perceived his talent. Sir James Mackintosh remarked, when he stayed at Maer, 'There is something in that man that interests me.' Similarly the botanist Professor John Henslow took him up and encouraged him. Even

Charles, modest though he was, himself realised that at that time he was 'something a little superior to the common run of youths'.

Impressed by Charles's ability, Henslow recommended him to Captain Fitzroy of HMS *Beagle* who was looking for a naturalist to accompany him on a five years' voyage round the world. His mission was to survey the coasts of Patagonia, Tierra del Fuego, Chile and Peru; to visit Pacific islands and to proceed around the world establishing a chain of chronometrical stations.

It was at Maer, on 1 September 1831, that the momentous decision was taken that would send Charles round the world. Dr Robert had strongly objected, but had added, 'If you can find any man of common sense who advises you to go I will give my consent.' When Darwin told his Uncle Josiah that he had refused the offer, Josiah immediately offered to drive him the thirty miles to Shrewsbury so as to persuade Dr Robert that Charles should not miss this opportunity. Charles was eternally grateful to his future 'uncle-father'. He left Plymouth in December, out of spirits 'at the thought of leaving all my family and friends . . . I was also troubled with palpitation and pain about the heart . . . and was convinced that I had heart disease. I did not consult any doctor . . . I was resolved to go at all hazards'.

Charles was away from 27 December 1831 to 2 October 1836, and during those years wrote long letters which were read with excitement and pride at Shrewsbury and recounted to the Wedgwoods at Maer. The families were dazzled by the vision of their easy-going Charles plunging into the primeval forests of Brazil or encountering naked savages in Tierra del Fuego and being shaken by earthquakes in Chile. They were fascinated by his fossil discoveries in Argentina and the coral reefs in the Pacific. But they were worried by his continual seasickness and the reports of his serious illness in South America, and they wished he would come home.

Charles's letters to Henslow so impressed him that he read them to the Philosophical Society of Cambridge, and Professor Adam Sedgwick was inspired to call upon Dr Robert to tell him that his son 'deserved a place among the leading men of science'. Charles, hearing this, wielded his geological hammer with renewed enthusiasm, delighted that his father at last no longer thought him a mere rat-catcher.

In his autobiography Charles claimed that this voyage determined his whole career, that to it he owed the first real education of his mind, and in particular that in those years he learned a 'habit of energetic industry and concentrated attention' which he always insisted was the secret of his scientific success. He was especially proud of his 'solution of the problem of the Coral Islands' and his geological studies, but most of all his discovery of what he called 'the singular relations of animals and plants inhabiting the several islands of the Galapagos Archipelago, and all of them to the inhabitants of S. America'. It was his observation of the similarities and differences in plants and animals in neighbouring islands that sowed the seeds of theories that more than twenty-five years later would blossom in *The Origin of Species*.

Meanwhile, in 1832, to Bessy's relief there were at last marriages in the family. Emma was a bridesmaid at the London wedding of her brother Hensleigh to her favourite cousin, the clever Fanny Mackintosh. This Fanny, though now officially Fanny Wedgwood, was henceforth known as Fanny Hensleigh in order to distinguish her from all the other Fannys in the family. Charlotte, Emma and their sister Fanny went down to London for the wedding, and a hilarious occasion it was. 'I was dressed up in a white silk wedding gown of Mrs Vicar's to enact one of the bridesmaids,' Emma's sister Fanny wrote home. 'The Thorntons had fished it out for somebody to wear and none of them would, so they made me and by intense squeezing I got into it.' But she was not allowed to wear her fine gown, for the bride's dress, a white poplin presented by Lady Holland, had not arrived, so Emma and her sister did their duty in two gowns of lilac silk and it was Fanny Hensleigh who wore the white silk wedding gown. Encouraged by Fanny's example, Charlotte agreed to marry the Rev. Charles Langton, and Emma stayed on in London to help buy Charlotte's trousseau. They were married in the same year. Frank, Emma's steady, plodding brother, who had now taken a responsible position in the family pottery, also married at this time; to add to the confusion of names in the Darwin-Wedgwood family tree, his bride was yet another Fanny.

A blank which will never be filled up

Then a blow fell which left the sunny Emma desolate. Her sister Fanny fell ill and died, probably a victim of the cholera that was sweeping the country in 1832. Throughout Fanny's illness Emma had nursed her patiently and lovingly. After her death she quietly wrote, 'Her loss has left a blank which will never be filled up.' Emma's prayer was that 'Fanny's sweet image should be a motive for holiness. What exquisite happiness it will be to be with her again, to tell her how I loved her who has been joined with me in almost every enjoyment in life.' It was her first real sorrow, and characteristically she refused to parade her grief. 'I do not like that you should be thinking of us as more unhappy than we are,' she wrote to Aunt Jessie. 'We all feel cheerful and susceptible of happiness. How faultless she was, hers has been a gentle, happy life.' Quietly Emma packed up all Fanny's careful lists and notes and kept them till the day she died.

When Emma lost her methodical sister there was a

void until she married Charles Darwin, who, like Fanny, gave order to her life. Fanny had needed the more outgoing Emma, but Emma had needed Fanny too; in the family she was 'Miss Pedigree' to Emma's 'Miss Slipslop'. Fanny's notebooks were meticulous, recording lists of temperatures, words, dates, weights, heights and distances. Emma's untidiness was, in fact, as her daughter Etty later wrote, 'the "*schatten-seite*" to a delightfully large-minded, unfussy way of taking life, which is more common among men than women'.

It was altogether a more serious Emma who emerged after the death of Fanny. This period marked the beginning of her real interest in religion. Josiah, like Jenny Marx's father, was something of an eighteenth-century freethinker, and Bessy took more interest in the mind than in the spirit, but Emma was a child of her age and influenced by the evangelical fervour of the time. She never indulged in extreme enthusiasm, unlike one of her friends, who took to speaking in tongues. 'Poor thing,' wrote Emma, 'I should think she would become quite mad soon.' But now Emma began to develop that profound and unshakeable faith that sustained her for the rest of her life.

Like her Allen aunts, she also became interested in politics in this exciting period. These were years of great unrest in Europe, but the more immediate concern in Britain was to secure the reform of a Parliament in which neither workers nor manufacturers were properly represented. There were so-called 'rotten boroughs' which sent back MPs from tiny hamlets, whereas the great and growing industrial cities had none. There were 'pocket boroughs', which were in the gift of their aristocratic patrons. When in 1831 the bill giving limited reform was passed at last in the Commons but thrown out by the Lords, rioting crowds broke windows and stoned their lordships in their carriages. Finally King William IV was forced to threaten to create more peers if the Lords continued to obstruct the Commons. So, on

4 June 1832, the Reform Bill was passed in both Houses, abolishing rotten boroughs, giving more seats in the new industrial towns, and extending the franchise. The Reform Bill took the heat out of the revolutionary movement in Britain. Men like Josiah Wedgwood could relax and get on with their own affairs.

Emma kept a keen interest in politics all her life, and she was an active supporter when her father was elected in December 1832 as the Liberal Member for Stoke in the new, reformed Parliament. Emma's politics were typical of her – moderate, progressive and humanitarian, though on the question of slavery she could be roused to unaccustomed passion. She was a little surprised that her father had done so well, 'as he has become too Tory for these Radical times'.

On her visits to her brother Hensleigh and his wife in London she frequently attended debates in the House of Commons, sitting in the ladies' gallery high up in what was known as the ventilator. Women were not allowed in the gallery at this time, so they peered down through a grille in the ceiling, claiming that they could hear better there than in the chamber itself. In August 1833 Emma, sitting in the ventilator, was highly incensed because Daniel O'Connell, furious with the *Hansard* reporters, had the gallery cleared. 'It was a most foolish, passionate thing to do,' Emma wrote with perception, 'as the Reporters are sure to gain the day in the end.' O'Connell was a Catholic lawyer who had led the campaign for Catholic emancipation and was now a Member of Parliament. Emma kept her interest in Irish affairs, first stimulated here, throughout her life.

In the early 1830s, while Jenny von Westphalen was enthusiastically supporting the Young Germany movement, Fanny Hensleigh had been equally passionate in the cause of the Italian patriot, Mazzini, and his Young Italy. He was then canvassing support while exiled in England, much to the fury of Jessie Sismondi. 'Mazzini', she declared, 'has been living on what he has duped from the poor Italian exiles, whom he has sent without number to death and dungeon, taking care to keep himself safe.' She was desperately concerned about Fanny. 'Underneath that refreshing quiet, that delicious calm,' she wrote to Elizabeth, 'Fanny has a lava of living fire that has made her do battle to all the Governments in Europe under the banner of Mazzini. She is of his Committee in London! How could Hensleigh permit it!'

Ever since her mother's death Fanny had entertained Sir James Mackintosh's literary and political friends with an easy grace. But Emma had little taste for high society. Her mother once described with despair how, when Emma arrived at the Mackintoshes' house in Clapham,

> she saw the dining room all lighted up as she drove into the court, and the Historian himself in full discourse (as she saw through the window) with a party of gentlemen. Emma desired to be shown up to Fanny's stepsister's room, where she had a very comfortable cup of tea and dish of chat with her. Fanny came up to ask Emma whether she would come down and see Mr Wilberforce . . . which she declined, and I daresay M [Mackintosh] thought her a great fool for doing so.

Emma was more detached and preferred to help in her own practical way, raising money at country bazaars for Spanish and Italian refugees. Jenny and Karl Marx, among the swarming émigrés in Soho, would have mocked, but Emma's embroidered purses and pen-wipers and Charlotte's paintings were a great success.

In her loneliness music now became more and more important to Emma; she visited music festivals at Manchester and Worcester, where she heard Clara Novello sing. Among all her relations only her cousin Fanny Hensleigh shared her knowledge and deep love of music. From Henwick, near Manchester, Emma wrote to Fanny: 'Last night we had Mozart's symphony in E flat and the Midsummer Night's Dream, and the night before Beethoven in C minor which I had only heard once before ages ago and I like it better than anything I ever heard I think, and tonight we have the Pastoral Symphony which I have never heard.' Emma's attitude to music was always cool and unsentimental, but her emotions, though controlled, ran very deep, as her daughter Etty remembered: 'One of the very few times in my life that I saw her lose her self-control was when Clara Novello sang the solo verse of God Save the Queen at the opening of the Crystal Palace. My mother broke down then and sobbed audibly.'

But Emma could not often get away. In 1832 her mother had fallen in what seems to have been a kind of epileptic fit and had broken a leg. From then onwards she was a chronic invalid, often comatose and seldom leaving her room. Elizabeth and Emma nursed her with devotion. Sometimes one of the family would take their place, and once Emma was able to take three months' holiday at Cresselly, the Pembrokeshire family home of the Allens. Here, Emma wrote, 'the country was bright and pretty as when I was a child', and she scrambled over the rocks at Tenby and thought with pain of her lost sister.

Perhaps because after Fanny's death she became more approachable, Emma suddenly had four or five proposals of marrige. There were young men who hoped to win her with music: one such claimed to be an expert flautist, but when he did not come up to her standards he and his 'tootlings' were dismissed. Emma laughed at her friends' efforts to get her married. At a party at the Tolletts' house 'two singing sisters and their brother, a perfect seraph by their account', were much admired. Emma, with mock regret, pronounced him too young for her. Once Bessy found a young curate walking round the lake, weeping with disappointment at his rejection.

At this time Charles Darwin's elder brother, Erasmus, was obviously much attracted to Emma. But Erasmus, gentle, scholarly and languid, never found enough energy to propose, to the relief of the Allen aunts who did not much like him. The poet Alice Meynell said of him: 'He never grasped at happiness.' Erasmus was always to be happier as *cavaliere servente* than as lover, and went on to divide his attentions between Jane Carlyle and Fanny Hensleigh. One of the reasons why there is always an edge to Jane Carlyle's references to the Wedgwoods is that Fanny was stealing her admirer.

As for Charles Darwin, he had shown no signs of interest in Emma in the years before he left for his voyage. As Emma later laughingly reminded him, he used to call her 'a little baggage'. In any case Charles was at that time smitten by a neighbour, the delectable Fanny Owen, and among the Wedgwood girls it was Charlotte whose paintings he had so admired and whose beauty and lovely voice had enthralled him.

Better than a dog

During Charles Darwin's long years of absence on the *Beagle* the Wedgwoods at Maer had eagerly awaited letters from him. They wrote to him of Charlotte's marriage, and he sent his sympathy on the death of Fanny. At last, in October 1836, he returned and took the earliest opportunity to visit Maer Hall, where Emma and her family waited with some impatience. She had, she confessed, not read up as much as she should have done for him, though she had skipped through 'Captain Head's Gallop i.e. Sir Francis Head's Rapid Journeys Across the Pampas'.

Her account of his visit was enthusiastic, and she confessed to Fanny in a letter on 21 November,

> We enjoyed Charles's visit uncommonly. We had been very handsome in inviting the outliers of the family to meet him and the last morning the chaise from Fern Hill did not come and we persuaded them to stay and had

just made ourselves comfortable and planned a walk
when the chaise arrived, however we got them to let us
send it off though Caroline felt it to be rather naughty
and we had a very nice snug day of them to ourselves.
Charles talked away most pleasantly all the time we
plied him with questions without any mercy. Harry and
Frank made the most of him and enjoyed him
thoroughly . . .

In the comfort of Maer Hall Emma listened enthralled
while Charles told them of his five years' journey. She
commiserated over his constant seasickness, marvelled
at his courage as he rode alone with the gauchos over
the pampas, and shared his wonder at 'the unforgetta-
ble sight of a naked savage in his native land'. Emma
particularly must have been much moved as he told of
his 'sense of sublimity which the great deserts of Patagonia and the forest clad mountains of Tierra del Fuego
excited in me'. This was a different man from the
carefree young sportsman who had revelled in the
shooting at Maer.

Emma had been much taken with Charles ever since
his return, and there was even an unusual touch of
jealousy in her comment when Charles, dismayed at
Charlotte's portrait, said, 'I hope to fate she is not like
that picture.' 'I suppose', she wrote to her sister, 'he
has rather a poetical idea of her for the picture is
certainly very like.'

But she saw very little more of him in his first months
at home. He was busy in Cambridge sorting his notes
and his geological specimens, and she spent most of the
winter of 1836 with one of her Allen cousins, Lady
Gifford, in Edinburgh. Hospitable though the Scots
were, inviting them to balls and dances 'as though they
were somebody', as Emma wrote, nevertheless the
season was too frivolous for her new, serious tastes.
She would have preferred, she said, 'the learned season
to the gay one'. So when she could get away from her

domestic duties at Maer she chose to visit Fanny and
Hensleigh in London. In March 1837 Charles too moved
to London, into lodgings in Great Marlborough Street
near his brother Erasmus, where he worked at his
Journal of Researches.

In May Emma joined the Sismondis and Darwin's
sister for a great family party in Paris. This was a trip
that Emma found very enjoyable, and she was delighted
when Aunt Jessie prolonged the party. Sunday, however, was a lost day. According to Emma, 'Aunt Jessie
went in the morning to Notre Dame' where 'the music
was very beautiful but the mummery quite wonderfully
foolish. The Archbishop performed and drank off two
such large goblets of wine that she expected him to be
tipsy [*sic*].' Emma herself went to 'a most tiresome
service' in the little American chapel, where she heard
'an extempore sermon which we thought would never
end'.

On Monday they braved the rain and sailed 'at the
tail of a shower' to St Cloud. The sun came out, the
gardens at St Cloud were very pretty, the view of Paris
from the top of the park was quite beautiful, and they
dined in 'a little room looking over the river and to
complete our good luck got on board the steamer again
just before a thunderstorm that came down like a
shower bath'. She enjoyed a ride to St Germain. 'The
railroad goes just the same pace as ours, 14 miles in half
an hour. It is a very pretty drive', she told Fanny
Hensleigh, 'as you cross the Seine three times.'

They visited friends there, took a two-mile ride on
donkeys and 'a very indifferent horse', and came back
through the woods listening to the nightingales. Emma
was less enchanted with a visit to Franconi's circus.
'Tricks by horses are disgreeable when you think how
much they have been teased to perform.' If Aunt Jessie
took them shopping in Paris Emma did not think it
worth mentioning to Fanny.

On her return she spent some time with Fanny and

Hensleigh in London and was obviously disappointed that Charles, who was a frequent visitor, appeared uninterested in her. But she hid her feelings even from Aunt Jessie, only later confessing to her,

> When you asked me about Charles Darwin, I did not tell you half the good I thought of him for fear you should suspect something, and though I knew how much I liked him, I was not the least sure of his feelings, as he is so affectionate, and so fond of Maer and all of us, and demonstrative in his manners, that I did not think it meant anything, and the week I spent in London on my return from Paris, I felt sure he did not care about me, only that he was very unwell at the time.

In July Emma's eldest brother Jos – the silent one – married Charles's sister Caroline, who, when he was a little boy, had taken the place of his dead mother. Perhaps it was the jolt of this unexpected union – after all, Caroline was thirty-seven and Jos forty-two – that made Charles seriously consider marriage.

Methodical as always, he made two columns of arguments, pro and con; 'MARRY' and 'NOT MARRY', he headed them, before first jotting down the arguments for marriage:

> Children – (if it please God) – constant companion, (friend in old age) who will feel interested in one, object to be beloved and played with – better than a dog, anyhow – Home, and someone to take care of house – charms of music and female chit-chat. These things good for one's health. Forced to visit and receive relations but *terrible loss of time*.

Among the disadvantages were 'the expense and anxiety of children . . . loss of time . . . cannot read in the evenings . . . fatness and idleness . . . if any children . . . forced to gain one's bread'. But then he remembered that for him it was 'very bad for one's health to work too much'.

At this time Darwin was merely considering the principle of marriage, and he obviously did not yet have anyone in mind. But the advantages were clearly out-weighing the disadvantages. 'Imagine living all one's day solitary in smoky, dirty London house – only picture to yourself a nice soft wife on a sofa with a good fire and books and music perhaps – compare this vision with the dingy reality of Great Marlborough Street.' So, having come to the conclusion that he needed a wife, he cheered himself: 'One cannot live this solitary life, with groggy old age, friendless and cold and childless staring one in one's face, already beginning to wrinkle.' The conclusion was clear, even if his notes were hap-hazard. 'Never mind, trust to chance, keep a sharp lookout, there is many a happy slave.'

Though the families had now also decided that Charles needed a wife, and that Emma was the obvious choice, he himself was only just beginning to consider this a possibility. He was perhaps not a little unnerved by Emma's apparent detachment, and was quite con-vinced that after all the lively minds at Maer Hall she would find him unstimulating, also he thought himself unattractive.

So although in August he was often at Maer, at this time in high spirits, he said nothing and Emma began to think they might 'go on in the sort of friendship we were in for years and very likely nothing come of it at all'. But she was, as she later wrote, 'very happy in his company and had the feeling that if he saw more of me he would really like me'. And no other man had so won her admiration. As she told Aunt Jessie,

He is the most open, transparent man I ever saw, and every word expresses his real thoughts. He is particu-larly affectionate and very nice to his father and sisters, and perfectly sweet tempered, and possesses some minor qualities that add particularly to one's happiness, such as not being fastidious, and being humane to animals.

In November Charles at last plucked up enough courage. On the comfortable sofa by the library fire at Maer Hall he asked Emma to marry him, and was astonished at her immediate acceptance. Sobered by the sudden decision, they sat in unaccustomed silence through the family dinner until a worried Fanny and Hensleigh called them into their room to know what was the matter. The excited talk went on until early morning, and then Emma, typically unsentimental and ravenously hungry, sent Hensleigh down 'to forage in the kitchen', as she wrote to Aunt Jessie. There he 'found a loaf and 2lb butter and a carving knife, which made us an elegant refection'. The match that the family had wanted so long had been at last arranged.

Where does your father do his barnacles?

The marriage was fixed for 29 January 1839, though Charles, in his eagerness, convinced himself that they had decided on the 24th. Now that he had made up his mind he could allow himself to fall deeply in love: all his hitherto undeveloped emotions were now centred on Emma. From Shrewsbury he wrote, exulting at his good fortune,

> Like a child that has something it loves beyond measure, I long to dwell on the words, my own dear Emma . . . My life has been very happy and very fortunate and many of the pleasantest remembrances are mingled with scenes at Maer, and now it is crowned. My own dear Emma, I kiss the hands with all humbleness and gratitude which have so filled up for me the cup of happiness. It is my most earnest wish that I may make myself worthy of you.

It took Emma longer to reveal the love concealed beneath her cousinly badinage. 'You will kindly mention any fault of spelling or style . . . ,' she teased him, 'as in the wife of a literary man it would not do you credit, anyhow I can spell your name right. I wish you could say the same for mine.' He was her 'old curmudgeon', her 'dear Nigger'. This last was a nickname that stuck; her later letters often begin: 'Dear N.'. When she could not make up her mind where they should live, she wrote, 'Here you remark, tiresome toad, why can't she tell me which she would really like.' 'Toad' in the Wedgwood vocabulary was a term of endearment. When she was sick it was 'not, I am sorry to say, at grief at parting with you, but all owing to that horrid little bit of stewed beef we had on Thursday and again on Friday and half poisoned two or three of us'.

After much debate they decided to rent a house in London, and Charles wandered up and down the streets looking for 'To Let' signs until Emma considered: 'It is as well I am coming to look after you, my poor old man, for it is quite evident that you are on the verge of insanity.' She threatened to insert an advertisement: 'Lost in the vicinity of Bloomsbury, a tall thin gentleman quite harmless.'

Finally Emma went down to London to help, staying with her brother Hensleigh and Fanny, and on her return to Maer was delighted to hear that Charles had secured the house in Gower Street that she wanted. Its hideous furniture, gaudy yellow curtains and azure blue walls reminded Darwin of a tropical parrot – Macaw Cottage, he called it. But they did not care – neither then nor at any time did Charles and Emma aspire to elegance. Emma's heart must have sunk when, remembering the rolling acres at Maer, she saw the little sooty garden with its black sparrows and a grisly dead dog. But she did not complain; she wrote lightly that they would remove the dog, and that she intended to plant laburnum trees to shelter them from the neighbours.

The house, Emma told her family, had a 'front drawing room with three windows and a back one, rather smaller, with a cheerful look-out on a set of little gardens, which will be of great value to us in summer to take a mouthful of fresh air'. Charles, as excited as a child with a new toy, moved straight into Macaw Cottage before they were married. Emma imagined his pleasure: 'I can fancy how proud you are in your big house, ordering breakfast in the front drawing room, dinner in the dining room, tea in the back drawing room and luncheon in the study, and occasionally looking through your window on your estate and plantation.' He and his manservant hauled his weighty geological specimens into place. A scientist's wife, Emma soon learned, may have to house a museum. 'Where', one of the Darwin children later gravely asked a friend, 'does your father do his barnacles?'

Meanwhile Emma prepared for the wedding. 'Mamma . . . amuses herself a good deal with planning about houses, trousseaux and wedding-cake, which last we were in hopes she would not have thought of, as it is a useless trouble and expense.' To Charles she wrote, 'Don't you wish you could be married like a royal prince without being at your own wedding?' And Charles undoubtedly did; he was already apprehensive. 'I wish', he confessed to her, 'the awful day was over. I am not very tranquil when I think of the procession: it is very awesome.' Emma was distinctly relieved that he resisted his tailor's desire to get him up in a blue coat and white stockings. January was not the month for such wear.

I am very glad you resisted the blue coat, you would have looked very unnatural in it. The white trousers were no great temptation in this weather. I wonder what extravangrincies (this word will not come right) you have been committing. A diamond pin for your stock or some such thing I should not wonder.

Emma was quite content for Charles's sisters to 'get up the linen'; and Fanny Hensleigh, the experienced hostess, engaged domestic staff – a little maid, a handsome butler and a cook at 'fourteen guineas a year and tea and sugar'.

But they each had more serious concerns. Emma wanted Charles to understand how important her Christian faith was:

> Will you do me a favour? Yes I am sure you will, it is to read our Saviour's farewell discourses to his disciples which begins at the end of the 13th Chap of John. It is so full of love to them and devotion and every beautiful feeling. It is the part of the New Testament I love best. This is a whim of mine, it would give me great pleasure though I can hardly tell why. I don't wish you to give me your opinion about it.

Characteristically she immediately followed these profound thoughts with:

> The plaid gown arrived safely yesterday and is unanimously pronounced to be very handsome and not at all too dashing so that I could write my thanks and compliments with a very good conscience. It is blue black and green with a narrow scarlet cross bar.

Charles, anxious that she should understand his preoccupation with his work, confessed that, though he was so fond of talking and 'scarcely ever out of spirits', yet his happiness depended entirely 'on quietness and a good deal of solitude'. During the five years of his voyage, he told her,

> which may be said to be the commencement of my real life, the whole of my pleasure was derived, from what passed in my mind, whilst admiring views by myself, travelling across the wild deserts and glorious forests, or pacing the deck of the poor little *Beagle* at night.

He asked her to excuse this egotism because he thought that 'you will humanise me, and soon teach me there is greater happiness than holding theories and accumulating facts in silence and solitude'. Emma reassured him that she did not want a 'holiday husband'. This acceptance of each other's different needs and views was to be the foundation on which the happiness of their marriage was so securely based.

So for three years they lived at Macaw Cottage, No. 12 Gower Street. 'Emma', wrote Elizabeth, 'was entirely happy in her lot with the most affectionate husband possible, upon whom none of her pleasant qualities are thrown away, who delights in her music and admires her dress.' Emma had evidently taken Aunt Jessie's advice. 'Always dress in good taste; do not despise those little cares . . . because you know you have married a man who is above caring for such little things. No man is above caring for them.' None of the Wedgwood girls had ever bothered about dress. 'Elizabeth's clothes', her mother had written, 'were as near to the unpermissible as possible.' But Charles was a Darwin and Aunt Jessie was right – he did notice these things. So to please him Emma duly bought a 'morning gown, a sort of clarety-brown satin turque, very unobjectionable'. 'The milliner's bill,' Emma told Aunt Jessie, 'would do your heart good.'

Charles in his turn accompanied Emma to the theatre, which she loved and he disliked, and though he swore he was tone deaf he was learning to appreciate the music that was so important to Emma. So she and Charles slopped happily through the snow on their honeymoon to choose the Broadwood grand piano that was to give them joy for the rest of their married lives.

Emma learned to adjust herself to Charles's love of order – but there was always something in her of the 'little Miss Slipslop' of her childhood. Charles laughingly said that if he wanted a pair of scissors he had to keep them in his study. But Emma understood that

beneath Charles's affectionate amusement there was
anxiety. The meticulous Darwins at Shrewsbury in their
apple-pie house made no bones about Emma's housekeeping. 'A thunderstorm is preparing to break on your
head', wrote Darwin from Shrewsbury,

> which has already deluged me about Bessy [the maid]
> not having a cap 'looks dirty' – 'like a grocer's maid
> servant', and my father with much wrath added 'the
> men will take liberties with her if she is dressed differ-
> ently from every other ladies' maid'. I generously took
> half the blame and never betrayed that I had beseeched
> you several times on that score. If they open on you pray
> do not defend yourself for they are very hot on the
> subject.

At Shrewsbury Charles still easily slipped back into his
apprehensive boyhood, always metaphorically raising
an arm to ward off the criticisms of his adoring but
censorious sisters.

When Charles and Emma's first two children, William
and Annie, were born his family kept close watch on
their upbringing. Emma laughed when Willy picked up
a cockney accent from the servants, calling himself
'Villie Darvin'. In distant Shrewsbury they were not
amused. So when they went north Emma often chose
to remain at Maer while Darwin took the children on to
Shrewsbury, so that he could bear the brunt of the
carping. Willy, the Darwins complained, had a cup of
cream before breakfast every morning – the worst thing
possible for him. He was allowed to set off for a journey
with wet feet – most dangerous. Years later Charles told
his grandson's nurse that children ought to be allowed
to run barefoot and eat green gooseberries. When the
Darwin sisters came to stay, Emma noticed with some
amusement that they found the disorderliness of the
children worrying and were always tidying up after
them. Emma, relaxed and serene, preferred to let them

play until the chaos became unbearable and then sent for the maid to clear it up.

As she adapted herself to Charles's needs she created a home which was calm and tranquil. Thoughout their married life they earned the devotion of their servants, foremost among whom was Parslow, their butler. Aunt Jessie had spotted his virtues when she stayed at Gower Street in 1840: 'Be it observed that Parslow is the most amiable, obliging, active, serviceable servant that ever breathed. I hope you will never part with him.' They never did, and Parslow remained with them as a friend and part of the family until their deaths.

The excessive labour of inventive thought

Happy though they were, neither Charles nor Emma enjoyed the social round. Visiting in Victorian London was time-consuming. Distances were long and so were the dinners, and one did not clatter across London merely to drink a glass of sherry. A dinner party involved one night or even two absent from work. But Emma learned to entertain and astonished Hensleigh and Fanny – and herself – by the success of her own first dinner party. To her mother she wrote of this first dinner, and of their other servants:

> Fanny's maids have been very uneasy at the shortness of our housemaid and are afraid that she is not tall enough to tie my gown. She is about the size of Betty Slaney, so I hope Fanny set their minds at ease on that point. Our dinner went off very well, though Erasmus tells us it was a base imitation of the Marlborough Street dinners, and certainly the likeness was very striking. But when the plum-pudding appeared he knocked under, and confessed himself conquered very humbly. And then Edward is such a perfect Adonis in his best livery that he is quite a sight.

As far as one can judge from Emma's recipe book she and Charles enjoyed plain fare. Her Irish apple charlotte was 'baked for six hours in a very slow oven'. They made their own ginger beer. Her soups were simple and wholesome – a very popular one was made of three cabbage lettuces, three onions, sorrel, spinach, celery and parsley, and 'at the end a little cream and yolks of two eggs'.

Emma often found Darwin's scientist friends hard going. Later, Darwin recalled with amusement her reply to his apology. 'You must find this all boring.' Emma cheerfully answered, 'Not more than all the rest!' But the scientific evening could be long. 'Mr Lyell', she wrote to Elizabeth after one of her early dinner parties,

> is enough to flatten a party as he never speaks above his breath, so that eveybody keeps lowering their tone to his. Mr Brown, whom Humboldt called 'the glory of Great Britain', looks so shy, as if he longed to shrink into himself and disappear entirely; however notwithstanding those two dead weights, viz, the greatest botanist and the greatest geologist in Europe we did very well and had no pauses. Mrs Henslow had a good, loud, sharp voice which was a great comfort and Mrs Lyell had a very constant supply of talk.

In fact there were some highly intelligent wives among their friends. The botanist J. D. Hooker's wife was the daughter of Henslow – Darwin's old tutor at Cambridge; and, Hooker claimed, she was 'much cleverer than I'. And Emma herself, although she never pretended to be a scientist, often understood the direction of Charles's thoughts. Before their marriage she had written,

> I believe from your account of your own mind that you will only consider me as a specimen of the genus (I don't know which, simia I believe). You will be forming theories about me and if I am cross or out of temper you

will only consider 'What does that prove'. Which will be a very grand and philosophical way of considering it.

Reporting to Maer on Emma's appearance in London society, Fanny Hensleigh remarked how endearingly unspoilt and unaffected she remained. Thomas Carlyle found her 'the nicest girl he had ever met', and Emma brought out the best in him. 'He was', she wrote, 'very pleasant to talk to . . . so very natural'. She only wished his writing had been equally so. Charles never was at ease with the Carlyles nor they with him; and Jane was, for once, out of her intellectual depth in the world of science. Charles, for his part, found her Scots accent unintelligible and her manner affected.

As his work became more demanding, Charles became stressed and was frequently ill. Late in life he remembered that 'I did less scientific work, though I worked as hard as I possibly could, than during any other equal length of time.' In fact during his three years and eight months in London he achieved a great deal, in spite of poor health which included in that period one serious illness. He managed to complete his work on *Coral Reefs*, wrote papers for the Royal Geographical Society, of which he was honorary secretary, and prepared his *Zoology of the Beagle*. In addition, he opened his first notebook for what he described in his autobiography as 'Facts in Relation to the Origin of Species about which I had long reflected and never ceased work for the next twenty years'. These facts were leading him to disturbing conclusions and shaking his belief in the Christianity he had once blindly accepted.

Emma watched and was concerned. Soon after their marriage she had written him a long letter, 'because when I talk to you about it I cannot say exactly what I wish to say'. She wanted to believe that while Charles was 'sincerely wishing and trying to learn the truth', he could not be wrong, but she could not always give herself this comfort. She felt that he was so busy following up his own discoveries that he could not give his whole attention to 'the other sort of thoughts'. Then she feared that Charles was too much influenced by his older brother Erasmus – who was an agnostic. 'May not', she wrote, 'the habit in scientific pursuits of believing nothing till it is proved, influence your mind too much in other things which cannot be proved in the same way, and which, if true, are likely to be above our comprehension?' She was apologetic for bothering him, but was sure her 'own dear Nigger' loved her and went on, 'I cannot tell him how happy he makes me and how dearly I love him and thank him for all his affection which makes the happiness of my life more and more every day.'

Visitors such as their old friend Maria Edgeworth praised Emma's sweet nature but noticed that Charles was often ill. In their years in Gower Street Emma had two children in rapid succession, and London brought on the migraines from which she was to suffer all her life. Charles, as his work grew more demanding, became stressed and was frequently ill. For the rest of his life he was to be dogged by long bouts of illness. Many medical experts have made different diagnoses, but the truth would seem to lie in a combination of psychological and physical causes.

He was driven by a powerful, obsessive need to search out the truth. But unlike many other driven men he possessed a natural sweetness of temperament which did not allow him the relief of bad temper or outbursts of rage with which others released their tension. Then his will and dogged determination often pushed him beyond his intellectual capacity. He wrote of 'the excessive labour of inventive thought', and that 'the whole effort consists in keeping one idea before your mind steadily and not merely thinking intently'. And though, as he claimed in his autobiography, he was capable of prolonged reasoning, he did not enjoy abstract thought. The stress of prolonged mental effort undoubtedly affected his nervous system: as he himself said, his 'noddle' and his stomach were often in conflict. His particular genius was for observing and collating detail, but the facts, meticulously collected over the years, were leading him to conclusions which he knew would be disturbing. To break through old barriers to a new philosophy demanded a power of intellectual concentration which constantly exhausted him.

This stress found out physical weaknesses which had probably always been there. Charles had seemed healthy enough as a boy, especially when he came for the shooting at Maer; but even then he had suffered from eczema of the hands and mouth, which Dr Darwin had treated with arsenic. Before he left Plymouth on the *Beagle* he had been worried by palpitations, had been afraid he had heart disease. Then, during the voyage, he had been constantly and violently seasick. 'Sea sickness', he wrote, 'is no trifling evil, cured in a week.' Though he was well enough to make punishing long journeys into the interior of South America he certainly had one long illness which made his sister Caroline urge him to return. In his *Journal of Researches* Charles refers to the 'great black bug of the Pampas', *Triatoma infestans*, which had bitten him in Argentina in March 1835. This, Professor Saul Adler and other experts believe, could have been the carrier which gave Darwin the so-called Chagas' disease, which can affect the heart muscle and destroy the nerves of the intestine. Emma's sister Elizabeth, observing to Emma how ill Charles looked after his return, decided that it was 'the effects of too much exertion in every way during the voyage'. The commonsense explanation may well be the correct one.

In October 1837 Emma had reported that, according to Aunt Sarah,

Charles Darwin is very unwell. Something is amiss in the circulation and he has palpitations, but Aunt Sarah is always so apprehensive about health that she always sees this in the worst light. She says he does not appear at all invalidish. He hopes to come to Maer . . . but is correcting proofs every day and sending back the sheets by return of post.

In December 1838 Emma had noticed that he looked over-tired and unwell. She had written, 'Tell me how you are, I do not like your looking so unwell and being so over-tired. When I come and look after you, I shall scold you into health like Lady Catherine de Burgh used to do to the poor people.' He was ill again before their wedding, dreading, he wrote, 'the procession'. After their marriage he had gradually become worse, until the mere thought of a dinner party brought on 'violent shivers and vomiting attacks'. Only, he wrote, in the 'excitement' of his scientific work did he forget his 'daily discomfort'. But it was not just a matter of discomfort – noisy, violent and uncontrollable retching made visiting a pain and an embarassment. This gave him a reason – or an excuse – for avoiding the social engagements that increasingly wasted his time.

There were also psychological reasons for his illness. Like both David Livingstone and Karl Marx, Charles was much influenced by his father. Dr Robert's attack on Charles for his youthful idleness certainly gave him a dogged determination to succeed and directed his drive. But to suggest, as some have done, that Darwin had a suppressed desire to kill his father, together with God, is ridiculous. His respect and love for his father lasted all his life, even if, like everybody else, he regarded him with awe. It is possible that he sometimes exaggerated his illness in order to excite his father's interest and sympathy. If so, he did not always succeed. When he complained to Dr Robert of the dreadful numbness in his finger tips all the sympathy he could get was, 'Yes, exactly, tut tut, neuralgia, exactly, yes, yes.' He trusted implicitly in his father's prescriptions.

In April 1840, when on a visit to Shrewsbury, he wrote to Emma, 'My father says I may often take calomel', as though he needed reassuring that it was safe. Like Karl Marx, he was frequently afflicted by skin eruptions, caused by mental stress; on one occasion he suffered a 'frightful succession of boils, five at once'.

It is possible, too, that he sometimes gave in to illness when he wanted Emma's comfort. For he was always insecure, and his mother's death when he was eight must have been traumatic. It is significant that he could remember nothing of her except her long black velvet dress as she lay in her coffin. Emma gave him back his security. Many years later Mrs Huxley said of her, 'More than any other women I ever knew, she comforted.' In 1848, when ill in Shrewsbury, Charles wrote to her, 'Without you when sick I feel most desolate. O Mammy I do long to be with you, and under your protection, for then I feel safe.' It was the forgotten cry of a bereaved child, and it needs no psychologist to see the relevance of the nickname 'Titty' that he sometimes gave her. Later she was always 'Our dear old Mother who must be obeyed'. Just as before they were married, he looked forward to a 'good strict wife who will send me to my lessons'. Darwin's studies were leading him to disturbing theories which were bound to cause Emma pain. And as he laboured through the dark it was essential for him to know that she was there, steady and serene in the sunlight at the end of the tunnel.

Whatever the causes, Charles's pain was very real. Dr Lane, who treated him in later years and had come across many cases of violent indigestion, said, 'I cannot recall any where the pain was so truly poignant as in his. When the worst attacks were on he seemed almost crushed by agony. 'Yet he bore it with singular sweetness and patience. 'What a life of suffering his is,' wrote Fanny Allen, 'and how manfully he bears it . . . Emma's cheerfulness is equally admirable. I am sure she is a chosen one of Heaven.'

He kept a careful record of his symptoms, but to suggest that he was a hypochondriac in the ordinary sense of the word shows a misunderstanding of his character. Emma's shrewd Allen aunts, who had no disposition to love the Darwins and who positively disliked Erasmus, would have noticed such a quality in Charles. Aunt Jessie, in particular, remarked on his healthiness of mind. Observant scientist that he was, he watched himself as patiently and carefully as he watched for forty years the activities of his earthworms. When his friend Hooker was ill in 1854 he advised him, 'Write down your own case . . . and then consider your case as a stranger.' Nor would Emma have encouraged morbidity – she was no frustrated nurse. It is true that she had cared for her dying sister with devotion, and she had shared with her eldest sister, Elizabeth, the care of a sick mother. But there is no mistaking the relief with which she left the sickroom before her marriage.

Everything there was different. And better

Emma had found their tiny Gower Street back garden amusing at the beginning, and had laughed at its dead dog – but the smoke and smell of Victorian London was no joke. Both longed for the quiet of rural England.

So in the summer of 1842 they looked for a place in the country and found Down House in Kent; it was to be their home for the rest of their lives. Emma had not at first been impressed. She carried always the image of Maer as the perfect country house; Down House was plain and somewhat bare, and the chalk hills bleak and waterless. She was also at this time pregnant with her third child and had toothache. But in time she turned Down House into a comfortable, roomy home, enlarged it to accommodate their growing family, planted climb-

ing shrubs to mask its bareness and set out flower
gardens as she had done at Maer.

Strangely, Down House was unadorned by Wedgwood pottery. When Darwin's friend, the botanist
Joseph Hooker, developed a passion for Wedgwood
plaques and pottery Charles had to confess that they
were 'degenerate descendants of old Josiah for we have
not a bit of the pretty ware in the house'. As for the
plaques: 'We had a whole box of small Wedgwood
medallions but drat the children, everything in this
house gets lost or wasted.' This was not surprising,
since her daughter Etty remembered what delight they
had had as children playing in Emma's bedroom, dress-
ing up in her silks and jewels, and how completely
unfussed Emma had been.

There had been a sandy path round the lake at Maer
and one of their first improvements at Down was the
Sand Walk, shady on one side and on the other open to
the sun and to the Downs. Here Charles paced every
morning with clockwork regularity. Along the borders
of the Walk Emma planted wild flowers – bluebells,
cowslips and anemones – paying a small boy to keep
the border weeded. She lost her temper only rarely, but
did so when Charles once laughed because she was so
upset that the boy had pulled up all the wild flowers
and left the weeds and the dog's mercury that she
hated. The regularity of Darwin's walk and the luxuri-
ance of Emma's country flowers were symbolic of a
marrige in which each complemented the other. In time
Down became a home like Maer, passionately loved by
the children and grandchildren. When Aunt Jessie came
to stay, she found this 'pretty, brilliantly clean quiet
house' utterly refreshing. She wrote to Elizabeth: 'The
repose and coolness of it is delicious, let alone the
sunny faces which met us so lovingly at the door.'

Emma had found Down House an unattractive square
building in an empty, windswept landscape. She had
turned it into a place of enchantment. Her daughter,

Etty, and years later her granddaughter Gwen Raverat, both loved it passionately. 'All the flowers that grew at Down were beautiful; and different from all other flowers,' Gwen remembered.

Everything there was different. And better. For instance the path in front of the verandah was made of large round water-worn pebbles from some sea beach. They were not loose but stuck down tight in moss and sand and were black and shiny, as if they had been polished. I adored those pebbles. I mean literally, adored; worshipped. This passion made me feel quite sick sometimes and it was adoration that I felt for the foxgloves at Down and for the stiff red clay out of the sandwalk claypit and for the beautiful white paint on the nursery floor. This kind of feeling hits you in the stomach and in the ends of your fingers and it is probably the most important thing in life. Long after I have forgotten all my human loves, I shall still remember the smell of a gooseberry leaf or the feel of wet grass on my feet; or the pebbles in the path. In the long run it is this feeling that makes life worth living, this which is the driving force behind the artist's need to create.

It was Emma who created at Down the environment essential for Darwin. Here, in calm and ease and order, he could direct that 'driving force' into the stubborn problems of existence.

At Down Darwin is said to have lived like a recluse. In his autobiography he himself had written that after his marriage he had 'nothing to record during the rest of my life except the publication of my several books'. Certainly it is true that the man who had galloped across the wild pampas of South America, who had braved the immensity of the ocean and had contemplated the vastness of nature in so many parts of the world, now found his horizon circumscribed by the boundaries of the little Kentish village. 'Few persons', he wrote at the end of his life, 'can have lived a more retired life than we have done. Besides short visits to the houses of relations and occasionally to the sea-side or elsewhere we have gone nowhere.'

But the Darwin–Wedgwood families were worlds in themselves. Family parties of fifty-three, with Emma playing galloping tunes on the piano for the children, were common, for her cousins too had large broods. Nor, indeed, did Emma have much time to miss a social life. She was thirty when she married, and starting at that late age she was to bear ten children, the last when she was forty-eight.

Two children, William and Annie, had been born in Gower Street. On 23 September 1842 Mary was born, but lived only until 16 October. After the death of the baby Emma wrote, with characteristically balanced judgement, to Fanny Hensleigh: 'Our sorrow is nothing to what it would have been had she lived longer and suffered more. Charles is well today and the funeral over which he dreaded much . . . With our two other dear little things you need not fear that our sorrow will last long though it will be long indeed before we either of us forget that poor little face.' Soon after the death of Mary Henrietta (Etty) followed, in 1843. There was just a two-year interval between the arrival of George and Elizabeth in 1845 and 1847, and only a year later Frank came, to be joined in 1850 and 1851 by Horace and Leonard. After what must have been a welcome gap of five years their last and saddest baby, Charles Waring, was born. It was an almost annual trial, more dangerous each year. Charles found her pain in childbirth unbearable to watch and was immensely relieved when the discovery of chloroform, first used as an anaesthetic in 1847, made the last three confinements more tolerable. Charles gave Emma chloroform for the first time in 1850 when she was about to give birth to her eighth child. As he wrote to his old tutor, Henslow, he administered it himself without waiting for the doctor, and put Emma soundly to sleep for two hours. When she awoke the new baby, Leonard, was kicking in the cradle.

Yet like other progressive and scientific men of the period Darwin had no time for family planning, and wrote in 1878:

> I have lately reflected a little on the artificial checks but doubt greatly whether such would be advantageous to the world at large at present, however it may be in the distant future. Suppose that such checks had been in action during the last two centuries or even a shorter time in Britain, what a difference it would have made to the world when we consider America, Australia, New Zealand and South Africa. No words can exaggerate the importance in my opinion of our colonisation for the future history of the world.
>
> If it were universally known that the birth of children would be prevented and this were not thought immoral by married persons, would there not be great danger of extreme profligacy amongst unmarried women and might we not become like the . . . societies in the Pacific. In the course of a century France will tell us the result.

Such breathtaking, bland complacency staggers the modern reader, but was typical of the age. Like Livingstone and others who travelled abroad, Darwin had returned from his voyage round the world with an unshakeable belief in the superiority of the British, and in the need to go forth and multiply.

So Emma continued, as permanently pregnant as it was physically possible to be, until she was forty-eight. Yet there are few complaints in her letters, though she suffered frequently from migraine. Etty remembered:

> My mother had ten children and suffered much from ill health and discomforts during those years. Many of her children were delicate and difficult to rear, and three died. My father was often seriously ill and always suffering, so that her life was full of care, anxiety, and hard work. But her perfect union with him, and the

sense that she made every minute of every weary hour more bearable to him, supported her . . . She was born good . . . her life was happy as well as blessed.

Uncomfortable though the constant child-bearing must have been, many Victorian women like Emma seem to have accepted it, and though she was quite prepared to listen to unconventional views she could not take the reformer Josephine Butler seriously.

'Children', Darwin wrote to a friend in 1862, 'are one's greatest happiness but often and often a still greater misery. A man of science ought to have none – perhaps not a wife; for then there would be nothing in this wide world worth caring for and a man might (whether he could is another question) work away like a Trojan.' So too said Livingstone and Marx, but it must be remembered that this was the age of cholera, typhoid, scarlet fever and smallpox epidemics. And three of the Darwins' children had died when he wrote this. When scarlet fever killed his last baby he was terror-struck, and on 18 December 1861 wrote to Hooker: 'To the day of my death I shall never forget all the sickening fear about the other children, after our poor little baby died of it.'

Nevertheless family life was essential to him, as it was to both Marx and Livingstone. All of them found great release from tension in playing with their children. In Darwin's case his careful observation of his babies also resulted in useful scientific information. Emma was once detailed to watch 'if ever Steevie [Charlotte's son] has a good roar to observe the outline of his mouth whether it is square'. Of a small niece she wrote to Darwin, 'A fact which I think quite worthy to go down in your book along with the baby's nods and winks' is 'that when she coughs very sharply in the dark sparks come out of her eyes.'

Their children were not, in the Victorian manner, shut away. The nursery, it was claimed, was the last place to find a child at Down; Etty always remembered being tucked up on the sofa in the study while Darwin worked. Down was also home for their friends' children. 'Few . . . would have housed a friend's seven children and two nurses for a fortnight,' Thomas Huxley's wife remembered many years later; but Emma had done so when Mrs Huxley wished to accompany her husband to a meeting of the British Association.

It was fortunate that they could afford the staff to look after this large family. Neither Emma nor Charles ever had any financial worry in their lives. Dr Robert was well off – when he died in 1848 he left a considerable fortune. On her marrige Josiah Wedgwood had given Emma an ample dowry and arranged a generous annual income, and when he died in 1843 Emma inherited her share of his wealth. Nevertheless Charles, as his son Frank remembered, 'kept accounts with great care, classifying them and balancing at the end of the year, like a merchant'.

So Emma always had the comfort, and the care, of a large household. The Darwins' earliest alterations at Down had been to make the servants' quarters more pleasant. 'It seems so selfish making the house so luxurious for ourselves,' Charles wrote to his sister, 'and not comfortable for the servants.' Their grandson Bernard, who was brought up at Down, remembered them. Even when their own children were grown up and Bernard was the only child there, the household was immense. There was Fred, the adored groom, Jackson the butler (who made a model of Down House with corks), and John the coachman whipping up his horses, Flyer and Tara and Druid. There were gardeners and under-gardeners, Mrs Evans the cook, six maids, Jane and the beautiful Harriet, and William the footman. And there was always Parslow, the uncrowned king of the household, though in Bernard's day he was too old to take full responsibility. Parslow was the pivot on which all turned. Throughout Charles's life he was valet, bath-man, friend and his indispensable right hand during sickness.

In the days when Charles and Emma's children were all still at home the staff was even larger, with governesses, tutors, innumerable temporary nurses and above all Brodie, their faithful Scottish nurse. Etty later remembered with affection the plain, red-haired Scotswoman and the click of her knitting needles as she watched over them. According to family tradition Brodie had been a children's nurse in Thackeray's family, but she gave her heart to the Darwins. Preventing discord in such a large establishment needed Emma's tact. Brodie once had to be protected from the pertness of a young maid, and when a maid had 'a fit of the blues' she was sent to a concert in Bromley. Emma knew how music could give solace.

Nor was the wider world shut out. Emma retained her lively interest in politics, stimulated by Fanny Hensleigh and her Aunt Fanny Allen. Many of the actors on the mid-nineteenth-century world stage were family friends and acquaintances. Flo Nightingale's career in the Crimean War was followed closely. Emma read about the disturbances in Europe with particular fascination. Sismondi had died in 1842 but she still remembered his teaching. So she watched the rise of Louis Napoleon with amazement, recalling that Sismondi had not thought much of him when as a young man he and his mother, Queen Hortense, had come to call in Geneva.

Although the Darwins certainly led a retired life, they were not cut off from reality. Both Charles and Emma were involved in village matters, and Emma, brought up in the good Whig country house tradition, felt responsible for the welfare of the villagers. When she saw the local women hauling their water up to dry, hilltop Down from Keston, a mile away, she organised a water cart for them three times a week. Her children rememberd their mother's 'poories' and the smell of sickness and poverty in their homes with some revulsion.

Like the Darwin sisters and her own sister Elizabeth, Emma could write prescriptions and make up medicines, and her children recalled the fun of rolling rhubarb pills: Emma held firmly the Victorian faith in 'opening medicines'. Charles, remembering his medical training and the times when he had prescribed for his father's patients at Shrewsbury, was equally prepared to play doctor to the village. Dr Darwin's book of medicines, labelled on the brown leather cover 'Receipts' and on the back 'Memoranda', was their bible. Many of the additional prescriptions are in Emma's handwriting: 'Citric acid', she confidently asserted, 'alleviates the pain of cancer.' Laudanum (dose one and a half drams) mixed with 'Tinct Benzoin, Tinct. Myrrh, Oxymel Squills' made a cough mixture suitable for her son Frank. Laudanum was again used in her remedy for 'Mrs Seymour Hill's bunions'. Mixed with 'goulard', it was 'kept on the joint with lint and oilskin'. Many a woman must have cheered at the sight of Emma with her bottle of gin cordial made up to Dr Darwin's own prescription and intended for 'poor women weak after lying or with pains in the back'. She also pasted into the book a newspaper clipping on how to trap wasps in a glass inverted over a plate filled with rum, beer and sugar. Emma was obviously concerned about the danger of lead contamination in the water supply at Down, and copied carefully a test recommended by a newspaper. Aware of the danger of 'arsenic in wreaths and dresses', she kept a note on how to detect its presence with a drop of liquid ammonia. So with these small domestic cares the years passed. Down was the eye of the storm, the still centre of a turbulent world.

*My only hope of consolation is to have you home and weep
together*

But there was also sadness in those years. In 1843 Josiah
Wedgwood died, and it was almost a relief when three
years later Bessy finally followed him. It was a gentle
death. Elizabeth had heard her last whisper: 'Lord, now
lettest thou thy servant depart in peace.' 'No one',
Elizabeth wrote, 'could wish her half extinguished life
to be prolonged. For us it was still a happiness . . . to
see a faint gleam now and then of the purest and most
benevolent soul that ever shone in a face.' Charles
Darwin's debt to Emma cannot be exaggerated, but it is
worth remembering too Bessy Wedgwood, whose letters even now reflect her rare light and who bequeathed
to Emma that serenity and brightness that illumined
Charles's life.

In 1848 Charles's father died, and his grief made him
ill. Though he went to Shrewsbury he did not arrive in
time for Dr Robert's funeral. This absence showed not
neglect but excessive sorrow – just as it had done in the
case of Karl Marx.

In the spring of 1849 Darwin decided to try the water
cure, and Emma did not discourage him, for, as he
remembered in his autobiography, 'all last autumn, my
health grew worse and worse, incessant sickness, trem-
ulous hands, and swimming head. I thought I was
going the way of all flesh'. So they took a house, The
Lodge, at Malvern and put Darwin in the hands of Dr
Gully.

In the 1840s hydrotherapy was the new cult and at
Great Malvern Dr Gully was its high priest. There,
many of the rich and famous of the time, among them
Florence Nightingale, Dickens, Macaulay, Tennyson,
Bulwer Lytton and Marx, underwent his rigorous
regime. Almost all diseases, he claimed, could be cured
by one or other or all of the treatments. Hot and cold
formentations, for example, cured constipation and
nervous headaches. The victim was packed in wet

sheets for an hour or so till the body heat produced a
steam bath of his own making. This was followed by
friction with a dripping sheet. There were sitz baths
and foot baths and douches and abdominal compresses.
Powerful cold showers battered the patients from a
great height, and they were made to drink gallons of
the pure, icy Malvern water. The hills were alive with
scurrying figures making their way up to the well,
mouths wide open to take in the raw air. Behind them
the urchins chanted: 'Shiver and shake! Shiver and
shake!'

Whether it was the keen air, or Dr Gully and his
ordeal by water, or the fact that Darwin was not
permitted to worry his brain there, certainly Malvern
seemed to have cured him. Fanny Allen met him in
London looking 'well and stout', and once again observing 'something uncommonly fresh and pleasant in him'.
But though Charles was undoubtedly better, his appearance could, even to someone as shrewd as Fanny, be
misleading. Malvern in fact brought only temporary
relief.

Pleased with Dr Gully's apparently successful treatment, Charles and Emma decided to place their ten-
year-old daughter Annie under his care. Charles settled
her there with her sister, Etty, their sensible young
governess, Miss Thorley, and their trusted nurse,
Brodie. Annie was Brodie's particular darling.

The child had been ailing for over a year, and other
treatments at Down and at Ramsgate had failed; so now
she was to undergo the water cure. How much was
inflicted on the delicate little girl one does not know,
but within three weeks she was taken ill with a sick
fever. Her fever was accompanied by vomiting and
diarrhoea and was frighteningly familiar to Charles.
Had she inherited his crippling disease? Charles rushed
down to Malvern, leaving Emma to agonise at Down.
Expecting her ninth child, she was not allowed to risk
the journey. This time it was Charles who had to be

strong. As always, the family moved in to give support.
Fanny Allen was already with Emma at Down, Elizabeth rushed back to her from Jersey, and Fanny and
Hensleigh Wedgwood immediately put their own children aside and took the train down to Malvern. Charles
was deeply grateful. Fanny was intelligent and sensitive, and her constant care in the sickroom was 'an
infinite comfort'. Emma was less anxious to have the
help offered by Susan and Catherine Darwin, though
she insisted that Charles should write a tactful refusal.
The solicitous but censorious sisters would only have
added stress to their situation.

Nothing better illustrates the love and understanding
between Charles and Emma than their daily letters in
that terrible week. Each was concerned for the other –
Charles for Emma in the last stages of her pregnancy,
and she for him, fearing that Annie's pain and sickness
would make him ill. Yet Charles was not afraid to spare
Emma the cruel details which he knew she would
desperately want to hear. 'Poor Annie is in a fearful
mess,' he wrote, 'but we keep her sweet with chloride
of lime; the doctor said we might change the undersheet
if we could but I dare not attempt it yet.' Even in his
misery the agonised sentences are precisely punctuated,
the observations meticulous, as though the framework
of science could make the pain more bearable. *narrator*

Emma found her comfort in walking to her 'poor
darling's little garden to find a flower of her'. On that
last Saturday she met the messenger at the garden gate.
He brought a telegram of hope, and all that weekend
she planned for Annie's convalescence. 'Wednesday
23rd before post-time,' she wrote to Charles,

> I have been thinking about a few slops that might suit
> her when she can take a little food but it is more for the
> pleasure of fancying I have something to do for her. If
> the bowels are too loose rice gruel is good innocent and
> binding flavoured with cinnamon or currant jelly. Whey

from milk is very digestible and a spoonful of raw yolk
of egg beat up in hot water and a little salt.

But before she had finished the letter Charles's tragic
message came that Annie was dying. She ended with a
heartbroken, 'Alas my own, how shall we bear it. It is
very bitter but I shall not be ill. Thank dear Fanny.'
Next day she waited by the gate for the post in vain,

> knowing too well what receiving no message yesterday
> means. Till four o'clock I sometimes had a thought of
> hope but when I went to bed I felt as if it had all
> happened long ago. Don't think it made any difference
> my being so hopeful the last day. When the blow comes
> it wipes out all that precedes it and I don't think it made
> it any worse to bear. I hope you have not burnt your
> letter I shall like to see it sometime. My feelings of
> longing after our lost treasure make me feel painfully
> indifferent to the other children but I shall get right in
> my feelings to them before long. You must remember
> that you are my prime treasure (and always have been)
> my only hope of consolation is to have you safe home
> and weep together. I feel so full of fears about you, they
> are not reasonable fears but my power of hoping seems
> gone. I hope you will let dearest Fanny or Catherine, if
> she comes, stay with you til the end. I can't bear to think
> of you by yourself . . . Your letter has just come. Do not
> be in a hurry to set off. You do give me the only comfort
> I can take in thinking of her happy innocent life. She
> never concealed a thought and so affectionate and for-
> giving. What a blank it is. Don't think of coming in one
> day. We shall be much less miserable together. Poor
> Willy takes it quietly and sweetly.

In their misery they reached out to each other, but
letters came agonisingly slowly. Charles eased the pain
by writing hourly as the child's life slowly faded. And
then on Wednesday came the pathetic letter:

My dearest Emma,

I pray God Fanny's note may have prepared you. She went to her final sleep most tranquilly, most sweetly at 12 o'clock today. Our poor dear child had had a very short life but I trust happy and God only knows what miseries might have been in store for her. She expired without a sigh. How desolate it makes one to think of her frank cordial manners. I am so thankful for the daguerrotype. I cannot remember ever seeing the dear child naughty, God bless her. We must be more and more to each other my dear wife – Do what you can to bear up and think how invariably kind and tender you have been to her – I am in bed not very well with my stomach. When I shall return I cannot yet say. My own poor dear dear wife.

Emma's anxiety for Charles was justified. He could not face the funeral and hurried back to Down and Emma, leaving Fanny and Hensleigh to arrange everything and to follow Annie's coffin to the grave in Malvern's abbey churchyard. Her tombstone was simple:

I H S

ANNE ELIZABETH DARWIN
Born March 2, 1841
Died April 23, 1851

A dear and good child

But a week later Darwin wrote his own memorial to her, so that, 'in after years if we live [we could] recall more vividly her chief characteristics'. He described her 'buoyant joyousness', the way she pirouetted before him on the Sand Walk at Down, the affectionate way 'when poorly she would fondle for any length of time one of her mother's arms . . . we have lost the joy of the household, and the solace of our old age . . . Oh, that she could now know how deeply, how tenderly, we do still and shall ever love her dear joyous face! Blessings on her!'

Emma carefully collected and kept Annie's treasures, as she had done with those of her sister Fanny. Annie's small box still is prized in the Darwin family. It contains her little thimble and beaded ribbons, her quill pens and embroidered pen-wipers, and a careful, childish letter to the sister of her governess. There are two folds of paper: in one is a lock of light brown hair, still shining; in the other are two withered crocuses, the flowers that Emma had picked from Annie's garden. They are the most loving mementoes of the heartache of that week.

The death of Annie left a deep scar; neither Emma nor Charles would ever be the same again. Some of that merriment and gaiety that Aunt Jessie had so frequently admired in Emma was slowly subdued. And Emma, who had never fussed over the children, who had allowed the boys to wander off through the woods alone, now became careful of their health.

She had reason. The scythe of cholera sweeping through Europe in those years cut great swathes through families. When Dickens killed off his Little Nell it was not just Victorian sentimentality that had the whole nation weeping – there were too many little coffins in too many darkened rooms. So when Gwen Raverat wrote of her grandmother Emma's 'dangerous hypochondria' she perhaps had not understood the mental climate of those years. Darwin's colleagues Hooker and Huxley each lost a beloved young child. Karl Marx lost three out of six children, and Livingstone, who only lost one of his six, was perhaps wiser than he knew to have taken them gypsying through the desert. Dickens lost a baby in the same month that Annie died. To his wife Kate, who was also taking the water treatment at Malvern and who was in a highly nervous state, Dickens wrote like a kind father to child: 'Now observe. You must read this letter, very slowly and carefully . . . if you have hurried on thus far without quite understanding (apprehending some bad news), I rely on your turning back and reading again. Little Dora . . . is suddenly stricken ill.' In fact the baby was already dead, but Dickens dared not tell Kate the truth. 'Mind,' he continued, 'I think her very ill . . . I do not think her recovery at all likely.' In contrast, so confident was Darwin of Emma's inner strength that he hid nothing from her, telling even the most distressing details of the child's illness.

For once it was Emma who found it difficult to recover her spirits. Horace was born a few weeks later; not surprisingly, he was always delicate. 'How gently and sweetly Emma takes this bitter affliction,' Elizabeth wrote. 'She cries at times but without violence, comes to our meals with the children and is as sweetly ready as ever to attend to all their little requirements. I do not think she will be made ill.'

There had been further sadness for Emma in the 1850s. In February 1853 Aunt Jessie died at Tenby. After the death of her husband, Sismondi, Jessie had returned to her native Wales to end her days with Fanny and Emma Allen. Childless, she had lavished all her frustrated maternal affection on her nieces, and Emma was saddened by her death. Aunt Sarah Wedgwood died at Down in 1856. Josiah's sister was a difficult woman, deeply religious and given to charities and good works. Only with Emma did she seem at ease, and for the last years of her life she had come to live near her. The Darwin children remembered her long bony fingers in their mittens and how she would stump through Down House calling for Emma in her harsh voice.

For five years after the birth of Horace Emma had a respite from child-bearing, but on 6 December 1856, when she was forty-eight, her last child, Charles Waring, was born. The baby was backward, and never learned to walk or talk. One might have thought that the great scientist would have noted the high incidence of mental illness in babies born late in their mother's life, or that the fond husband would have seen that Emma had had enough. But, like Karl Marx and many other progressive men of the age, he could be astonishingly blind.

His health is always affected by his mind

In the dark days after Annie's death, Emma had the consolation of religion. But Charles found the tragedy easier to explain as an instance of the survival of the fittest. How could a God be both loving and yet so cruel? As he watched under the microscope the nightmare of cruelty involved in the struggle for life he felt he could make out a better case for the devil than for God. Once, he had thought he might be happy as a country parson, but in fact he was not by nature religious – his father and his grandfather were sons of the age of reason, and his elder brother Erasmus was an agnostic, so the gradual loss of faith in these years did not disturb him unduly. But Emma, watching his anguish over Annie's death, wished he could share her faith to alleviate his grief. Once again, she found it easier to write to him.

> When I see your patience, deep compassion for others, self command and . . . gratitude for the smallest thing done to help you, I cannot help longing that these precious feelings should be offered to Heaven for the sake of your daily happiness. But I find it difficult enough in my own case. I often think of the words, 'thou shalt keep him in perfect peace whose mind is stayed on thee'. It is feeling and not reasoning that drives one to prayer.

Ever since 1837, when he had opened his first notebook for *The Origin of Species*, his doubts had been growing. But while he was worrying at this problem, from 1846 he worked for eight years studying in meticulous detail the world of barnacles. It was as though, in the careful collation of detail, he could control the disturbing thoughts which his deeper studies awakened. That apart, he needed to have some thorough piece of scientific research behind him before presenting his new ideas to the academic world. Like Karl Marx, he was reluctant to bring research to its conclusion.

Now he had become convinced that species of animals and plants were not, as was generally believed, fixed and immutable, unchanged from the pairs that had gone into the Ark. Stimulated by reading the economist Malthus's *Essay on the Principle of Population*, he was now formulating his theory that in the struggle for existence 'favourable variations would tend to be preserved and unfavourable ones destroyed'. The result of this would be the formation of a new species. These dominant and increasing forms themselves 'become adapted to many and highly diversified places in the economy of Nature'.

The sequence of events leading to the publication of *The Origin of Species* is well known. In June 1842, three years after he had clearly formulated his theory in his own mind, Darwin wrote a brief summary, on which he enlarged two years later. By 1856 he had, with difficulty, persuaded Hooker and Lyell that his views were valid, and they in turn urged him to publish them. But early in the summer of 1858 a devastating letter came from Alfred Russel Wallace, a zoologist then working in Borneo. He had independently come to the same conclusions and outlined them almost exactly in Darwin's words.

After twenty years' painstaking work Darwin was in danger of being forestalled. Thunderstruck, he was almost ready to recede into oblivion. But with a generosity rare in academic life the two men agreed to publish Wallace's essay with Darwin's summary in the *Journal of the Linnean Society.* Their work passed almost unnoticed, and the President that year noticed that 'Nothing of particular moment has been published.' Spurred into action, Darwin now worked flat out and in November 1859, after what he describes as 'thirteen months and ten days hard labour', *The Origin of Species* was published. Darwin always measured his working time exactly.

Less well known is the human suffering that lay behind the academic crisis. Throughout this time Emma, weakened by the birth of their last baby, grew more and more distressed as it became obvious to her experienced eyes that there was something wrong with the child. Bessy, born in 1847, had been slow, but this little boy was clearly retarded.

The summer of 1858 brought much illness. The baby caught scarlet fever and died on 28 June; Etty, too, was taken seriously ill and for a year her life was in danger. Remembering the tragedy of Annie, Charles and Emma were distraught, and the apparent collapse of his scientific hopes at this time was the last straw. Like Marx, Darwin could anaesthetise himself by work. It was more difficult for Emma, but, just as Jenny Marx found relief in working at the proofs of Marx's *Critique*, she immersed herself in reading the proofs of *The Origin of Species*, though that could hardly have reassured her.

The Origin of Species was an immediate success. John Murray sold out the first printing before publication, and almost immediately translations were begun into many languages. Darwin started work straightaway on the second, revised, edition. Friedrich Engels read the book as soon as it came out and enthusiastically wrote to Marx in December, 'Never before has so grandiose an attempt been made to demontrate historical evolution in Nature, and certainly never to such good effect. One does, of course, have to put up with the crude English method.' And Marx, reading the work a year later, echoed Engel's opinion in almost exactly the same words. He was so impressed that when, in 1867, *Das* *Kapital* was published, he sent Darwin an autobiographed copy.

It is difficult for the modern reader fully to understand the furore that Darwin's theories caused at the time. Most believers accepted in blind faith the literal truth of Genesis: at the Creation, God made each species distinct and immutable; two by two, the animals marched into the Ark, and centuries later were still unchanged. The idea that species would evolve led to the uncomfortable conclusion that man was an animal improved, not uniquely made in the image of God. That evolution was caused by 'natural' selection was even more alarming. If it were so, blind chance, not God, ruled the world. In *The Origin of Species*, Darwin was careful to omit man from his speculation. It was not until he wrote *The Descent of Man* in 1871 that he dealt with this problem, and by that time the idea was accepted. But the inference that man was descended from the animal world was clear.

For simple churchgoers in 1859 these ideas were as earth-shaking as the earlier theories of Galileo, as a result of which the earth lost its place as the centre of the universe. Now man was no longer the unique work of God. It was not that Darwin's ideas were new. In the freethinking eighteenth century his own grandfather, Erasmus Darwin, had suggested in *The Temple of Nature* that

> Organic life beneath the shoreless waves
> Was born, and nurs'd in ocean's pearly caves,
> First forms minute, unseen by spheric glass
> Move on the mud, or pierce the watery mass;
> These, as successive generations bloom,
> New powers acquire, and larger limbs assume;
> Whence countless groups of vegetations spring,
> And breathing realms of fin, and feet, and wing.

But now the time was ripe for such ideas; scientists and mathematicians were already casting doubts on the truths of the Old Testament. Improved microscopes and telescopes were transforming what had originally been called 'natural philosophy' into science based on careful observation. Even the new railways helped, for as cuttings were dug they revealed the earth's different strata, encouraging a positive mania for geology. There was much speculation, too, about the antiquity of the earth and the development of man. Many scientists and churchmen were nevertheless outraged by Darwin's theories, and even intellectuals like Carlyle mocked them.

All this, and the agony of waiting for publication, had proved too much for Charles. Throughout 1858 he had had frequent bouts of sickness, and had retreated again and again to Dr Lane's hydrotherapy establishment at Moor Park. Malvern held too painful memories. As Fanny Hensleigh once remarked, 'His health is always affected by his mind.' Now, unwilling to face the uproar that his book was producing, Darwin retreated to York-shire, to a chilly water cure in Ilkley; Emma and the children followed later. But though they took splendid rides over the windswept moors to Bolton Abbey, Ilkley did little to cheer them. The children remembered it as the coldest, most miserable time they had ever spent, and Emma's migraine returned with a vengeance.

Charles was incapable of taking up arms himself in the battle over *The Origin of Species*, but luckily he had a doughty champion in Thomas Huxley. At the famous meeting of the British Association in Oxford in 1860, when Darwin's opponents turned out in full force to demolish him, Huxley defended him with devastating brilliance. Professor Owen and the egregious Bishop of Oxford, 'Soapy Sam' Wilberforce, were completely routed.

But the criticism rumbled on for the rest of Darwin's

Emma had to endure that.

life. He would frequently be equated with Satan, and there were endless silly jokes about men and monkeys. Emma's sense of humour saved her; she collected the most outrageous cartoons and letters and sent them to their children. Emma was too balanced to be upset even by the occasional vicious attack. She was sustained by her love for Charles and a belief in his essential goodness. However, for one whose religion was simple, undogmatic but profound, they were disturbing months.

Emma had an additional worry at this time. Like Charles, her brother Hensleigh tended to take to his bed in times of stress – it was only with difficulty that he got to his own wedding. He, too, had been through the throes of authorship and at last his great volume on etymology was due to appear. The strain was too much; he took to his bed once again, and later he and Fanny came to Down, where Emma helped Fanny nurse him. So the noise of the battle over *The Origin of Species* came muffled into the sickrooms at Down.

As good as twice refined gold

Darwin considered his *Origin of Species* to be his life's work, but he continued to work on steadily for the remaining years. Emma did not like his *Descent of Man*, considering that it took Charles 'further from God'. But his books on orchids and climbing plants gave her great pleasure – she had no objection to him elevating plants and animals in the scale of existence. She did it herself, talking of the climbers 'twitching their little ears'. She watched his painstaking observations of worms with amused tolerance: when they went to Stonehenge it was 'chiefly for worms'; unfortunately, she wrote, 'the worms seemed to be very idle out there'. Emma always talked of their dogs as though they were human. 'F. wants to put Polly in his Man book,' she wrote. Much to his disgust, Charles had now become 'F' to the family. He would, he growled, rather be called 'Dog'. When Darwin died, Polly pined and had to be put down.

At Elizabeth's house in Hartfield, away from scientific battles, to Emma's relief Darwin immersed himself in botany. Yet even here his ever-curious mind led him into the nightmare world where even plants were 'red in tooth and claw'. He found specimens of the sundew in Ashdown Forest and watched the tiny plants trap insects in their talons, digest them and open again to release the dust that remained of their prey. Once again Emma was clever enough to see where his researches were taking him. 'Charles is too much given to anxiety, as you know,' she wrote to Lady Lyell, 'and his various experiments this summer have been a great blessing to him . . . At present he is treating *Drosera* just like a living creature, and I suppose he hopes to end in proving it to be an animal.'

The strain of the past years was now telling on Emma. At Hartfield she said they had had 'the bad luck to fall in with a desponding doctor', and only her natural optimism saved her from acute depression. The visit of Mrs Huxley and her children in March 1861 could not have raised her spirits. The Huxleys were still stricken after the death of their son, and their grief must have opened old wounds. But Emma, as Fanny Allen observed, 'of all others, blends cheerfulness with consolation', and in restoring them she restored herself.

A month in Torquay in the summer of 1861 revived them all. At this time the Devon resort was new, bright and fresh. They had a magnificent view over the rocky cliffs from Hesketh Terrace, which was far enough from the town to give them peace. The local scientists were delighted: 'The great Darwin is here', wrote the brilliant Torquay geologist, Pengelly. It is probable that the Darwins visited the scientific Institution there, where the Friday lectures were exceptionally interesting. There were geologists working on the excavations at Wookey Hole, and botanists collecting seaweeds and studying the fossil flora of the coalmines. Darwin would remember Torquay and its bright scientists with pleasure. Here he worked on his current book, on the fertilisation of orchids. Emma had the rare luxury of a tour of Devon without the children. They returned to Down refreshed, to face new trials in the coming years.

Their twelve-year-old son Leo caught scarlet fever in 1862, and after weeks of nursing him Emma herself was stricken and retreated to Bournemouth to recover. It was altogether a black year. Charlotte, who had been ill since autumn 1861, went to St Leonards to convalesce in January 1862, but died there. Her clear, pure voice that had enchanted them all on those faraway magical evenings at Maer was now silenced for ever. She had spent her last summer with Elizabeth. 'Her patient, calm and thoughtful look is every present to me,' wrote Fanny Allen. 'It was the same countenance that has gone with her from her childhood and has the stamp of an heavenly birth on it.'

Charlotte's marriage to the rather colourless Charles Langton had been surprisingly happy. In recent years they had lived at Maer and he had shown a rare understanding of Charlotte's mother, looking through the comatose old lady to the brilliant Bessy of the past. After Charlotte's death Langton married Charles Darwin's younger sister Catherine, to the astonishment of Wedgwoods and Darwins alike.

In the next years Charles himself was dangerously ill with the old sickness and new fainting fits and dizziness. They again took a house in Malvern in 1863 and Charles tried unsuccessfully to persuade Emma to undergo the treatment. It was her first visit since Annie's death, and she had to endure the agony of searching for the overgrown grave in the churchyard.

Emma rarely gave in to self-pity, and in the garden at Down she found solace. 'I often felt surprised,' she wrote, 'when I was feeling sad how cheerful a little exercise like that was.' Distinguished scientists, who now made pilgrimages to Down, would often find her 'cutting and carving among the shrubs' in her faded lilac cotton gown. Never one to fuss over her appearance, she was, however, glad when one distinguished botanist visited that she was wearing her new gown. 'Rags do not look well in the sunshine'. When Elizabeth had left Maer and built herself a house on the edge of Ashdown Forest, Emma had cheerfully dug up her most prized shrubs to give to her beloved sister – much to Charles's amusement.

February 1866 brought tragedy. Charles's sister Susan was taken ill at Shrewsbury, where she had lived after her father's death caring for four adopted nephews and nieces. Charles's younger sister Catherine, who came to nurse her during her illness, suddenly died, and Susan followed her in the autumn. Charles felt deeply the loss of the sisters who had been so close to him in childhood. Now it was 'sad, sad Shrewsbury,' as Fanny Allen wrote, 'which used to look so bright and sunny'. But neither Emma nor her aunts were completely at ease in the formal atmosphere at Shrewsbury. Even the clever Fanny Allen confessed, 'I did dread the Doctor a good deal and yet I saw his kindness.'

Many years later, Charles and Emma called in to see the new owner of his old home in Shrewsbury, and Charles was sad that he was not able to wander alone among his ghosts, to remember the past, the exquisite order of the rooms, and the neat garden. Had he done so, he wrote, he was sure his father would have reappeared in his wheelchair among the flowers.

In this year, in spite of the loss of his sisters, Charles's health improved under the care of Dr Bence-Jones, who managed to make him well enough to brave London again. In April Emma described his triumphal appearance at a soirée at the Royal Society. Few of his old friends recognised the hollow-eyed old man with the white beard. 'He was obliged to name himself to almost all of them,' Emma wrote, 'as his beard alters him so much. The President presented him to the Prince of Wales . . . the Prince looks a nice good-natured youth and very gentlemanlike. He said something Charles could not hear so he made the profoundest bow he could and went on.'

Emma was for once sufficiently concerned about her own health to consult Dr Bence-Jones. He 'is to do me some good too. I am to drive every day and Charles to ride'. So encouraged, she shook off the migraine that always dogged her in London and trudged round the galleries. 'We did one set of pictures which is staring unwholesome work and did not suit either of our heads.' As always, music was balm. She took her sister Elizabeth to hear 'our dear old Mozart D Minor at the Philharmonic. It was very charming and we used to play it quite fast enough (and very well) and gave it quite the right air'. But as for the singing in *Arabella* – 'It was hideous – Mlle Sinico sang *"Vedrai Carino"* as slow as a psalm tune and as loud as she could.' She was glad to return to Down and her growing family.

There was an affectionate warmth and ease in the relationship between Charles and Emma and their family. They were immensely proud of them all. 'Oh Lord, what a set of sons I have, all doing wonders!' Darwin wrote; and again to his son George, then studying astronomy. 'What a lot of swells you have been meeting . . . Hurray for the bowels of the earth and their viscosity and for the moon and for the Heavenly bodies and for my son George (F. R. S. very soon).' One of them later recalled:

the delightful playmate he made for us as children. In later life he always treated us with entire trust and freedom, and all our opinions or views or desires he would discuss and consider almost as if we were his equals; and it is touching to recall, though it almost

makes one smile, the tone of admiration and gratitude
with which he would acknowledge any little help we
could give him in botanical or other matters.

Nothing delighted Emma more than when, in 1880,
the family clubbed together to buy Darwin a fur coat.
Francis reported to Etty,

> I left it on the study table furry side out and letter on top
> . . . so that he would find it at 4 when he started his
> walk. Jackson [the butler] was 2nd conspirator, with a
> broad grin and the coat over his arm peeping through
> the green baize door while I saw the coast clear in the
> study.

Emma let into the secret, was there to enjoy the fun. 'I
do not feel my sons are my sons,' Etty remembered
Emma saying, 'only young men with whom I happen
to be intimate.'

His granddaughter Gwen Raverat remembered them
as 'a solid block of uncles – each more adorable than the
other'. William became a banker. He was so wholesome
that 'Uncle Frank once said you could eat a mutton
chop off William's face.' He married late, and went to
live in what the family considered a hideous house at
Bassett near Southampton; but here Darwin could visit
him and be comfortable. George, Gwen's father, had
his father's intellectual energy and a passionate interest
in history. Frank was a scientist, a botanist and a
musician. It was he who wrote his father' biography
and returned to live with his parents, helping Darwin
with his last books. Frank brought his charming wife
Amy to live at Down, and her death on the birth of her
son Bernard rocked Emma. 'I feel I can bear your
father's loss,' she said to Etty after Charles's death. 'I
felt I *couldn't* bear Amy's.'

Bernard, who later became a writer and a great golfer,

was brought up at Down. He remembered how he used to be allowed to slide down the stairs on a polished strip of wood as his father had done. And Emma, just as she had done with her own chilren, often bribed him with sugar plums. 'She had', he wrote, 'an odd habit of enforcing the law in insignificant matters.' But she was, he claimed, 'one of the wisest people I have ever known' and on 'important questions she was firm enough and was one with whom nobody old or young could take a liberty'. She was of all people the least subject to any form of fuss. Indeed, she had allowed her own children to do some adventurous things such as letting a small boy of eight, his Uncle George, ride nearly twenty miles alone on his pony from Down to Hartfield in Sussex.

Amongst the younger generation Horace's chief claim to fame, according to Gwen Raverat, was 'that he used to amuse us by standing on a chair in the dining room, holding a tin of treacle and demonstrating that syrup always fell in a perfectly straight line . . . into a saucer on the floor'. Nothing delighted them more than when his theory and the syrup slurped together on the carpet.

Henrietta – Etty – was clever: 'Miss Rhadamanthus,' Huxley called her. Bessy was large, slow, affectionate and not very bright. While Etty corrected her father's proofs, Bessy sat placidly knitting. In 1871 Etty was married in the village church at Down – even that quiet ceremony totally exhausted Charles. Her husband, Richard Litchfield, was a quiet, dedicated scholar and one of the founders of the Working Men's College. He was devoted to Emma and she enjoyed his wide-ranging intellect. 'I am glad you are reading Plato,' she wrote to him. 'Do you think I could endure any of it?' Litchfield, who loved nothing better than sitting quietly with Emma on the sunlit lawn, wrote after one after-noon, 'Her presence always gives me a feeling of a beautiful and tranquillising spirit.' Charles wrote to Etty on her honeymoon: 'I have had a happy life notwithstanding my stomach and this I owe almost entirely to our dear old mother who is as good as twice refined gold. Keep her as an example and then L. will love and worship you as I worship our dear old Mother.'

Litchfield brought academic and literary colleagues from London to Down. One of his close friends was Arthur Munby, the extraordinary Victorian whose passion for working girls culminated in his secret marriage to his housekeeper; he found Emma 'comely'. The annual outing of the Working Men's College was often held at Down; there were picnics on the law and full-throated singing in the evening under the lime trees. Neither Emma nor Charles was particularly easy on these occasions, but Etty remembered her mother's gracious welcome. Her working-class friends fascinated Emma: 'Henrietta has been to a working man's ball and danced with a grocer and a shoemaker who looked and behaved exactly like everyone else and were quite as well dressed.'

I sometimes feel it very odd that someone belonging to me should be making such a noise in the world

In the late 1860s and 1870s Charles's health improved and they made several expeditions. In 1868 Charles and Emma, accompanied by Erasmus, spent six weeks at Freshwater in the Isle of Wight, renting a house belonging to the photographer, Julia Margaret Cameron. She took her famous photograph of Darwin at this time, but refused to take Emma. 'No woman', she maintained, 'between eighteen and seventy is worth photographing.' Darwin and Erasmus were captivated – Emma less so. Nor was she particularly impressed with Tennyson, who visited them at this time. 'His absurd talk', she wrote to Fanny Allen, 'is a sort of flirtation with Mrs Cameron.' The invalid Mrs Tennyson was, however, 'very pleasing and gracious'.

They visited William at Bassett, where, to Emma's delight, Charles's pleasure in the beauty of landscape was reawakened. They were particularly comfortable with relatives: Lord Farrer, at Abinger Hall in Surrey, was Fanny Hensleigh's son-in-law, and Charles and Emma enjoyed wandering round the grounds there and visiting Jos and Caroline at Leith Hill Place. In January 1874 Emma and Charles were present at a party at Erasmus's house in London where a medium, a Mr Williams, was to demonstrate his skills. The other guests included George Eliot and her husband George Lewes, who nearly wrecked the performance by making jokes. There were satisfactory manifestations, Etty claimed, 'sparks, wind-blowing and some rappings and moving of furniture'. What Charles Darwin's reaction was, Etty does not say, but Emma, she claimed, 'maintained an attitude of neither belief nor unbelief'. Was she half hoping to hear the thin voice of a child long dead?

In 1879 they made the long journey to Coniston in the Lake District and called on Ruskin. They were depressed by the clouding of his mind but they dutifully admired his Turners, for once faking an enthusiasm which they did not feel. Emma enjoyed rowing on the lake and climbing the hills, until Charles was taken with what Emma called 'a fit of dazzling'.

They both preferred the peace of Down. Emma had more time for music now and had Frank and Litchfield to accompany. Each evening she and Charles played two games of backgammon; 'Bang your bones!' he would shout when he lost.

Darwin was now world-famous, though that never went to Emma's head. 'I sometimes feel it very odd', she wrote to Fanny Allen, 'that someone belonging to me should be making such a noise in the world.' Visitors from all over the world made the pilgrimage to Down. There were Scottish students, a strange Canadian and an odd Australian who rushed in, shook

hands and fled. One week Emma thought they were
'rather overdone with Germans'. Lyell and Huxley and
Hooker were their favourite guests.

A less welcome visitor to Down in 1883 was Dr
Aveling. Now he is chiefly remembered for his unhappy
relationship with Marx's daughter Eleanor, but it was
as a leading atheist and Vice-President of the National
Secularist Society that he came to see Darwin, whose
open support of atheism would have been a feather in
his cap. He had written to Darwin in 1880, asking him
to read the proofs of his book on Darwin's thought and
offering to dedicate it to him. Courteously, Darwin
refused, in a letter long assumed to have been
addressed to Marx. Though he was, he wrote, a 'strong
advocate of free thought', he had always avoided writing on religion. 'I may, however, have been unduly
biased by the pain which it would give some members
of my family, if I aided in any way direct attacks on
religion.' He was, he apologised, 'old and have very
little strength and looking over proof sheets . . . fatigues
me much'. As a result of their discussion Aveling
published an article that year entitled 'The Religious
Views of Charles Darwin', in which he assumed that
Darwin's views were similar to his own. In fact Francis,
Darwin's son, refuted this in an appendix to his father's
autobiography. Darwin's unaggressive agnosticism,
according to Francis, distinguished him completely
from the class of thinkers to which Dr Aveling
belonged. For, as Darwin himself wrote, 'In my most
extreme fluctuations I have never been an Atheist in the
sense of denying the existence of God.' It was not
merely that he would have been reluctant to wound
Emma by publicly declaring his scepticism; he was
profoundly convinced, as Francis wrote, 'that a man
ought not to publish on a subject to which he has not
given special and continuous thought'. Emma had long
ago accepted his views, and although over the years her
own faith had become, in Etty's words, 'less vivid', it

was still the source of her serenity, and as such Darwin was grateful for it.

Nothing better illustrates Emma's relaxed attitude to fame than the account written to her son William of the Cambridge ceremony on 16 November 1877 when Charles was made a Doctor of Laws.

My dear William,

It was a great disappointment your not coming yesterday to witness the honours to F., and so I will tell you all about it.

Bessy and I and the two youngest brothers went first to the Senate House and got in by a side door, and a most striking sight it was. The gallery crammed to overflowing with undergraduates, and the floor crammed too with undergraduates climbing on the statues and standing up in the windows. There seemed to be periodical cheering in answer to jokes which sounded deafening; but when F. came in, in his red cloak, ushered in by some authorities, it was perfectly deafening for some minutes. I thought he would be overcome, but he was quite stout and smiling and sat for a considerable time waiting for the Vice-Chancellor. The time was filled up with shouts and jokes, and groans for an unpopular Proctor, Mr——, which were quite awful, and he looked up at them with a stern angry face, which was very bad policy. We had been watching some cords stretched across from one gallery to another wondering what was to happen, but were not surprised to see a monkey dangling down which caused shouts and jokes about our ancestors, etc. A Proctor was foolish enough to go up to capture it and at last it disappeared I don't know how. Then came a sort of ring tied with ribbons which we conjectured to be the 'Missing Link'. At last the Vice-Chancellor appeared, more bowing and hand-shaking, and then F. was marched down the aisle behind two men with silver maces, and the unfortunate Public Orator came and stood by him and got thro' his very tedious harangue as he could, constantly interrupted by the most unmannerly shouts and jeers; and when he had continued what seemed an enormous time, some one called out in a cheerful tone 'Thank you kindly'. At last he got to the end with admirable nerve and temper, and then they all marched back to the Vice-Chancellor . . . in scarlet and white fur and F. joined his hands and did not kneel but the Vice-Chancellor put his hands outside and said a few Latin words, and then it was over, and everybody came up and shook hands.

Of all days in the year I had a baddish headache, but managed to go and enjoyed it all. F. has been to Newton's Museum today and seen many people – also a brilliant luncheon at George's. J. W. Clark did me a good turn, as I followed his lead in tasting galantine – which is very superior.

I felt very grand walking about with my LL.D. in his silk gown.

The juxtaposition of silk gown and galantine was typical of Emma. It was her way of staying sane.

In the autumn of 1879 Emma's sister Elizabeth died. She had lived in a house nearby in her last years and had become almost blind, relying more and more on Emma, tapping with her stick through the sunlit rooms, her voice echoing, 'Where is Emma?' Erasmus died in 1881. Francis remembered his father's sad figure at the graveside, a scattering of snow on his long black cloak.

In October that year they went to see Horace and his bride in their new house in Cambridge. 'Joyous arrival,' Emma recorded, 'admiring the house'. Charles was 'pretty well all the time'. They went to see his portrait in the library of the Philosophical Society. Emma thought it 'quite horrid . . . so fierce and so dirty. However it is under a glass and very high up so nobody can see it'.

Charles was quite set up by the visit to Cambridge and the good talk with old friends, but it was his last expedition. In December Emma, very worried, quietly went up to London and consulted Dr Andrew Clark. This time it was Charles's heart that was weak, and she knew now that the end was near. But there were still some happy days, and her diary recorded the visit in January of 'the tramps – Leslie Stephen, Virginia Woolf's father, and his walking party. He was an old friend, and Virginia herself was to be a friend of their granddaughter, Gwen Raverat.

The entries in her journal for the following weeks, however, were brief and poignant. In February she took 'one walk with him to the terrace on a beautiful still, bright day'. March was 'a peaceful time without much suffering – exquisite weather often loitering out with him'. On 10 March Dr Clark came to see him and for a while he rallied. On 7 April she noted: 'Good day, a little walk out in the orchard twice.'

But for 18 April her entry was simple. 'Fatal attack at 12.' He had wakened her at midnight saying, 'I have got the pain and I shall feel better or bear it better if you are awake.' They sent for Etty, who arrived on the morning of the 19th and found her father 'being supported by my mother and my brother Frank'. Emma was persuaded to take an opium pill and get some rest while they stayed with him. During that time, Etty remembered he said to them: 'You are the best of dear nurses.' Emma did not rest for long: she was awakened in the afternoon and was at his side when, as Etty recorded, 'He peacefully died at half past three on the 19th of April.'

Poor mother, you have time enough now

Throughout the days that followed Emma remained calm, natural. 'She came down to the drawing-room to tea', wrote Etty in amazement on the day of her father's death, 'and let herself be amused at some little thing, and smiled, almost laughed, for a moment as she would on any other day.' She had never in the past made a parade of grief, and though this was the greatest deso-

lation of her life she did not do so now. She had
anticipated Charles's death for a long time, and found
it bearable in a way that Annie's had not been. Bernard
remembered how that day she helped him with his
French lessons, and how she comforted his tearful Aunt
Bessy.

But the structure of Emma's world was shattered.
Her whole life had revolved around Charles, and the
regular rhythm so essential to him had made the pattern
that her own easy-going nature needed. Wisely, she
now recreated her own life, gradually reviving interests
which she had neglected when her work was Darwin's.
The family was the framework of her new life.

They were there for the funeral in Westminster
Abbey, the sons – so like their father – sitting in the
front pews. William, unselfconscious as always, sat
through the whole ceremony with his two black gloves
on top of his head to protect his bald pate from the
Abbey draughts. The Darwins were always careful of
their health.

But Emma was not there. Needing obscurity, she hid
her grief alone. Did she walk on that day along the
Sand Walk, as they so often had done together? Did she
sit at her piano and play, as she had done for him every
evening of their lives? If so, it would have been even
then with a control that always soothed her most
profound emotions. She was not at the unveiling of the
monument to him at the Natural History Museum,
preferring, she wrote, 'to avoid all greetings'. But she
went quietly afterwards to see the statue, admiring its
looks of dignity and repose even though she did not
find it a good likeness. Leo's deep grief had helped her
to cry. 'It is always easier to write than speak,' she
wrote to him afterwards. 'I will tell you that the entire
love and veneration of all you dear sons for your Father
is one of my chief blessings and binds us together more
than ever.'

Poor Bessie needed comforting, but to Etty, the closest of all her children, she could unburden her grief. 'I am trying', she wrote later to her,

> to make stages in the day of something special to do. It often comes over me with a wave of desolate feeling that there is nothing I need do and I think of your true words, 'poor Mother, you have time enough now'. The regularity of my life was such an element of happiness and to be received every time I joined him by some word of welcome and to feel that he was happier that very minute for my being with him . . .

As Charles himself had done after the deaths of his children, she wrote in her diary memories she wanted to fix, 'for fear I should forget if I live long': the happiness of their first visit to Horace in their new home in Cambridge; Charles's pleasure in Etty's picture by his chair; his constant delight that the boys had given up the billiard room to give him a better study. Above all she remembered his gracious words when she came into the sickroom. Again and again he had said, 'It's almost worth while to be sick to be nursed by you.' She wrote of their last walks together in the exquisite February sunshine, how they had loitered down to the terrace looking for the first crocuses. 'The last ten or twelve years', she wrote, 'have been the happiest, overflowing with tenderness.'

She could not bear to sell Down House and still spent the summers there, but now she jotted in her diary, each time she came, 'black and dark'. Huxley visited her there in 1891. His visit was 'very pleasant if rather sad. Mrs Darwin is wonderfully well, naturally aged but bright and cheerful as usual. Parslow turned up on Sunday – just eighty but still fairly hale.' The winters she spent at The Grove, a house she had bought on the Huntingdon road in Cambridge. Her sons had a house on either side and the unfenced gardens ran together.

Francis and Bernard lived with her until Francis married again; then, wisely, she decided it would not be fair to Ellen, the new wife, to share Bernard with her, so Francis and Ellen moved to their own house. Her children and grandchildren kept her interested. Once again she played her old galloping tunes, and guiltily bribed them as she had done her own children; when the noise at lunchtime deafened her, she secured quiet by paying pennies for low voices. Of her eleven-month-old grandson Erasmus she wrote that he 'sits every day in his chair at luncheon and insists upon having a great deal of pudding beside his own broth, flapping his fins between each mouthful'.

Her chief joy in the years after Charles's death was in writing letters – for which she had considerable talent. As Aunt Jessie had once written, Emma was poetical without knowing it. She wrote in relief after the great heat of the summer of 1893, 'I feel quite tipsy looking out at the dear black sky and drizzled windows.' A friend's rendering of Brahms was so bad that it 'satisfied me never to wish to hear another, though there were grand sort of North Wind gleams in it'. And when she read her son Frank's *Life and Letters*, 'A little mention of me . . . sent me to bed with a glow about my heart coming on it unexpectedly'.

Now she read more than ever before, often keeping two books on the go at the same time – a demanding one and an easy one. In 1888, for example, she was reading 'Paradise Regained' and Rousseau's *Confessions*, and Henry James sandwiched with Leslie Stephen's *Hours in a Library*. In 1894, well into her eighties, she confessed, 'I am rather ashamed to find I use up rather more than a volume a day of novels.' Even since girlhood she had read widely on religion and philosophy; now in her old age she was reading Milner's *History of the Jews* and strongly recommending to Leonard the *Life of Henrietta Ker – a Nun*. Scott and Mrs Gaskell she read over and over again, but Jane Austen was her favourite; she had always rather identified with Jane's Emma.

Bernard, her grandson, remarked on the quality that is so noticeable even in her early letters. 'She had a genius, quite indescribable by me, for dry and definite statements of her own particular flavour. "I dislike all poetry, especially good poetry" is attributed to her, though it certainly did her an injustice.' Emma had never pretended to care for poetry, though she exaggerated her distaste, disliking gush. Stanley's *Darkest Africa*, which she read in 1888, she found 'the most tiresome book in the world – he observes nothing'. Emma dealt with her old enemies with energy – Rousseau's odious vanity and Louis Napoleon's presumption filled her with fury.

Politics continued to fascinate her. She had always been a Whig–Liberal and an admirer of Gladstone, though she parted company with him over his Home Rule policy for Ireland. The Gladstones had visited them at Down, and their daughter was a friend. When Emma was eighty-four she 'boiled over with excitement' when Leo stood as a Liberal candidate for Lichfield. She followed the campaign fervently, colouring a map of gains and losses. 'I am so intensely interested in the debates,' she wrote, 'I must put myself on stoppages or I shall wear out my eyes.' The only shadow over their celebrations of Leo's success was the absence of Charles. 'How your father would have enjoyed it!' she said. When Leo lost Litchfield in 1895 her disappointment was correspondingly great: 'I have hardly the heart to go on with the map.'

In these last years her wide range of interests and her mental alertness made her the best of listeners to all ages. Like Fanny Allen, she 'enjoyed a youthy age'. Something of the gay radiance of her youth had gone – her daughter, reading old letters, was surprised at the young Emma's liveliness – but the tranquillity which had always been there was now remarked upon by all who met her.

Emma enjoyed the house at Cambridge, especially in the spring when the nightingales sang along the Backs. 'The east wind and bright sun are just what I like,' she wrote to Etty, 'and our old nightingale sang 8 or 9 hours at a stretch yesterday. I wonder whether it is the same – he is louder and more tipsy than ever.' Even the sharp winds she found invigorating. She was still observant, noticing that in early spring the elm buds along the Backs had 'taken a purplish glow'. Later in the season she wrote, 'The day was perfect . . . and it is the first time that the tulips have really opened their eyes. I am always divided at this time of the year between the wish to stay on to enjoy the spring and early summer here and the opposite wish to be at Down before the trees have become dark and summer-like.'

Each summer she looked forward with excitement to the return to Down, yet on each first day the sense of blankness depressed her. But she was resilient and there were honied summer days with tea on the verandah, or haymaking and tennis. 'Life is not flat to me,' she wrote to Etty, 'only all at a lower pitch and I do feel it an advantage not to be grudging the years as they pass and lamenting my age.'

In the last years of her life her health improved, though her eyesight failed. 'It is a surprising thing', she wrote, 'that at 87 I should feel stronger and better in every way than I did at 85.' Matheson, her devoted maid and friend, read aloud to her. Once, in 1887, she hired a prim pupil-teacher to read. 'I embarked with her on such a frivolous novel all about flirtations and lovers that I have changed it for Miss Young – all about scarlet fever and drains.' Her old attendants were as faithful as ever. Parslow was part of the family and refused to be retired. She regarded the new ones with amused tolerance: 'Nurse's manner to me is like one housemaid to another a little beneath her, but I am not in the least offended.'

The whole family were with her during the last summer at Down, and she still played her galloping tunes for the little ones, even though now it exhausted her. Early that September she was wheeled in her bathchair for a long tour of the surrounding lanes. The roads now seemed deeper and the hedges and trees had grown high, but she 'felt the sharp wind over the bare field quite like an old friend'.

Three weeks later, on Sunday, 27 September 1896, she was taken ill, and when Etty arrived the following Thursday Emma was already fading fast. On the evening of the next day Etty watched her wind up her watch for the last time and then fall back on her pillow.

Hers had been a life which had had its share of tragedy, but even now she radiated a rare light. Clear and confident, her character shines through her letters. Married to a man whose life work had disturbed the world, whose ill health had been a constant strain, she had kept her own faith and her own personality. She had remained tranquil and loving. Above all, she had never been lost in the shadow of her great husband. Neither fame nor controversy rocked her. In her life with Charles she was supportive, yet when he had gone her mind continued to develop and grow. Darwin's debt to her can never be fully estimated. Without her he might – like her brother Erasmus – have been a clever man who yet achieved nothing. Or like his Uncle Tom, who discovered photography but never fulfilled his promise, he might have been a great scientist destroyed by poor health. Emma kept Charles Darwin alive, and he knew her value.

In his autobiography he wrote to his sons,

> You all know your mother, and what a good mother she has ever been to all of you. She has been my greatest blessing and I can declare that in my whole life I have

never heard her utter one word which I would rather have been unsaid. She has never failed in kindest sympathy towards me, and has borne with the utmost patience my frequent complaints of ill-health and discomfort. I do not believe she has ever missed an opportunity of doing a kind action to anyone near her. I marvel at my good fortune, that she, so infinitely my superior in very single moral quality, consented to be my wife. She has been my wise adviser and cheerful comforter throughout life, which without her would have been during a very long period a miserable one from ill-health. She has earned the love and admiration of every soul near her.

Under the date February 1893 Emma had copied these lines from Tennyson's 'In Memoriam' into her book of extracts:

> Not all regret: the face will shine
> Upon me, while I muse alone;
> And that dear voice, I once have known,
> Still speak to me of me and mine:
>
> Yet less of sorrow lives in me
> For days of happy commune dead;
> Less yearning for the friendship fled,
> Than some strong bond which is to be.

Epilogue

When the fire of genius strikes, it often blasts the ground around. It destroyed Mary Livingstone and scarred Jenny Marx; Emma Darwin survived, protected by her own serenity and sheltered by material comfort. The children of exceptional men and women do not go unscathed; for it is not easy to live under the shadow of a great name. The crackling energy of the driven genius often enervates the children; many sons of famous men throughout history have been discouraged, as young Charley Dickens was by a schoolmaster's chilling 'Consider what name you bear.' To be uprooted time and time again, like the children of Marx and Livingstone, imposes psychological and physical strains.

David Livingstone rightly praised his wife for having brought up their five children so well under such difficult circumstances. Certainly, with the exception of Robert, they surprised their English friends with their gentleness and modesty. After Mary's death they were left in the care of David's sisters, Agnes and Janet, who gave up their bonnet shop to make a home for them. Although the aunts did not complain, they often found it hard to make ends meet. The daughter of Livingstone's wealthy friend William Webb remembered them, at their brother's funeral in Westminster Abbey, as two nice, sensible-looking, elderly women, square and solid, with dark, strong faces, who spoke broad Scots but carried themselves with dignity. Young Agnes's respect for her aunts, her Spanish good looks and bearing attracted the sympathetic attention of all in the crowded congregation.

Livingstone had sent Agnes to Paris after her mother's death, where she spent a year studying French and music at a small Protestant school. This was not so surprising as it might seem, since Mary's sister Ann had married a French missionary and Agnes had French cousins. After her father's death she spent much of her time with the Webbs at Newstead Abbey. Wiliam Webb had known her as a little girl in the Kalahari desert, 'sitting under the old camelthorn trees at the turn of the Zouga River, playing at making tea with the pods and seeds as tea-things'. William Cotton Oswell, too, remembered her from those years and was as kind and generous to her as he had been to the family in Africa. He would go, he promised her, to the ends of the earth should she ever need him. Agnes married a wealthy husband and later returned on a visit to Africa, following the family's old mission route in a comfortable railway carriage.

Anna Mary was like her grandmother, Ma Mary – pretty, fair-haired, with blue eyes. As a little girl she had kept up a touching correspondence with Hans Andersen. She had been educated at the Quaker School in Kendal, where she met and married Frank Wilson, a nephew of Mr C. Braithwaite, her father's friend. She and her husband spent their summers in little mission ships to deep sea fishermen and then became missionaries in Sierra Leone, where Frank died of yellow fever. Anna took care of the old aunts at her home in Kendal until they died in 1895.

Tom and Oswell studied medicine, as Livingstone had recommended to his trustees. Oswell was remembered at the time of his father's funeral as a young doctor, slight and very silent. He had gone in search of his father in 1871 with a government-sponsored search and relief expedition, but they met Stanley on the return journey from his famous meeting with Livingstone and the search was called off. Though he wanted to go on alone, Oswell was advised that he was not strong enough to brave the dangerous journey. He never quite

forgave himself for not over-riding this opinion, and
Livingstone himself bitterly complained that Oswell had
rejected the opportunity to prove that he was not
merely David Livingstone's son. Old Robert Moffat was
a striking figure at Oswell's wedding, as he had been at
the funeral in Westminster Abbey.

The two sons who walked before their father's coffin
looked strained and ill. Thomas had never lived up to
his nickname – Tau, the lion. Too delicate to face the
rigours of a Scottish school, he had been taken away, to
be taught by Mary at home. When Livingstone heard
the news in Africa he was annoyed – though he was
careful not to blame his wife. 'The Livingstons [sic]', he
wrote, had been 'rather famous for quick learning
among Highland Chieftains' sons'. Poor Tom, who had
to bear not only the weight of his father's fame but the
reputation of generations of hardy Scots, had a chronic
disease, possibly bilharzia. This was a legacy from his
African childhood – though Livingstone blamed the
Scottish drains. Tom worked in Egypt where he contracted yellow fever and died at the age of twenty-
seven.

As for the problem eldest son, Robert, his story is a
classic example of the burden of a famous father's name.
After his mother's death Robert tried to join his father
on the Zambesi, but Livingstone discouraged him.
Robert wrote to his sister Agnes that he had been
drugged by sailors and taken off to America. Certainly
he fought in the Civil War in the 3rd New Hampshire
Regiment under the name of Private Rupert Vincent,
and, fatally wounded in battle near Richmond, died in
hospital on 5 December 1864 at Salisbury, North Caro-
lina. He had assumed another name so that he should
not disgrace his family. In fact he had shown great
courage, fighting in his own way against the slavery
that his father so abhorred.

* * *

It was as well that Jenny Marx was not to know the fate of her three adored daughters. Two years after her mother's death, Jennychen died of cancer; her children survived to continue the Marx line into this century. Then in 1898 warm-hearted, vital Tussy committed suicide. A competent interpreter and translator, she was responsible for the first English translation of Flaubert's *Madame Bovary*. She was also a good actress, an eloquent lecturerer, a writer and editor of her father's work, and much loved in the working-class movements to which she devoted her life. Tussy idolised her father and idealised his love for Jenny, remembering how he had told her of his visit to Trier twenty years after their marriage, and of the pilgrimages he had made to Jenny's old house. The news that Freddy Demuth was Marx's son shattered that idyll. Her second and mortal blow was the discovery that Edward Aveling, with whom she had lived for eleven years, had not only bankrupted her but also secretly married a young woman. No longer wishing to live, she sent her maid to the chemist with Dr Aveling's prescription – possibly with his knowledge – took chloroform and prussic acid and died alone.

In 1911 Laura and her husband Paul Lafargue also killed themselves. With their inheritance from Engels they had bought a magnificent house with a park and orangery at Draveuil, near Paris. In the true Marx manner they squandered their bequest, and having nothing – as they believed – to live for since their children had all died, they made a suicide pact.

The full story of Frederick Demuth, Marx's natural son, may never be known, and perhaps he should be left in quiet obscurity. When he grew up he became a skilled fitter and a member of the Amalgamated Engineering Union. Tussy and Laura knew him after their mother's death as the son of their 'dear Nymmy' – Lenchen. She had gone to take care of Engels after Marx's death, and there, at his comfortable home in

Regents Park Road, Freddy visited her regularly, always coming to the kitchen door – the proper entrance for a Victorian workman. When Lenchen died in 1890 she left all her worldly goods – and ninety-five pounds – to Frederick Lewis Demuth of 25 Gransden Avenue, Hackney. Lenchen kept her secret to the end. In fact it was not until Engels was dying of cancer of the throat that he decided to leave the record straight, in case historians should blame him for neglecting Freddy, who had always been assumed to be his son.

His lawyer, Sam Moore, broke the news to Tussy, who refused to believe it until she heard it from Engels himself. Unable to speak, he wrote the devastating truth on a slate. Overcome with guilt, Tussy tried to make amends for the injustice to Freddy, who, quiet and reliable, became her closest friend during her last tragic days. Freddy died in Upper Clapton in 1929 in the house he shared with a Miss Laura Payne, leaving his possessions and the surprisingly large sum of £1971 12s 4d to Harry Demuth, whom he mysteriously named as his nephew, though he had always called him his son.

Freddy's own marriage had been unhappy; as Tussy said, they had both been strangely dogged by misfortune. It is rumoured that Karl Marx called on him after Jenny's death; if this was so, he must have been haunted by remorse and regret, hearing his father's warning echoing from the past.

The Darwin children, brought up in the calm security of their Kentish home, had a better chance. It is a great tribute to the ease and affection of their family life that none of the sons appears to have been in any way checked by his father's fame, each achieving distinction in his different field. William was a successful banker; George a Fellow of Trinity College, Cambridge, and Plumian Professor of Astronomy. Leo, for twenty years a soldier in the Royal Engineers, later became President of both the Royal Geographical Society and the Eugenic Society. Frank, a naturalist, collaborated with his father and later edited his *Life and Letters*. Even Horace, the least ambitious, became a scientific engineer, his 'shop' developing into the Cambridge Scientific Instrument Company. Etty, like many daughters of famous men, flourished in her father's shadow; she was her husband's biographer, read the proofs of Darwin's books, and in her *Life of Emma Wedgwood* preserved the memory of her mother as Frank had done for his father.

Emma had the pleasure of seeing and encouraging in her grandchildren and their cousins the talents that would later emerge. Young Ralph Vaughan Williams, the grandson of Jos and Caroline, shared her love of music; Snow Wedgwood, Fanny Hensleigh's daughter, was a writer and came to Down House, knowing that there she could write her philosophical works in peace. Later she was to become the close friend of Robert Browning; their platonic love affair lasted for years. George's daughter, Gwen Raverat, was to become a skilled artist and write movingly of her Cambridge childhood. Emma, seeing her come home to Down with shining eyes, her arms full of flowers 'and one strawberry' knew that there was something special in the child. Watching her grandchildren racing around as she played her old galloping tunes, seeing them growing up, gave Emma happiness and comfort until her death. She had seen difficult and tragic times, but she had never been torn apart by conflicting calls of husband and family as Mary Livingstone and Jenny Marx had been. Though three of her children had died young, she had never had to watch them suffering hunger and hardship.

Would these three wives, given a second chance, have married the same husbands? Would they have thought their sacrifice worthwhile? Mary Livingstone had gone to Africa at the end, as her mother wrote, 'as a lamb to the slaughter', knowing in her heart that she would not survive. But she would have taken comfort from the fact that in changing and turbulent Africa Livingstone is still revered. Salisbury and Rhodesia have disappeared from the map, but Blantyre and Livingstonia remain. Jenny Marx would have exulted in the triumph of Marxism across the world. As a girl she had been inspired by Shelley's 'Prometheus Unbound', but like Shelley's wife she saw the other side of the Prometheus story. Frankenstein, the hero Mary Shelley created, challenged God and created, not a superman, but a monster. To half the world Marx is Frankenstein. To the rest he is Prometheus still. As for Emma, she would have been amused at the arguments that still rage around Darwin's name. But her rare anger would be aroused by those who would use Charles's arguments to justify totalitarian doctrines. The world cannot forget Livingstone, Marx and Darwin as it has forgotten their wives.

But all three women had learned to understand and accept that the men they loved had to push their way beyond discovered frontiers by the rockiest of roads. As Marx said, he could not have lived 'like an ox', and Emma, though she often wished it, knew that she could never get Charles to 'ruminate like a cow'. Livingstone, Marx and Darwin were driven by a force that was both creative and destructive. Under its remorseless pressure each was to open a road which led to both good and evil. None of them could dam up the energy which drove them to sacrifice themselves and those around them for the mission to which they believed they were called.

Bibliography

Andreas, B. (ed.), *Briefe und Dokumente der Familie Marx aus den Jahren 1862–1873*, Hanover 1962.

Atkins, E., *The Religious Views of Charles Darwin*, London 1884.

Atkins, Sir H., *Down: The Home of the Darwins*, London 1976.

Awdrey, F., *An Elder Sister*, London 1878.

Baines, E., *Explorations in South West Africa*, London 1864.

Barlow, N. (ed.), *Charles Darwin and the Voyage of the Beagle*, London 1945.

Barzun, J., *Darwin, Marx and Wagner*, Boston 1946.

Berlin, Sir Isaiah, *Karl Marx, His Life and Environment*, Oxford 1939.

Blaikie, W. G., *The Personal Life of David Livingstone*, London 1880.

Blumenberg, W., *Karl Marx*, London 1971.

Bottigelli, L. and D., *Lettres et Documents de Karl Marx 1856–1883*, Milan 1958

Brent, P., *Charles Darwin*, London 1981.

Briggs, Asa, *The Age of Improvement*, London 1944.

Butler, Marilyn, *Maria Edgeworth: A Literary Biography*, Oxford 1972.

Campbell, J., *Travels in South Africa*, 2 vols, London 1959.

Carlyle, Jane W., (ed. J. A. Froude), *Letters and Memorials*, 3 vols, London 1883.

Carlyle, Jane W., *Letters to Her Family*, London 1924.

Carlyle, Jane W. (ed. A. Carlyle), *New Letters and Memorials*, 2 vols, London 1903

Carlyle, T. (ed. C. E. Norton), *Reminiscences*, London 1887.

Chadwick, O., *Mackenzie's Grave*, London 1959.

Chamberlin, D. (ed), *Some Letters from Livingstone 1840–1972*, London 1940.

Chancellor, J., *Charles Darwin*, London 1974.

Chapman, J., *Travels in the Interior of South Africa*, 2 vols. London 1868.

Cole, G. D. H., *What Marx Really Meant*, London 1934.

Colp, R., *To Be an Invalid*, Chicago 1977.

Collins, H. and C. Abramsky, *Karl Marx and the British Labour Movement*, London 1965.

Comyn, Marian, 'My Recollections of Karl Marx', *The Nineteenth Century*, vol. 91, no. 539, January 1922.

Coupland, R., *Kirk on the Zambesi*, Oxford 1928.

Cumming, R. G., *Five Years of a Hunter's Life in the Far Interior of South Africa*, 2 vols. London 1850.

Curle, Richard, *Robert Browning and Julia Wedgwood*, New York 1937.

Darwin, B., *Life is Sweet, Brother*, London 1940.

Darwin, B., *The World That Fred Made*, London 1955.

Darwin, E., *The Botanic Garden*, London 1924.

Darwin, E., (ed. D. King-Hele), *Essential Writings*, London 1968.

Darwin, E., *The Temple of Nature*, London 1825.

Darwin, F. (ed.), *Charles Darwin: Life and Letters, Including an Autobiographical Chapter*, London 1887.

Darwin, F. (ed.), *More Letters of Charles Darwin*, 2 vols, London 1903.

Devereux, W. C., *A Cruise in the Gorgon*, London 1869.

Dickson, Mora, *Beloved Partner*, London 1974.

Dodds, John W., *The Age of Paradox*, London 1953.

Dornemann, Luise, *Jenny Marx*, Berlin 1968.

Engels, F., *The Conditions of the Working Class in England*, London 1892.

Fay, Margaret, 'Did Marx Offer to Dedicate *Capital* to Darwin?' *Journal of the History of Ideas*, New York 1978

Foskett, R. (ed.), *The Zambesi Doctors*, Edinburgh 1964.

Foskett, R. (ed.), *The Zambesi Journal and Letters of Dr John Kirk*, 2 vols, London 1965.

Frazer, Alice Z., *Livingstone and Newstead*, London 1923.

Gelfand, M., *Livingstone the Doctor*, Oxford 1957.

Glendennan, G. *David Livingstone. A Catalogue of Documents*, Edinburgh 1979.

George, Wilma, *Darwin*, London 1962.

Goodwin, H., *Memoir of Bishop Mackenzie*, Cambridge 1865.

Gruber, H. E. and P. H. Barrett, *Darwin on Man*, London 1974.

Hawkins, E., *Filio Desideratissimo*, Oxford 1862.

Henderson, W. O., *The Life of Friedrich Engels*, vol. II, London 1976.

Herzen, Alexander, *My Past and Thoughts*, vol. III, London 1968.

Himmelfarb, G., *Darwin and the Darwinian Revolution*, New York 1959.

Hobsbawm, E. J., *The Age of Revolution*, London 1962.

Hockley, H. E., *The Story of British Settlers of 1820 in South Africa*, Cape Town and Johannesburg 1948.

Huxley, E., *Livingstone and His African Journeys*, London 1974.

Huxley, Sir J. and H. G. B. Kettlewell, *Charles Darwin and his World*, London 1965.

Huxley, L. (ed.), *The Life and Letters of Joseph Hooker*, 2 vols, London 1918.

Huxley, L. (ed.), *The Life and Letters of T. H. Huxley*, London 1900.

Irvine, W., *Apes, Angels and Victorians*, London 1955.

Jeal, Tim, *Livingstone*, London 1973.

Kapp, Yvonne, *Eleanor Marx*, vols 1 and 2, London 1979

Kapp, Yvonne (ed.), *Karl Marx: Letters to Kugelmann*, London 1954.

Karl Marx Haus, Trier, *Bilddokumente über das Geburtshaus*, Trier 1977.

Karl Marx Haus, Trier, *Zur Persönlichkeit von Marx'*

Schwiegervator Johann Ludwig von Westphalen, Trier 1973.

Kettle, A. G., *Karl Marx, Founder of Modern Communism*, London 1963.

King-Hele, D. G., *Doctor of Revolution – The Life and Genius of Erasmus Darwin*, London 1977.

Krause, E. (with introductory essay by Charles Darwin), *Erasmus Darwin*, London 1879.

Lichtheim, George, *Marxism*, London 1961.

Liebknecht, W. (ed. G. Eckert), *Briefwechsel mit Marx und Engels*, The Hague 1963.

Liebknecht, W. *Selected Works*, vol. 1, London 1942.

Litchfield, H. (ed.), *Emma Darwin: A Century of Family Letters*, 2 vols, London 1915.

Litchfield, R. B., *Tom Wedgwood*, London 1903.

Livingstone, D., *Journeys and Researches in South Africa*, London 1905.

Livingstone, D., *Missionary Travels and Researches in South Africa*, London 1857.

London Missionary Society, *London Missionary Magazine and Chronicle*, vols 4–20, 1840–56.

Long, Una (ed.), *The Journals of Elizabeth Lees-Price 1854–82*, London 1956.

Lovett, N., *The History of the London Missionary Society*, 2 vols, London 1899.

Lyell, Sir C., *The Antiquity of Man*, London 1863.

Lyell, Sir C., *Principles of Geology*, 2 vols, 10th edn, London 1867.

Lyell, Sir C. (ed. Lady Lyell), *Life, Letters and Journals*, 2 vols, London 1881.

McLellan, David, *Karl Marx, His Life and Thoughts*, London 1972.

McLellan, David (ed.), *Karl Marx – The Early Texts*, Oxford 1971.

Magarshack, D. (trans.), *Turgenev's Literary Reminiscences*, London 1959.

Marx, Karl, *The 18th Brumaire of Louis Bonaparte*, London 1926.

Marx, Karl, *Letters 1835–1871*, Moscow 1983.

Marx, Karl and Friedrich Engels, *Collected Works*, London 1975–83.

Marx, Karl and Friedrich Engels, *Reminiscences*, Moscow n.d.

Medawar, Sir P., 'Darwin's Illness', *New Statesman*, 3 April 1964.

Meier, Olga (ed.), *The Daughters of Karl Marx*, London 1982.

Merriweather, Alfred, *Desert Doctor*, Guildford and London 1969.

Meteyard, Eliza, *A Group of Englishmen*, London.

Meteyard, Eliza, *The Life of Josiah Wedgwood*, 2 vols, London 1865.

Moffat, J. S., *The Lives of Robert and Mary Moffat*, London 1885.

Moor, James, *The Post-Darwinian Controversies*, Cambridge 1979.

Moorhouse, G., *The Missionaries*, Philadelphia and New York 1973.

Müller, M. (ed.), *Familie Marx in Briefen*, Berlin 1966.

Oswell, W. E., *William Cotton Oswell, Hunter and Explorer*, 2 vols, London 1900.

Owen, R., *The Life of Robert Owen*, 2 vols, London 1894.

Padover, Saul K., *The Letters of Karl Marx*, Princeton 1979.

Payne, Robert, *Marx. A Biography*, London 1968.

Payne, Robert, *The Unknown Karl Marx*, London 1972.

Pickering, Sir G., *Creative Malady*, London 1974.

Popper, K. R., *The Open Society and Its Enemies*, London 1952.

Prawer, S.S., *Karl Marx and World Literature*, Oxford 1978.

Raddatz, Fritz, *The Marx-Engels Correspondence*, London 1981.

Ransford, Oliver, *David Livingstone: The Dark Interior*, London 1978.

Raverat, G., *Period Piece*, London 1952.

Schapera, I. (ed.), *Apprenticeship at Kuruman: Being the Journal and Letters of Robert and Mary Moffat 1821–1828*, London 1951.

Schapera, I. (ed.), *David Livingstone Family Letters*, 2 vols, London 1959.

Schapera, I. (ed.), *Livingstone's Private Journals 1851–1853*, London 1960.

Schapera, I., *Married Life in an African Tribe*, London 1940.

Schofield, Robert, *The Lunar Society*, Oxford 1963.

Seaver, G., *David Livingstone: His Life and Letters*, London 1957.

Sedgwick, A. (ed. Clark and Hughes), *Life and Letters*, 2 vols. Cambridge 1890.

Seigel, J., *Marx's Fate*, Princeton 1978.

Sillery, A., *Sechele: The Story of an African Chief*, Oxford 1954.

Sorge, F. A., *Correspondance Engels–Marx*, Paris 1950.

Speake, Robert (ed.), *Betley, a Village of Contrasts*, Keele 1980.

Stewart, James, *Dawn on the Dark Continent*, Edinburgh and London 1903.

Torr, Donna (trans.), *Marx–Engels – Selected Correspondence 1846–95*, London 1934.

Trevelyan, G. M., *English Social History*, introduction by Asa Briggs, London 1973.

Turgenev, Ivan, *see* Magarshack.

Venables, V., *Human Nature, the Marxian View*, New York 1945.

Vinogradskaya, P. S., *Documentary Life of Jenny Marx*, Moscow 1969.

Wallis, J. P. R. (ed.), *The Matabele Journals of Robert Moffat 1929–1860*, 2 vols, London 1945.

Wedgwood, Barbara and Hensleigh, *The Wedgwood Circle*, London 1980.

Wells, James, *Stewart of Lovedale*, London 1908.

Winslow, J. H., *Darwin's Victorian Malady*, Philadelphia 1971.

Woodard, Sir L., *The Age of Reform*, Oxford 1961.

Manuscript Sources

Mary Livingstone

The British Library, London.
Burdett–Coutts papers.
Livingstone Memorial, Blantyre: diaries, journals and notebooks.
National Archives of Zimbabwe, Harare: family letters, journal of James Stewart, Mary Livingstone's letters to Mrs Fitch.
National Library of Scotland, Edinburgh: Acc. 6396, Braithwaite papers, Harryhausen Collection, Wilson Collection.
Rhodes House, Oxford: Thornton papers, Waller papers.
School of Oriental and African Studies (University of London): London Missionary Society Archives, Mary Livingstone's letters, Moffat and Livingstone papers.

Jenny Marx

Institute of Marxism–Leninism, Moscow.
International Institute of Social History, Amsterdam.
Karl Marx Haus, Trier.

Emma Darwin

Cambridge University Library: Darwin Archives.
Down House, Kent, and the Royal College of Surgeons of England.

Keele University: letters to Fanny Wedgwood.
Professor Keynes, Cambridge: journals and miscellaneous papers in his possession.

Picture Acknowledgements

Mary Livingstone

BBC Hulton Picture Library: 1 above and below
Congregational Council for World Mission (Weidenfeld and Nicholson Archive): 2 above
Hamilton District Museum: 2 below
United Society for the Propagation of the Gospel: 3 above and below

Jenny Marx

Communist Party Picture Library: 6
Down House, Kent, and the Royal College of Surgeons of England: 6
Karl Marx Haus, Trier: 4 above and below, 5 above left, 5 below left, 5 right

Emma Darwin

Cambridge University Library: 7
Down House, Kent, and the Royal College of Surgeons of England: 8

Index

Adler, Professor Saul, 236
Algiers, 189
Allen, Baugh, 202
Allen, Emma, 202, 203, 254
Allen, Fanny, 207, 208, 238, 246, 249, 250, 254, 261, 262, 263, 268, 276
Allen, Harriet, 202
Allen, Jane, 202
Allen, John, 202
Amalgamated Engineering Union, 283
American Civil War, 282
Andersen, Hans, 281
Anglican Church, 64, 65–6
Argenteuil, 186, 188, 190
Argyll, 3rd Duke of, 85
Austen, Jane, 201, 205, 275
Austria, 93
Aveling, Dr Edward (1851–98), 177, 269, 283

Bad Kreuznach, 83–4, 107, 108
Baden, 121
Baines, Thomas, 56
Bakwain tribe, 23, 24–8, 31, 78
Barmen, 112, 121
Barthelemy, 130
Batlaping tribe, 3, 9–10
Bauer, Karl, 132
Bax, Ernest, 191
Beagle, HMS, 15, 195, 214, 221, 229, 236

Beckwith, General, 85
Bedingfeld, Commander Norman, 55, 59
Beltz, Peter, 84
Bence-Jones, Dr, 263
Bennett, Sir J. Risdon, 50
Berlin, 160–1, 162–3
Berlin University, 96, 97–9, 104
Bible, 13, 15, 258–9
Bismarck, Prince Otto von (1815–98), 173
Blaikie, W.G., 49
Blanc, Louis (1811–82), 122, 129
Boers, 28–9, 31, 47, 58–9
Bonn University, 96, 104
Born, Stephen, 115
Boulton, Matthew, 200
Boynell, Miss, 154
Braithwaite, Anna, 45, 58
Braithwaite, Charles, 45, 281
Braithwaite, Mrs, 45–6, 55
British Association, 259
British East India Company, 6
British Museum, 134, 139, 151, 169
Brodie (nurse), 246, 249
Brontë, Charlotte, 114
Brown, Lancelot 'Capability', 203
Brown, Mr, 233
Brown, Mrs, 50

Browning, Robert, 191, 285
Brunswick, 93
Brunswick, Duke of, 85
Brussels, 92, 109, 114–16
Buchanan, Professor, 55
Bürgers, 136
Burns, Lydia (1827–78, Lizzie), 133, 170
Burns, Mary, 107, 112, 116, 133, 163, 170
Burrup, Mr, 72
Burrup, Mrs, 43–7, 64, 71–2
Bushmen, 11
Butler, Josephine, 244
Byron, Lady, 207
Byron, Lord, 207, 213

Caldwell, Emma, 205
Camberwell, 145
Cambridge, 274, 277
Cambridge Scientific Instrument Company, 285
Cambridge University, 213, 270–1
Cameron, Julia Margaret, 267
Campbell, John, 5, 6–7
Cape of Good Hope, 6
Cape Town, 14–15, 38–9, 63–4
Carlyle, Jane, 135, 221, 234
Carlyle, Thomas, 135, 234, 259
Cavaignac, General, 122
Charles X, King of France, 92
Chartists, 115, 121, 181
Chelsea, 125
Chobe river, 36–7
Chonwane, 23–4, 25
Clark, Dr Andrew, 271
Cluss, 136
Coleridge, Samuel Taylor, 201, 207

Cologne, 105, 109, 120–1, 135
Communist Correspondence League, 115
Communist International, 172, 174, 177, 182, 191
Communist League, 191
Communist Manifesto, 118
Confederation of Rhineland States, 93
Congress of The Hague (1872), 178
Coutts, Miss, 50, 53, 55, 57, 58, 59, 61
Coutts, Thomas, 50
Coutts and Co., 59
Cresselly, Pembrokeshire, 201, 220
Crimean War, 246

Dana, Charles Anderson (1819–97), 142, 151
Daniels, 136
Darwin, Amy, 265
Darwin, Annie (1841–51, Emma Darwin's daughter), 231, 242, 249–53, 254, 262, 273
Darwin, Bernard (Emma Darwin's grandson), 245, 265, 275, 276
Darwin, Catherine (1810–66, Charles Darwin's sister), 201, 250, 263,
Darwin, Charles (1809–82), 169, 190, 195–7, 205; family background, 211–13; early life, 212, 213; Variation of Animals and Plants under Domestication, 212; education, 213; Beagle expedition, 15, 214–15, 221–2, 229, 236;

autobiography, 215, 235, 241–2, 248, 269, 278; Emma falls in love with, 221–5; *Journal of Researches*, 223, 236; marriage, 195, 198, 202; ill health, 225–33, 234–9, 248, 259, 262, 263, 278; *Coral Reefs*, 234; Zoology of the Beagle, 234; character, 235–6; relations with his father, 237, 263; at Down House, 239–41, 245–6; children, 242–4, 262–4; hydrotherapy, 248–9, 259, 262; and Annie's death, 249–53; *The Origin of Species*, 60, 212, 215, 255–60; *The Descent of Man*, 258, 260; fame, 268–71; religious views, 269; death, 271–2

Darwin, Charles Waring (1856–8, Emma Darwin's son), 242, 254, 257

Darwin, Elizabeth (1847–1926, Bessy, Emma Darwin's daughter), 242, 257, 262, 266, 273

Darwin, Ellen, 275

Darwin, Emma (1808–96), 135; family background, 198, 200–3; character, 201, 203; childhood, 203–8; education, 204, 210; religious beliefs, 209, 217, 229, 255, 269–70; in Switzerland, 209–10; and Fanny's death, 216; political interests, 217–19, 246, 276; love of music, 219, 230, 264, 268; in love with Charles Darwin,

222–5; marriage, 195, 198, 225–33, 278; children, 231, 235, 242–4, 249–53, 263–4; ill health, 235, 243, 259; at Down House, 239–41, 245, 262–3, 264; and Annie's death, 249–53, 262, 273; and *The Origin of Species*, 257–8; scarlet fever, 262; and Charles's fame, 268–71; and Charles's death, 271–2; last years, 274–8; death, 278

Darwin, Erasmus (1804–81, Charles Darwin's brother), 200, 205, 207, 213, 221, 223, 235, 255, 267, 271, 278

Darwin, Erasmus (1731–1802, Charles Darwin's grandfather), 195, 200–1, 258

Darwin, Erasmus (Emma Darwin's grandson), 275

Darwin, Francis (1848–1925, Frank, Emma Darwin's son), 242, 245, 246, 265, 269, 271, 272, 275, 285

Darwin, George (1845–1912, Emma Darwin's son), 242, 265, 266

Darwin, Henrietta (1843–1927, Etty, Emma Darwin's daughter), 205, 217, 220, 241–5, 249, 266, 268, 269, 272–8, 285

Darwin, Horace (1851–1928, Emma Darwin's son), 242, 254, 266, 271, 274, 285

Darwin, Leonard (1850–1943, Leo, Emma Darwin's son), 242, 262, 273, 276, 284

Darwin, Marianne (1798–

1858, Charles Darwin's sister), 201
Darwin, Mary, 200
Darwin, Dr Robert (1766–1848, Charles Darwin's father), 195, 198, 201, 206, 214–15, 242, 245, 247, 248, 263
Darwin, Susan (1765–1817, Charles Darwin's mother), 200, 238
Darwin, Susan (1803–66, Charles Darwin's sister), 201, 250, 263
Darwin, William (1839–1914, Emma Darwin's son), 231, 242, 265, 268–72, 284
Davies, Captain, 67
Demuth, Fredrick (1861–1929, Karl Marx's son), 138, 283–4
Demuth, Harry, 284
Demuth, Helene (1823–90, Lenchen), 113, 116, 121, 122, 123, 128, 138–9, 142–4, 153, 155, 158, 162, 185–6, 190, 283
Devereux, Cope, 67–8
Dickens, Charles, 50, 135, 248, 253–4
Dickens, Charley, 280
Dickens, Kate, 253–4
Dogberry club, 183
Donkin, Dr, 186
Down House, Kent, 239–41, 245–6, 254, 262, 264, 268, 273, 277
Draveuil, 283

Edgeworth, Maria, 235
Edinburgh University, 213
Edward, Prince of Wales, 264

Edwards, Mrs, 20
Edwards, Roger, 20, 22
Edwards, Sam, 32
Eisdell, Misses, 17, 47
Eliot, George, 268
Engelmann, Dr, 84
Engels, Friedrich Sr, 168
Engels, Freidrich (1820–95), 142–3, 161; meets Marx, 105, 111–12; *Conditions of the Working Class in England*, 112; Communist Correspondence League, 115; Baden insurrection, 121; work for German refugees, 128–9; financial help for Marx, 129–30, 145, 149, 155, 162, 169; and Lenchen's baby, 138–9; and Mary Burn's death, 163; mistresses, 170; on Jennychen, 170; and *Das Kapital*, 171–3, 174–5; and Jenny Marx's death, 188; and Marx's death, 190; reads *The Origin of Species*, 257; Lenchen takes care of, 284; death, 284
Engels, Marie, 106
Ermen Brothers, 106
Etruria Hall, Staffordshire, 203
Eugenic Society, 285

Farrer, Lord, 268
Fawkes, Guy, 125
Fenians, 171
Feuerbach, Ludwig (1804–72), 182
First International Working Men's Association, 174
Fitch, Frederick, 51

Fitch, Mary, 51, 62, 63
Fitzherbert, Mrs, 205
Fitzroy, Captain, 214
Flaubert, Gustave, 283
Fleckles, Dr Ferdinand (d.c. 1894), 185
Flocon, 120
Florencourt, Wilhelm von, 105
Florencourt family, 94
Frankfurter Zeitung, 179–81
Free Kirk of Scotland, 60–64
Freiligrath, Ferdinand (1810–76), 115, 126, 131, 136
French Revolutions, 92, 95, 191
Freund, Dr, 144, 145
Friedrich Wilhelm, Prince of Prussia, 153
Friedrich Wilhelm IV, King of Prussia, 160

Galapagos Archipelago, 215
Galileo, 258
Garibaldi, Giuseppe, 129
Gaskell, Mrs, 212, 275
Geneva, 209–11, 246
George III, King of England, 200
George IV, King of England, 205
German Workers' Educational Society, 134
Gifford, Lady, 222
Girsch, Karl, 179
Gladstone, William Ewart, 276
Gorgon, HMS, 67–8, 71, 72
Gray, Sir George, 57
Grenville-Murray, 181
Greville House, 204–5

Grey, Bishop of Cape Town, 64
Gricqua Town, 7, 11, 39
Guiccioli, Countess, 207
Guizot, Francois Pierre Guillaume (1787–1874), 113
Gully, Dr, 248–9
Gumpert, Dr Edward, 185

Hackney, 44–5
Hadley Green, 49
Hallé, Charles, 185
Hamilton, Scotland, 42–3, 49
Hampstead Heath, 142, 150
Hannan, James, 55
Hanover, 93, 172
Hansard, 218
Harney, George Julian (1817–97), 116, 121
Harney, Mrs, 116
Haverstock Hill, 150, 154
Hawkins, Rev. Edward, 66
Hegel, Georg Wilhelm Friedrich (1770–1831), 101, 106, 159, 182
Heine, Heinrich (1797–1856), 109, 110, 132, 136, 149
Helmore, Holloway, 58–9
Hensleigh, Fanny (Fanny Wedgwood, *née* Mackintosh), 135, 215, 218–27, 242, 246, 250, 259, 260, 268, 285
Henslow, Professor John, 213–14, 215, 233, 242
Herwegh, Georg (1817–75), 109, 122, 132
Herzen, Alexander (Alexandre Ivanovich, 1812–70), 129
Hesse-Cassel, 93
Hetty Ellen, 61, 65–7

Highgate Cemetery, 190
Holland, Lady, 216
Homer, 91
Hooker, Joseph, 233, 239, 244, 253, 256, 269
Hortense, Queen, 246
Hottentots, 6, 7
House of Commons, 218
House of Lords, 218
Howitt, William, 143
Huxley, Mrs, 238, 245, 261
Huxley, Thomas, 135, 182, 245, 253, 259

Imandt, Peter, 145
Indian Army, 40, 42
Indian Ocean, 79
Irving, Henry, 178, 180
Italy, 93, 204, 209, 218–19

James, Henry, 275
Jews, 90–1, 108, 161
Jones, Ernest Charles (1819–69), 115, 182
Journal of the Linnean Society, 256–7

Kalahari desert, 29, 30, 31, 35–6, 39, 59, 281
Kendal, 45–6, 55, 281
Kirk, Dr John, 55–6, 72, 73, 74, 79
Kolobeng, 24–8, 31, 33–4, 46, 78
Krosigk, Adolf von, 86
Kugelmann, Gertrud (1839–?), 172
Kugelmann, Dr Ludwig (1830–1902), 172, 173
Kuruman, 3–4, 7–15, 17, 18, 22, 29, 30, 34, 57

Lady Nyasa, 61, 63, 66, 69, 70, 79
Lafargue, Etienne (Schappy), 176
Lafargue, Paul (1842–1911), 169–70, 176, 283
Lancet, 27
Lane, Dr, 238–9, 259
Langton, Rev. Charles, 216, 262
Lassalle, Ferdinand (1825–64), 160–1, 162, 164
Lattakoo, 5, 7, 9, 12
Lennox, Jessie, 64, 72
Lewis, George, 268
Liebknecht, Wilhelm (1826–1900), 130, 132, 138, 142, 157, 158, 190
Lincoln, Abraham, 155
Linnean Society, 256–7
Lissagaray, Prosper Olivier (1838–1901), 176
Litchfield, Richard, 266, 267
Livingstone, Agnes (David Livingstone's sister), 26, 55, 280, 281
Livingstone, Agnes (1847–1912, Mary Livingstone's daughter), 24, 30, 32–3, 37, 42, 45, 55, 74, 280–1
Livingstone, Anna Mary (1858–1939, Mary Livingstone's daughter), 58, 60, 79, 281
Livingstone, Charles (David Livingstone's brother), 26, 42, 56, 75
Livingstone, David (1813–73), 237, 243, 253; decides to become a missionary, 16; marriage,

3–4, 18–19, 40–1; on the
British character, 116;
missionary life, 22–8;
explorations, 30–7, 46;
opposition to slave trade,
31; reunited with Mary, 48;
Missionary Travels, 51–2, 59,
60, 63; Zambesi expedition,
51–9, 67–78; and Mary's
death, 73–8; death, 79;
funeral, 280, 282
Livingstone, Janet (David
Livingstone's sister), 26,
55, 280, 281
Livingstone, John (David
Livingstone's brother), 42
Livingstone, Mary (1821–62),
family background, 4–10;
birth, 7; childhood in
Africa, 9–13; education,
13–14; ill health, 14, 34, 46,
65; goes to England, 15–16;
marriage, 3–4, 18–19,
40–2, 46; missionary life,
22–8; children, 23, 26, 30,
33, 37; explorations with
Livingstone, 31–7; leaves
Africa, 38–42; courage,
39–40; difficulties in
Victorian society, 42–3, 45,
49–50; life in Scotland,
42–3; poverty in England,
43–5; reunited with
Livingstone, 48–51; poetry,
48; and the Zambesi
expedition, 52–9, 60–78;
returns to Scotland, 59–60;
friendship with James
Stewart, 60–8; death, 73–8
Livingstone, Neil, 44, 49
Livingstone, Oswell
(1851–92, Mary

Livingstone's son), 36, 37,
42, 45, 55, 79, 282
Livingstone, Robert (1846–
64, Mary Livingstone's
son), 23, 25, 30, 32, 37, 42,
45–6, 60, 280, 282
Livingstone, Thomas Steele
(1849–76, Mary
Livingstone's son), 27–8,
30, 32, 33, 43, 46, 55, 60,
282
London Missionary Society,
6, 16, 20, 39, 43–5, 52
Longuet, Charles (Jenny
Marx's grandson), 190
Longuet, Charles (1833–
1903, Jenny Marx's son-in-
law), 176, 186, 191
Louis Napoleon, Emperor
(Napoleon III), 123, 129,
140, 175, 246, 276
Louis Philippe, King of
France (1773–1850), 113,
119, 120
Lower Silesian Railway, 149
Lunar Society, 200–2
Lutheran Church, 90
Lyell, Charles, 233, 256, 269
Lyell, Lady, 261
Lytton, Edward Bulwer, 248

Ma Robert, 55, 61
Mabotsa mission, 19–20, 22
Macaulay, Thomas
Babington, 206, 248
Macaw Cottage, Gower
Street, London, 227–8, 230
Mackenzie, Bishop Charles,
63–8, 72
Mackenzie, Miss, 64, 66, 72
Mackintosh, Sir James, 202,
207, 211, 213, 219

Mackintosh, Lady (Kitty, *née* Allen), 202, 207, 211

Maer Hall, Staffordshire, 195, 198, 203–8, 211–12, 221, 239–40, 262

Magomero mission, 68, 71

Makololo tribe, 29, 36, 58–9

Malthus, Thomas, 39, 256

Malvern, 248–52, 259, 262

Manchester, 45, 111, 115, 131, 138, 142, 145, 171, 185

Mantatee tribe, 11

Marjoribanks, Mr, 59

Markheim, Bertha, 165

Martineau, Harriet, 39, 207

Marx, Edgar (1847–55, Jenny Marx's son), 118, 127, 144, 153

Marx, Edward (Karl Marx's brother), 103

Marx, Eleanor (1855–98, Tussy, Jenny Marx's daughter), 133, 144, 150, 152, 155, 167, 169, 176, 177, 178, 182–7, 190, 191, 269, 283, 284

Marx, Franziska (1851–2, Jenny Marx's daughter), 137, 139, 141

Marx, Heinrich (1777–1838, Karl Marx's father), 84, 90–1, 96–7, 101, 103, 108

Marx, Heinrich (1840–50, Jenny Marx's son), 125, 128

Marx, Henrietta (1787–1863, Karl Marx's mother), 84, 90–1, 98, 104, 110, 118, 128, 166–7

Marx, Jenny (1814–81), 218, 219; childhood, 85, 86–7; family background, 85–6; character, 88, 103–4, 191;
political views, 88, 90, 92–4; education, 90, 104; courtship and marriage, 83–4, 94–103, 104–5, 145–6; *Short Sketch of an Eventful Life*, 85, 178; life in Paris, 109–10, 113; children, 110, 116–17, 125, 136, 141, 144, 152, 158; in Brussels, 114–19; relations with Engels, 116, 162; arrest, 119–20; in Cologne, 120–1; returns to Paris, 123–4; life in England, 124–59, 162–90; and Lenchen's illegitimate child, 137–8; personal assistant to Marx, 140, 156, 166, 257; isolation, 151; smallpox, 158–9; legacies, 166–7; and the publication of *Das Kapital*, 173; and the Paris Commune, 175, 178; journalism, 178–82; last years, 182–90

Marx, Jenny (1844–83, Jennychen, Jenny Marx's daughter), 110, 114, 118, 151, 160, 162, 169, 170, 176, 184, 186–90, 283

Marx, Karl (1818–83), 202, 207, 219, 237, 244, 248, 253, 255; early life, 90–1; at university, 96–104; courtship and marriage, 53–4, 94–104, 105, 145–6; financial problems, 96, 101, 118, 133, 141–2, 149, 155, 162; character, 97; poetry, 99–100; edits *Rheinische Zeitung*, 105–6, 107; meets Engels, 106, 111; anti-

Semitism, 108, 161; life in Paris, 109–10, 113; friendship with Engels, 111–12, 133–4; *Das Kapital*, 112, 132, 157, 166, 171–3, 174, 177, 182, 258; in Brussels, 114–20; Communist Manifesto, 118; arrested in Brussels, 119–20; *Neue Rheinische Zeitung*, 121; sedition trial, 121; returns to Paris, 123–4; life in England, 124–59; illegitimate son, 137–8; ill-health, 141, 165–6, 174, 188, 189, 237, 248; *Critique of Political Economy*, 156–7, 257; and Jenny's smallpox, 158–9; visits Lassalle in Germany, 161, 162; legacies, 166–7; and his daughters, 169–70, 176; and the Communist International, 172, 177, 182, 191; and the Paris Commune, 175; reads *The Origin of Species*, 257; last years, 182–91; and Jenny's death, 185–90

Marx, Laura (1895–1911, Jenny Marx's daughter), 118, 133, 145, 152–3, 172, 174, 188, 189–90

Marx, Sophie (Karl Marx's sister), 91, 98–9, 168

Matabele tribe, 4, 15, 29, 36, 58

Mazzini, Giuseppe (1805–72), 93, 129, 135, 218

Meynell, Alice, 221

Modena, 93

Moffat, Ann, 13, 14–15, 23, 281

Moffat, Elizabeth (Bessie), 16, 29

Moffat, Emily, 57

Moffat, Helen, 12, 17, 45

Moffat, James, 12, 16

Moffat, Jane, 17, 30, 49

Moffat, John, 12, 15, 18

Moffat, John Smith, 24, 57

Moffat, Mary (Mary Livingstone's mother), 3–19, 23, 31, 34, 41, 62, 282

Moffat, Robert (1795–1883, Mary Livingstone's father), 3–18, 29, 36, 39, 57–8, 79, 282

Moffat, Robert (1827–62, Mary Livingstone's brother), 10, 11–12, 13, 65

Mokateri, John, 15

Moore, Sam, 185, 284

Moore, Thomas, 208

Mozambique, 67

Munby, Arthur, 267

Murchison, Lady, 50, 78

Murchison, Sir Roderick, 53

Murchison Falls, 61, 68

Murray, John, 49, 212, 257

Mzilikatze, chief of the Matabele, 4, 15, 36, 58

Napoleon I, Emperor, 93, 207

Napoleonic wars, 93

National Secularist Society, 269

Natural History Museum, 273

Neue Rheinische Zeitung, 121

Neuenahr, 184

New American Cyclopaedia, 151

New Testament, 15

New York Daily Tribune, 142, 151

Ngami, Lake, 30, 31, 33,

Nightingale, Florence, 207, 210, 212, 246, 248

Novello, Clara, 220

Nyasa, Lake, 61,. 78

Nyasaland, 72

O'Connell, Daniel, 218

Old Testament, 258–9

Oswell, William Cotton, 29–40, 49, 79, 281

Owen, Fanny, 221

Owen, Mrs, 53–4

Owen, Professor, 50–1, 53, 259

Oxford and Cambridge Mission to Central Africa, 52

Pall Mall Gazette, 181

Palmerston, Lord, 121

Pannewitz, Second Lieutenant Karl von, 93–4

Papal States, 93

Paris, 109–10, 113, 119, 120–4, 186, 204, 223

Paris Commune, 175, 178, 191

Park, Mungo, 205

Parma, 93

Parslow (butler), 232, 245, 274, 277

Pearl, 55–7

Pengelly, William, 261

Philip, Dr, 7

Philips, Lion (d. 1866), 128, 160, 162, 167

Philips, Nanette, 160, 161

Philosophical Society of Cambridge, 215, 271

Pieper, Wilhelm (c. 1826–?), 132, 140, 149, 154

Pioneer, 61, 68–73

Plato, 266

Poland, 93

Price, Mrs, 59

Price, Roger, 58–9

Proudhon, Pierre Joseph (1809–65), 129

Quakers, 45–6, 52, 281

Rae, George, 56, 61, 65, 72, 74

Ratzfeldt, Countess, 161, 162

Raverat, Gwen, 241, 253, 265, 266, 272, 285

Reform Bill, 218

Rentsch, Miss, 154

Rheinische Zeitung, 105, 106

Rickes, Johann, 84

Robey, Sarah, 11, 15, 17

Robey, William, 6

Rothschild family, 132

Rousseau, Jean Jacques, 90, 204, 276

Rovuma river, 61

Royal Geographical Society, 30, 49, 53, 234, 285

Royal Society, 263

Ruge, Arnold (1802–80), 108, 120, 171

Ruskin, John, 268

Russia, 93, 173, 181

Salem, 13

Saxony, 93

Schiller, Johann Christoph Friedrich von, 207

Schöler, Lina, 123, 168

Schramm, Conrad (1822–58), 130

Scotland, 42–3, 59–60
Scott, Sir Walter, 276
Sebituane, chief of the Makololo, 29, 33, 36–7
Sechele, chief of the Bakwain, 23–9, 35
Sedgwick, Professor Adam, 215
Senegal, 55
Sesheke river, 37
Shaftesbury, Lord, 49, 51
Shaka, chief of the Zulus, 11
Shakespeare, William, 90, 91, 115, 154, 155, 178, 179–80, 181, 213
Shaw, Rev. William, 14
Shelley, Percy Bysshe, 95–6, 106
Shire river, 68, 71, 78
Shupanga, 71, 72
Sierra Leone, 57
Sismondi, Jean-Charles Simonde de (1773–1842), 202, 207, 209–11, 223, 246, 254
Sismondi, Jessie (1777–1853, née Allen, Emma Darwin's aunt), 202, 207, 209–10, 216, 218, 223–4, 230, 232, 239, 240, 253, 254
Skinner, Marian, 183
Smith, Dr Andrew, 15
Smith, Rev. Sydney, 208
Soho, 127–8, 135, 142–4, 151
Sorge, Friedrich Adolf (1828–1906), 184
South America, 214, 222, 236, 241
South Hampstead College for Ladies, 153
Staël, Madame de, 207, 210

Stanley, Henry Morton, 276, 281
Steele, Colonel, 49, 79
Stephen, Leslie, 272, 275
Stewart, James, 60–77
Storch, Wilhelm, 87
Strauss, David Friedrich (1808–74), 106
Switzerland, 121, 190, 204, 209–10

Tenge, Frau, 172
Tennyson, Alfred, Lord, 248, 267, 279
Tennyson, Mrs, 267
Thackeray, William Makepeace, 246
Thorley, Miss, 249
Thornton, Richard, 56
Tidman, Rev. Arthur, 20, 39, 42–3, 47
The Times, 50, 52, 180
Tollet, Ellen, 198, 212
Tollet, George, 212
Tollet, Georgina, 212
Tollet family, 203, 212, 220
Torquay, 261
Trier, 83, 85, 86–92, 93, 107–8, 110, 117
Trinity College Cambridge, 284
Turgenev, Ivan, 122
Turner, J.M.W., 268

Universities' Mission to Central Africa, 63

Vaughan Williams, Ralph, 285
Vavassour, James, 45
Veltheim, Louise von, 86
Victoria, Princess, 153

Victoria, Queen of England, 27, 53, 153

Victoria Falls, 37

Vogt, Karl (1817–95), 158

Wallace, Alfred Russel, 256

Waller, Rev. Horace, 72, 79

Watt, James, 200

Webb, Captain, 40, 79, 280

Wedgwood, Caroline (1800–88, Charles Darwin's sister), 200, 201, 211, 222, 268, 285

Wedgwood, Charlotte (1797–1862, Emma Darwin's sister), 202, 206, 211, 215–16, 219, 221–2, 262

Wedgwood, Elizabeth (1764–1846, Bessy, Emma Darwin's mother), 198, 202, 204, 208–10, 217, 220, 248, 262

Wedgwood, Elizabeth (1793–1880, Emma Darwin's sister), 198, 202–5, 211, 219, 230, 236, 239, 246–8, 254, 260–1, 271

Wedgwood, Fanny (1806–32, Emma Darwin's sister), 203, 209–11, 215–17, 219, 220, 252

Wedgwood, Fanny (Frank Wedgwood's wife), 215

Wedgwood, Fanny (Hensleigh Wedgwood's wife), see Hensleigh, Fanny

Wedgwood, Frank (1800–88, Emma Darwin's brother), 202, 216

Wedgwood, Harry (1799–1885, Emma Darwin's brother), 202, 203

Wedgwood, Hensleigh (1803–91, Emma Darwin's brother), 202, 215, 218–19, 223–6, 232, 250–2, 260

Wedgwood, Josiah I (1730–95), 143, 198, 200, 240

Wedgwood, Josiah II (1769–1843, Emma Darwin's father), 195, 198, 200–2, 204–7, 214, 217–18, 245, 248

Wedgwood, Josiah III (1795–1880, Jos, Emma Darwin's brother), 198, 202, 224, 268, 285

Wedgwood, Sarah, 254

Wedgwood, Snow, 285

Wedgwood, Tom, 201, 207, 278–9

Weerth, Georg Ludwig (1822–56), 115, 125, 132, 136

Weitling, Wilhelm, 110

Wellington, Duke of, 54, 132, 133

Westminster Abbey, 75, 79, 273

Westphalen, Caroline, Baroness von (1776–1856, Jenny Marx's mother), 83–4, 85, 94, 104–5, 110, 118, 146, 148

Westphalen, Edgar von (1819–c. 1890), 83, 86–7, 90, 114, 123, 168

Westphalen, Ferdinand Otto Wilhelm von (1799–1816), 83, 86, 87–8, 90, 94, 105, 106, 122, 130, 149, 165

Westphalen, Franziska von, 86

Westphalen, Karl von, 86

Westphalen, Laura von, 86

Westphalen, Lisette von, 86, 88

Westphalen, Louise von, 90, 94, 105, 152–3, 155

Westphalen, Ludwig, Baron von (1770–1842, Jenny Marx's father), 83, 85–8, 90–1, 94, 105, 155

Westphalen, Philipp, Baron von, 85–6

Weydemeyer, Josef (1818–66), 115, 126, 136, 139, 140, 158

Weydemeyer, Louise, 150, 158, 159

Whigs, 208

Wilberforce, Samuel ('Soapy Sam'), Bishop of Oxford, 259

Wilhelm I, King of Prussia (1797–1888), 161

William IV, King of England, 217

Williams, Mr, 268

Willich, August (1810–78), 129, 130

Wilson, 32

Wilson, Captain, 67–72

Wilson, Frank, 281

Wishart, Jean, 85

Wolff, Ferdinand (1812–95, Red Wolf), 135

Wolff, Wilhelm (1809–64, Lupus), 115, 135, 168

Woolf, Virginia, 272

Wordsworth, William, 207

Working Men's College, 266

Young, James, 53, 55

Young Europe, 93, 94

Young Germany, 90, 93, 218

Young Italy, 93, 218–19

Zambesi river, 37, 47, 50, 52–3, 57–8, 60, 63, 67–79

Zouga river, 31, 34, 37, 281

Zulus, 6, 11–12, 13

MARGARET CROSLAND
PIAF

More than twenty years after her early death, the legend that was Piaf is still remembered.

Born in Paris in 1915, Edith Gassion's rags to riches life held many tragedies – desertion by her mother, the death of her own daughter and then later her lover, a fatal dependence on drink and drugs. But above all this, her talent soared.

PIAF is the story of an extraordinarily talented artist, a woman world-famous for her records, but equally at home on stage and screen. Margaret Crosland's fascinating biography sheds new light on this most complex of stars, one whose fame has continued to grow over the years.

POST A LITTLE HAPPINESS

Post·A·Book

A Royal Mail service in association with the Book Marketing Council & The Booksellers Association.

Post-A-Book is a Post Office trademark.

ANNE EDWARDS

MATRIARCH

Queen Mary, born Princess May of Teck, was the consort of George V, mother of Kings Edward VIII and George VI, and grandmother of Elizabeth II.

Haughty, resolute and supremely Royal, Queen Mary was for sixty-one years intimately linked with the House of Windsor. Through the tumultuous years of the twentieth century – spanning two world wars, the toppling of many European monarchies, and the Abdication crisis – Queen Mary stood as a symbol of an enduring England, a staunch defender of the values of God, King and Empire.

An yet, as Anne Edwards' vivid biography shows, the course of twentieth-century history itself might have been very different – had the young Princess May married the man to whom she was first engaged and who died, perhaps fortuitously, only weeks after their betrothal: the weak, ineffectual Prince Eddy, a man rumoured to be mad, homosexual and linked with Jack the Ripper.

HODDER AND STOUGHTON PAPERBACKS

SHERIDAN MORLEY

DAVID NIVEN: THE OTHER
SIDE OF THE MOON

'If you want to know about my father's life you won't
find it in his autobiographies. They're all about other
people'

DAVID NIVEN JNR.

DAVID NIVEN – actor, author, ultimate English gentleman is a legend – a legend of carefree elegance, of time-
less charm, of Hollywood's glittering silver screen.

Yet legends often hide the truth.

'An excellently researched analysis . . . Head and should-
ers above the average showbiz biography . . . He under-
stands many of Niven's deeper feelings'

John Mortimer. The Sunday Times

'A well-told story . . . giving us the darker side as well as
the mask of a complex and perhaps desperate character.
He was a life-enhancer off-screen as well as on'

J. W. Lambert, The Times

HODDER AND STOUGHTON PAPERBACKS

JOHN H. DAVIS

THE KENNEDY CLAN –
DYNASTY AND DISASTER 1848–1984

The Kennedy saga, complete.

From early Irish roots, through the decades of struggle and the rise to power in the rough-and-tumble of Boston politics, to the arrival on the world stage with the Presidency and the flowering of Camelot. Then, tragedy, striking again and again.

John Davis, first cousin to Jacqueline Kennedy, tells the story of the Kennedy family from the inside. Personal observation and an eye for the vivid, revealing incident enliven an enthralling story. For behind the glittering public image lies an often darker private reality.

'Carefully researched and highly readable'
Financial Times

HODDER AND STOUGHTON PAPERBACKS

MARY CRAIG

THE CRYSTAL SPIRIT

In August 1980 something extraordinary happened. Out of the chaos and turmoil of Poland, there emerged the first modern free trade union in the Communist bloc. The movement was called Solidarity. One man personified its indomitable spirit.

Lech Wałęsa, electrician from Gdansk, spoke out for his fellow workers. He became a national figure and world hero. He was awarded the Nobel Peace Prize in 1983. The movement now outlawed, yet its spirit still uncrushed, he has returned to the factory floor.

Mary Craig went to Poland to meet him. THE CRYSTAL SPIRIT is not only a remarkable biography. It also places the emergence of Solidarity in its historical context to give a rare picture of a country both in the past and the present.

HODDER AND STOUGHTON PAPERBACKS

ALSO AVAILABLE FROM HODDER AND STOUGHTON PAPERBACKS